Wide Eyes in
Burma and Thailand
Finding Your Way

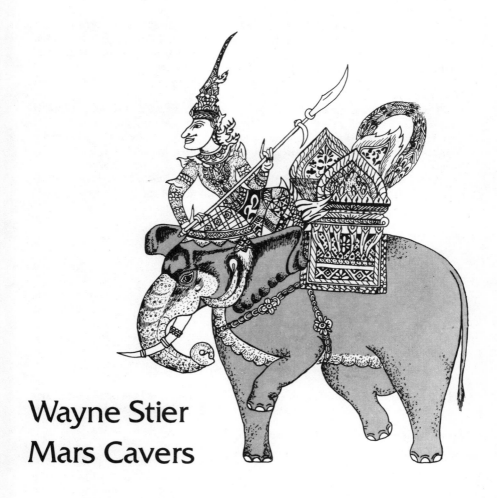

Wayne Stier
Mars Cavers

Meru Publishing

Acknowledgements

Thank you for the hands and eyes that produced your art: Vic Mancilla, Connie Bethards, Bruce Takang Kuo, John Beagle, Maung Aye Myint, Diane Catterall, Laurel Rain, Dave Hurst.

Thank you for helping us with the languages and for giving us a first sense of the countries: Pra Panom, Maung Kyaw (David Gee) and family, Gilbert Nathen and family, Pra Smai Khamhung, Pat Richardson, Praky Suttiboon, Nangbahn Nuamprasert, Pornchai Methakajornkul (Paul), Lin Barnett.

Thank you for your comments and suggestions: Elizabeth Albrecht and Mary Eade.

Thanks to all the travelers we met for testing out travel in Asia and telling us your stories: Bangkok Bob, Teresa Lozito, Stephanie Lee, and many more.

Our thanks too, for the equipment and information made available to us by Al Beck, Bill Dalton, Cliff White, Tourist Authority of Thailand, and Tourist Burma.

And finally, our thanks to Barb and Gordon Sheridan of Sheridan Publications Services for their editing, design, and production of the book.

Cover design is adapted from a nineteenth-century painting in Thonburi, Thailand.

Paperbound: ISBN 0-911447-00-8
Hardcover: ISBN 0-911447-01-6

Contents

Southeast Asia Overview

Echoes and mirrors and dreams and fears, illusion encrusted fact, and tangible fantasy: Asia.

This book comes from Asia. It's about traveling wide-eyed with amazement, traveling with eyes wide open to the scintillating differences from and startling similarities to what you once called reality.

> *A rice farmer's wife leaves the chipped lacquerware on the crude wooden shelf. Instead, she serves a traditional home-cooked meal to you, her honored guest, on a treasured, new plastic plate.*

Because the writers lived for five years in Asia, *Wide Eyes in Burma and Thailand* reflects a learned compromise between East and West. For instance, there are maps and suggestions on places to see, where to stay, foods to try, buses, trains, and ox carts to ride. In short, there is enough information in this book for you to find your way. But often, the facts—if they haven't already changed to history—have been embedded in the story of the road. For to go to Asia with an eye for facts is to miss the best part of travel there: the surprises.

An informal one-handed *wai,* a friendly Thai "hello."

The Ticket

Travel is dream fulfillment. You participate. First you fall into a photograph of a SE Asian scene and you find you can't get yourself out. You reach for the phone to book the ticket. Wait. There's some planning to do and some ticket shopping.

The newspaper has ads on discount tickets to Asia. Many kinds are available: budget fares with one-year open tickets (good for a full year), group fares (for groups as small as four), excursion rates (for round-trip tickets with a limited number of days), tours, and add-ons (for example, a stop in Tokyo for an extra $25). The challenge of finding the cheapest ticket can get entertaining when you start considering value. For instance, some tickets sell for around $400 from the west coast of the United States to Bangkok. What are the cancellation fees and rescheduling fees? How many days advance purchase are necessary? Are there cheaper routes or some with more stops? There are so many questions, some travel agencies limit the amount of time an agent can spend with each customer. With a great deal of digging you might discover that an obscure airline in Minnesota has a university tour to Asia and needs a likely-looking "varsity member" to fill the vacancy. You might get lucky and run across a super-agent who gets totally into your trip and does the digging for you. Many first-time travelers have regretted buying too much air ticket after they discover land travel in SE Asia.

____Getting Around Southeast Asia

Waiting: Most of your travel time is spent waiting. You wait for buses to load up while, to lure in more passengers, the driver edges forward as if he's leaving. Eventually, they pile in with bundles that fill the aisles and you're off. You wait in bus company restaurants while the driver eats. You wait while the conductor fills the radiator with water dipped from a roadside rice paddy.

The bus stops when the rain drowns out the windshield wipers. It stops for the driver and several of the male passengers to make a quick run into the bushes. It stops to pick up someone who is waving beside the road in the middle of nowhere. In some places, "rapid transit" means anything that could beat an ox cart in a drag race two out of three times.

Occasionally, you decide to splurge, giving up local experience and some money for air-conditioned, cushioned comfort, which sometimes includes meals and a video movie. These are usually long distance "express" buses that don't stop at every town or for passengers en route (except in major cities). You pull out of the bus terminal and speed down the road to the nearest gas station, where there's a line of buses waiting.

By Air: Sometimes land travel isn't worth the pain and adventure. When you're sick, a long, Lomotil-popping bus run looks less than inviting. When you've been riding on a burning Naugahyde seat for a few days and your behind takes each bump as a personal insult, a cool, quick airflight may be worth the extra dollars (figure about twice the price of surface travel). Sometimes when you include the expense of meals and hotels along the way, air travel may actually be cheaper.

Often there are package deals that are hard to pass up. For example, one ticket out of Bangkok allows you to take a year to fly from Singapore, Jakarta, Australia, New Caledonia, New Zealand, and Tahiti en route to Los Angeles for around $750. Another ticket out of Bangkok goes via Hong Kong, Manila, Sidney, and back to Hong Kong for around $700. A ticket out of Singapore allows stops in Jakarta, Bali, Yogya, and Jakarta once more before returning to Singapore for a little over $300. Bangkok still sells the most discount tickets at the cheapest prices, although Penang is becoming competitive. Singapore travel agents are often able to quote the best prices on flights out of Singapore. Shop around and make sure you are buying what you need. Remember to bring your student ID card for additional discounts.

Traveling for Free: Hitching varies from country to country, largely dependent on the number of private vehicles on the road. To wave a car down don't thumb; wave your hand at the driver, bending it at the wrist (a gesture that means "come here" in Asia). Men with short hair and neat looking clothes will have the best luck. Many travelers try their luck at the yacht clubs in Manila, Hong Kong, Singapore, Penang, and Phuket. Both men and women are often signed on as crew (no experience needed), and given food and transportation in exchange for a few hours work each day on board a yacht.

Other Ways to Travel: Cars are for hire in every major city. You keep your personal space at the expense of personal contact with the locals and a great deal of money. Motorbikes are often available for rent; but for your own safety, don't learn to ride in SE Asia. The speed, narrow roads, and intuitive Asian driving style can be deadly to even the most skillful foreign biker.

___Travel Documents

Passport: In 450 B.C., Nehemiah asked the Persian king for a letter guaranteeing safe passage on his junket to Judah and the travel document was born. We're stuck with it. Now you must hold a valid passport to pass any legal port of entry into most countries.

Ask for a business passport; these have more pages and so you'll avoid a bothersome trip to the embassy in a foreign country when your pages fill up with official stamps.

The passport was designed in the twenties by the League of Nations. The International Civil Aviation Organization is considering using computer card passports soon.

Visas: Burma permits only seven-day tourist visas. The Burmese embassy in Bangkok will have your visa ready in one day if you show an air ticket in and out of Burma. Thailand gives you fifteen days to leave the country if you arrive without a visa. You can get one-, two-, or three-months' tourist visas if they are applied for outside the country. They grant few extensions.

___Health

Preparation: It's simple. The body wants to be healthy; all it needs is a little help and those diseases that take you on tours to the doctor, the bed, and the bathroom won't stand a chance. Start with the basics: good food, plenty of rest, a calm mind, and an already healthy body.

You no longer have to go through an injection needle gauntlet before you travel to SE Asia. Smallpox has been eradicated. Neither cholera nor yellow fever immunization is required unless you were recently in an infected area (parts of Africa and South America). Diphtheria-tetanus shots don't need boosters; you probably already have lifetime protection. A typhoid fever shot is recommended by some doctors, but none of the countries in SE Asia require it. A hepatitis vaccine became available in 1982.

Pack a small health kit for convenience. However, remember that most of the normal medical supplies you may need are available in the larger cities and in a large share of the smaller towns. Throw in a few bandaids, some aspirin, an ace bandage, PABA lotion for a natural sunscreen, and some old-fashioned Mercurochrome antiseptic for tropical ulcers. Tropical ulcers are open sores that otherwise don't dry up enough to heal in the damp climate.

Buy medical drugs in your first Asian city where they're cheaper and you often don't need a prescription. Some places require a passport to prove you're not a resident. For malaria, buy Fansidar; get one tablet for each week you plan to travel plus four more for after you return home. As for intestinal diseases such as Gardia with its rotten-egg burps, preventative caution over what you ingest is a lot easier on your kidneys and liver than last straw drug cures.

Jet Lag: Tests have shown that you lose nothing in your capacity to do physical work and only a small loss (ten to fifteen percent) of your mental efficiency during a long distance air flight. Psychologically, however, you feel tired from being out of sync with local time. To decrease the effects, drink a lot of liquid during the flight (but not coffee, tea, or alcohol). This will compensate for the dry cabin air. Do stretch exercises. Unless you plan to sleep for a few days after you arrive (not a bad idea), forego one of the in-flight movies and close your eyes. Get a blanket—it gets cool—and a pillow from the overhead compartment when you board.

Sun: Take the intense midday tropic sun seriously. It's too easy to underestimate its power. Too much sun will microwave your brain causing headaches, dizziness, and strokes. Reduce the risk by wearing a hat and sunglasses and avoiding alcohol while out in the direct noonday sunlight. If you do feel dizzy, put your head between your knees and eat some cool watery fruit (not necessarily at the same time). If you want to be certain to keep from getting sunburned, use PABA sunscreen or get in the shade when your pulse rises two counts per minute. Many people try to escape the heat by going into air-conditioned rooms, thus asking their bodies to make energy-sapping adjustments.

Globetrotter Trots: The Thai call it the walking stomach, but for foreigners it's the runs. If your body is in good shape, you should be able to adapt to the change in diet with only minor discomfort. There are some things to avoid. Water is generally not purified, especially in more rural settings. It's best to drink only boiled water. Some travelers carry water purification tablets, but they're expensive and take about thirty minutes to work. It's much easier to drink the weak tea available at restaurants—often it's offered free. Remember ice is as likely to be impure. It's best to do without, but when the sun is frying the bus you're in and the vendor holds up a cold sweating drink, it's hard to resist. You must balance your need for relief with a fair assessment of the potential danger. Most of the time you give in.

As for food, meats are harder to digest. Pork, if not done well, may contain trichinosis. Shellfish, too, should be avoided, especially oysters and clams. Raw vegetables and fruits are often washed in impure water; peel them first—even grapes! In truth, almost everything you ingest could cause you stomach disorders whether it's from the food stall on the street or the flash restaurant.

As a rule of thumb, look at the cook. If he is healthy, chances are the food is too. (*Side note:* Men tend to lose weight traveling in SE Asia, but women gain an average of four kilograms because they more readily retain rice carbohydrates.)

It happens. Sometimes you are humbled by the runs. Locals say chili peppers combat bacteria. But this cure can be worse than the disease—causing irritation in the intestinal tract. Large doses of garlic are also said to be helpful, and peppermint is supposed to reduce stomach gas. Some older Asians claim betel nut cures hunger pangs, intestinal worms, and protects tooth enamel (while it rots the gums and gives a mild euphoria so you don't really care). Yogurt bacteria is also said to be helpful. Recently, scientists have discovered a more effective purge for stomach disorders—the cucumber, peeled. If all fails and you come down with a bad case, a few days' regimen of weak tea and plain rice should clear up the problem. If your colon is highly irritated, take Lomotil for a day and give the muscles a few hours off work. Chances are, in a few days you'll be able to hang up a vacancy sign outside the toilet. If not, see a doctor.

Malaria: The female Anopheles mosquito is a carrier of fever chills, coma, and death from malaria. She is recognizable by the way she flies low and bites ankles with her head down and her legs in the air. The disease can last for up to forty years. The Anopheles mosquito thrives in SE Asia, yet foreign aid to fight malaria has decreased.

Spiders and gecko lizards are your allies; they dine on the femme fatale. Screens and nets make see-through sanctuaries, although one non-malaria-carrying species can light on the net, stick its head through the tiny holes, and squeeze through to visit you. Where nets can't be hung, incense coils, readily available in most places, will fill the air with smoke more foul-smelling to mosquitos than to you (hard as that may be to believe).

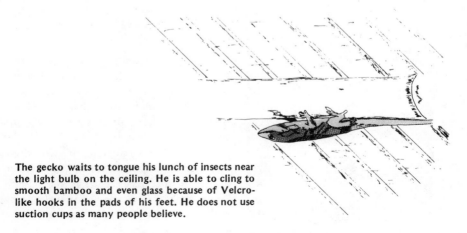

The gecko waits to tongue his lunch of insects near the light bulb on the ceiling. He is able to cling to smooth bamboo and even glass because of Velcro-like hooks in the pads of his feet. He does not use suction cups as many people believe.

Outside, insect repellent is your armor along with long sleeves and pants in the early evening. It may be best to assume you'll get bitten and take a weekly dose of Fansidar (*Pyrimethamine-sulfadoxine*). Fansidar, effective in most cases, isn't available in the United States or Canada.

In the rare instance that you become ill despite these precautions, bring along some chloroquine, the most common antimalaria drug. Use a few tablets to cut back a severe fever fast before it can do brain damage. Otherwise, avoid use; it damages the kidneys. Neither Fansadar nor chloroquine should be ingested on an empty stomach. After leaving the infected area, continue to take Fansidar for four to six weeks to guard against latent parasites lurking in your liver. If you feel ill, tell your doctor that it might be malaria. This avoids a waste of time and testing. Don't donate blood while on the malaria pills.

Miscellaneous Health: To remove leeches, touch them with a burning match or cigarette; don't pull them off. Leeches hate the smell of moist tobacco. Tiger Balm, Asia's cure-all, relieves mosquito itching, sunburn irritation (although plain vinegar works better), muscle aches, and, when rubbed on the temples, headaches. Even drowsiness from the monotony of a long bus ride can be chased away with a little balm below your nose. To escape the heat on your skin, buy some prickly-heat talcum powder, readily available in Thailand. With it on, the hotter you get, the cooler it feels. For beach safety, wear footgear in the shallows to protect your feet from the knife-sharp spines of stonefish, almost invisible in the sand.

——*Money*

Tarnished silver coins dangle from the headdress of an Akha tribeswoman in northern Thailand. An Indian merchant in Rangoon will pay double what you

paid for your black-market, brand-name whiskey. Banks in Bangkok have walkup windows for currency exchange. A fisherman in south Thailand barters part of the morning catch for a bag of rice. In Burma and Thailand, concepts of money vary more than the weather.

Carrying Money: Traditions are breaking down in SE Asia as the young look to the West for role models. Some strata of the cultures, such as the Chinese, see no hope of rising to the top echelon of their society. They, therefore, have become less reluctant to suffer the humility of wealth. Gradually, wealth is taking on the status it has in the West. Some of the young are impatient. They make a special effort to learn English for the sole purpose of making more money. A few take a more direct route by relieving you of your shoulder bag or accepting the gift of an unguarded camera. To be safe, carry only as much cash as you plan to spend in the day. (*Note:* Daily expenses depend on how you want to travel. Figure a minimum of $3 per day for a very basic budget.)

Traveler's checks are a valuable insurance. American Express and Thomas Cook have offices in the capitals of most SE Asian countries. Both have good records for replacing checks that are lost or stolen. It helps to have a police report to verify your claim. (Often the police charge you to write one up.) Keep the receipts of your traveler's check purchases and the check numbers with your passport, but separate from your checks. Without the receipt you'll be unable to redeem the lost traveler's checks except at the place where you purchased them.

Many travelers keep their valuables in a money belt. Wrap your traveler's checks in plastic to protect them from getting wet. They will void themselves with a chemical change caused by anything foreign passing through them in order to protect the company from photocopy fraud. The best rates of exchange are in the major cities. It takes about seven weeks to recover your money.

Miscellaneous: American Express offers free mail service to anyone holding one of their checks. Use their offices for your road mail or use c/o post restante. Credit cards, though convenient, are generally honored only at more expensive places, or you must pay a seven to ten percent service charge to use them.

Having Money Sent: You'll get your money the quickest by having the receiving bank in Asia send a wire to your home bank. Figure $20 for that and the return cable (also called wire or money transfer), plus a bank fee of about $6.50 for any amount up to $5000. You can have it sent in United States currency or in the currency of the country you're in. Allow a minimum of five working days for the transaction.

____Weather

The inevitable rain closes toward you and the treetops disappear. Then the world is water, gray. You stop to watch under a thatched roof. A native girl in a soaked sarong carrying a banana leaf for an umbrella scurries past you. You drink the air. The rain continues, and time sleeps. Silence. Then a few chirps. The sun is shining, and there's a cool breeze. The dust over the road has disappeared; the vibrant green around you is varnished with sparkling wet. Your clothes dry in a few minutes. Invisible steam thickens the air and blankets your skin. You hop on a vehicle and dive into the drying, cool ocean of air.

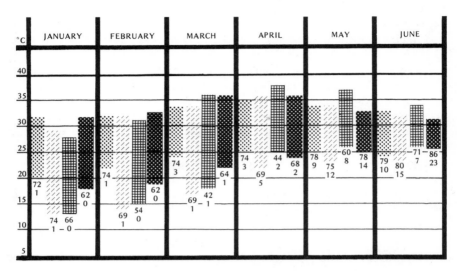

Temperatures are in Celsius at the left and Fahrenheit at the right and give the average daily range. Below each column is the mean relative humidity, with the usual number of days of rain for the month written beneath.

There are two seasons: wet and dry. The dry winds blow out of the northeast between October and February, bringing in cool air. Then there's a period of hot calm. By mid-May the daily rains have begun, although they rarely last a whole day. Bring a poncho. In general, cotton clothes are the most comfortable in tropic climates. Bring along some warm late autumn clothes if you plan to go to any mountain areas.

___Customs

Things aren't done this way in your home country. Men don't normally walk hand in hand back there. Here they walk with their arms draped over each other. But if a man touches a woman here, it's considered a lewd sexual invitation. Just to be seen in public with a foreign man is enough to ruin a woman's reputation—or to help advertise her profession. A proper woman is deeply insulted if a man's eyes slip below her neck. A woman-watcher must develop peripheral vision to save face.

Saving face is the art of giving a discount to reality while raising the value of interpersonal harmony. Take the word *yes*; it means something different in SE Asia. They believe a positive answer will make you feel better. So when you ask, "Is this the way?" you may five hours later find yourself a hundred kilometers "happy" in the wrong direction. Perhaps the aversion to *no* came from the days when a negative at the wrong moment to the wrong monarch would mean the sacred head of the speaker would roll in the mud. That's losing face!

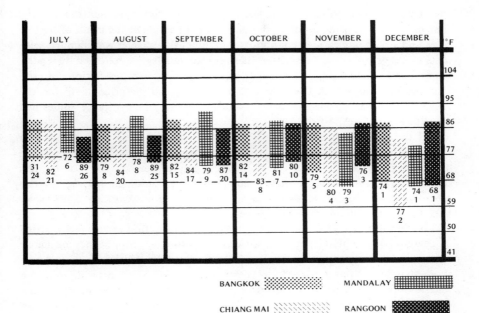

| | JULY | AUGUST | SEPTEMBER | OCTOBER | NOVEMBER | DECEMBER | °F |

BANGKOK   MANDALAY

CHIANG MAI   RANGOON

Whereas the head is sacred, the feet are vile. You can't get much lower than the bottom of your foot, and pointing it at someone's face implies that he is more loathsome than your feet. When he gets angry, he smiles. The ideal person never displays negative emotion in public. He is supposed to be detached from this life where nothing is permanent. Pride, fear, anxiousness, anger: all conjure up a smiling mask. To embarrass someone is to expose his surface calm as merely a mask. That's dangerous, for without *face* he has nothing to lose by expressing his anger. After a few months you begin to recognize the emptiness of an angry or embarrassed smile. It's a handy culture cue to have. It beats walking into a home with your shoes on and being welcomed by the smiling, red-faced family lined up at the door. Sometimes when the smiling at temples and shrines visited by unknowing foreigners becomes too bad, the elders decide to put a man at the threshold pointing at the shoes of the forgetful one. "You, shoe off."

After awhile you develop the Asian art of smiling yourself. You get plenty of practice over matters concerning privacy. In the Asian families there are often too many people for such a luxury as individual space. On a crowded city bus you're offered lessons when people step on your toes. They're too embarrassed to excuse themselves, so they giggle. It's not the way things are done in your home country.

Bargaining: "How much is that?" asks the traveler looking at some fruit. The vendor squatting behind her mangos eyes the bargainer's camera and lets a smile leak onto her lips. Her mangos are worth what she can get balanced by what the buyer is willing to pay. "You, how much?" She tries to get him to make the first offer and the game begins with righteous indignation at the insult of his low price and a ridiculously high counteroffer in hopes the traveler isn't familiar with local prices or currency. Teasing insults about the quality are followed by reports about family sicknesses, gossip about the village headman, predictions of crop size, renegotiations with two items, and references to the price of oil and the rising cost of transportation. All the while the grand joke of "price" hides just beneath the surface.

If the mango lady gets to know you, she'll squirrel away some of her best fruit until you come along and bargains more easily as a sign of friendship. If she can't understand English and you don't speak any of her language, she has less fun and wants some extra money as compensation. For all she knows, you can afford to pay a lot more. You're in her country and not working. She's never been farther from home than the village market.

It's not only the price of mangos that is negotiable. Taxi drivers feel justified in charging quadruple fare if no price was set before the trip. Money exchange rates vary; the more you exchange the better the rates will be. In shops—even those that have "fixed prices"—an automatic discount is given to anyone who asks. A hotel clerk usually has cheaper rooms than the one he first shows you and a special rate for a several-night's stay. Even the cost of visas sometimes varies with the bureaucrat who is trying to survive on his beggar wages.

How much is it? That depends.

Gifts: Traditionally, only merchants handled money. It was considered beneath the dignity of nobility and a sacrilege for a priest to be seen receiving money. To handle currency in public became a symbol of vulgarity. Gifts of money are discretely placed in envelopes.

Many of the families who offer you a place to stay would be deeply insulted by the crudeness if you offered them money, whereas a gift, especially from abroad, would be graciously accepted—but not as payment. Symbolically, golden items such as oranges or mangos are sufficient. (It's a good idea to bring some along when you visit a home.) If you eat their meals or are in any other way a burden, a more substantial gift will be reluctantly accepted. In remoter villages, bring tobacco, matches, nuts (peanuts are less prized), Aji No Moto (MSG; despite the potential harmful effects, they love it), and photos, colored brochures, and marbles for the children.

All giving and receiving should be done with the right hand. Touch your elbow with your left hand to be extra courteous.

_____Conduct

Sometimes the exotic is more than you can handle. Your mind throws the automatic circuit breaker just before your certainties burn up. Time deserts you in surroundings where transportation systems work on "maybe tomorrow" schedules, and where daytime here is nighttime at home. Your prejudices lurk in the dark, menacing, sensual eyes staring back at you. You begin seeing a smile as a cover for some sinister intent. Every phrase in the strange tongue spoken around you seems to be about you. You find yourself stripped of all certainty, and, just as you would if you were standing naked at a busy intersection, you tend to block out certain areas. This is paranoia.

Paranoia is uncomfortable at first, but it gives a form of relief to confusion. You start finding fault with the Asian ways instead of with yourself. You begin smelling the open sewers, the tobacco smoke, the uncomfortably pungent aromas of fermented fish paste frying. Even the incense and unfamiliar flowers seem too heavily sweet. You curl inside the safety of a culture bubble by sticking to the hotels and restaurants where other like-minded foreigners hang out. You travel from city to city as though going through mined enemy territory. Of course, those who wish to rob you, or to take advantage of the "looser sexual mores" of western women are drawn to the places where travelers most often frequent. They look for those who are most nervous, who probably have the most to lose.

If you don't want to be eaten, don't look like food. Relax. If you can't relax, fake it. Show a calm face. Walk away from the tourist touts and travelers traps. Adjust your priorities. Put adventure over comfort. Smile. You'll see what you're looking for and it looks good.

CROSS CULTURAL SPINNING

You sit in a restaurant at a table covered with linen. A single rose in a vase decorates the center. It's slow and easy here in Asia. The people are friendly, smiling. They giggle with embarrassment when they can't understand you. You recall the family you stayed with a while back. They gave you meals, a place to sleep and presents you couldn't refuse. They didn't understand a word of English. Of course, the bed was only a thin mat on the teakwood floor, but it was the best they had.

You look at the elegance around you. This isn't your everyday fare on the road. You love the contrasts.

You notice young locals in the dark outside the restaurant, peering at you and your camera on the table. They think you're a rich man. They can't understand why you wear plastic thongs if you can afford to own a camera. They've never traveled.

Buddhism

In 563 B.C., Gautama Buddha* was born a royal prince on the border between Nepal and India. He led a fairly sheltered existence until as a young adult he saw first a sick man, then someone starving, then a man wrinkled with age, and finally a corpse. Prince Gautama was horrified.

He left his wife and his newborn child, sneaked out of the palace, and cut off his hair, a symbol of his noble class. He began to look for the sense inside the madness of suffering.

---

*Buddha, the enlightened one, usually meaning Gautama Buddha although there have been others before and since who have attained the state of *Buddha*.

Buddha preferred that his followers not worship his likeness. Until 143 B.C., the wheel or the deer represented Buddha's teachings.

Through enlightenment he discovered the eight paths out of the apparent mess of life. 1) A person should be willing to adjust his theory about the make-up of the universe (Right Understanding). 2) A person should admit when his old theory is bunk (Right Thought). 3) He should keep his mouth closed unless what he says is pleasing, for words are too powerful to be wasted on a negative idea (Right Speech). 4) Don't step on a neighbor's toes (Right Actions). 5) He should give the fisherman enough rice for his catch (Right Livelihood). 6) He should keep trying and be patient (Right Effort). 7) What are you doing now? (Right Mindfulness). 8) It doesn't matter (Right Concentration).

In addition to the eight paths, he also suggested 227 precepts to help his followers in everyday life. To some it seemed a little strict: no swimming, no sex, no eating after noon. Even Buddha didn't think they were all absolute laws. In fact, one day he called a few of his close disciples together and told them only six precepts were absolute. The other 221 were merely spiritual exercise drills. Buddha never got around to saying which six were important.

Mahayana Buddhists (the larger vessel) believe that they know which six he was talking about. They allow for much more flexibility of action. When they went to China, Japan, Sumatra, and Java they quickly adapted so that old deities and ancestor-gods could continue to be worshipped as Boddhisattvas. These saints could intercede in human affaris. Thus, the old mother god of China became Kuan Yin, the Goddess of Mercy for Chinese Buddhists.

Meanwhile, other Buddhists were beginning to become concerned about the purity of their doctrine. They went back to the original 227 suggestions for the righteous life. They knew that laymen couldn't keep all the rules all of the time, so they allowed each man to go into the monkhood to practice being Buddha-like for at least some portion of his life. This branch of the Buddhist faith-philosophy is called Hinayana or Theravada Buddhism (the lesser vessel).

Buddhism spread throughout India primarily because of Asoka (ca. 245-207 B.C.), the king who conquered the subcontinent of India. Near the end of his life he repented his wars by becoming a monk-like ruler. Later, the Moslems came pouring in from the northwest to conquer the north of India. In the Tamil south, Hinduism had a resurgence. Buddhism remained strong only in Ceylon (Sri Lanka) where a theological university became the arbitrator of Theravada dogma.

Mon monarchs in Burma (who in turn taught the Thai in Sukotai), sent for priests to help them purify the faith. Abuses were common in blasphemous monasteries. Monks led ribald lives that they claimed were to the glory of Buddha. Both the Burma and Thai brotherhood of monks have gone through successive housecleaning and schisms. When the Tamil destroyed the Ceylon university library and much of the monkhood, Ceylon had to request a copy of the holy documents from Thailand. Thus, Thailand claims to be the preserver of the truest form of Buddhism as taught by Gautama. And Burma was host to the worldwide Sixth Buddhist Synod in 1954, on the twenty-five hundredth anniversary of Buddha's enlightenment.

___Ready for Takeoff, Even if Only in Your Mind

"Prease fasten you seatbelt," smiles the Asian stewardess having trouble with her *r*s and *l*s. At last the trip you've been planning for so long is about to begin. In your mind, the idea of travel has taken such a firm root in the realm of the future that finding it happening in the present seems unreal.

Unreality. That's something you're going to have to learn to live with. Deep down you know that no matter how much you've read about Asia, you are in for a jolt. There's no turning back now.

You've packed everything you'll need and probably some things you don't need. Your mind starts fumbling over the list one last time: backpack, check; rain gear, check; ticket and passport, *passport!* Only after your heart has started to race do you discover it in your shirt pocket.

Your pulse pounds out a heavy rhythm to accompany the end of the narrated life-jacket dance being performed by the stewardesses in front of you. The plane accelerates down the runway. *"Prease put you seat in an uplight position. Have a present fright."*

Burma

*Slow down. Set your watch back thirty minutes from Bangkok
time and your mind back a century. The Buddhists of Burma believe
that to hurry is to show a lack of trust in fate—a sure sign of insufficient
merit for the good life. Here in this human sanctuary speed has been
filtered out of time. It's always now and it feels like forever. In the
short eternity of your alloted seven days, you'll experience many
moments that aren't in pace with the rest of the world.
A horse-drawn cart becomes the most sensible means of transport
to the Mandalay airport. A passenger-tricycle driver carries a vase of
flowers on his handlebars. The driver of your jeep righteously refuses
to exceed the legal limit of twenty passengers. An Indian merchant
implores you to smuggle in Testoviron, an aphrodisiac, to sell to
him when you return from India. The black market whiskey
buyer suggests that you go into the government-run Tourist
Burma office to be sure his money isn't counterfeit. A
book vender refuses to sell his favorite books.
Temple roofs are a filigree of floral swirls in tin. In the midst
of the babble of a temple market countless Buddhas sit in serenity.
And always the stares are punctuated with smiles so genuine you
feel as though you must have met before. Don't take your
time; leave it on the plane when you fly into Rangoon.*

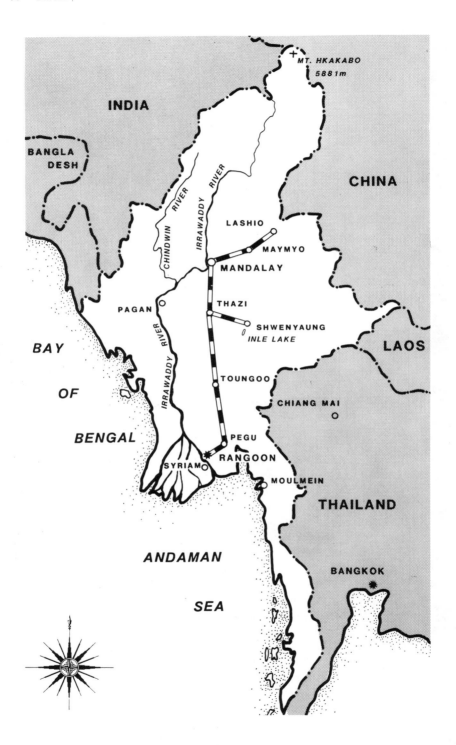

___Getting There

Routes: Flying is about the only legal way to enter the country. Aeroflot, Thai Air, Bangladesh's Biman Airlines, and the Burma Airways Corporation (UB, known in the country as BAC), are the main carriers landing at Mingalado Airport, twenty-three kilometers from Rangoon. UB flies twice weekly from Singapore, and stopovers are possible en route between Nepal and Bangkok or Calcutta and Bangkok. But most travelers buy the round trip ticket from Bangkok ($122). The Thursday flight on Thai Air arrives at 1140 and departs at 1720, thus giving you an extra four and a half hours in Burma. Avoid Saturday arrivals if you plan to travel out of Rangoon on the same day. Tourist Burma Office, where you must book your express train and plane tickets, closes on Saturday at 1200 and doesn't reopen until Monday.

Arriving: The plane angles down toward the flat, far-reaching plains of Central Burma and taxies along the runway. You walk to the airport terminal. No hurry. Unless you're first in line, there's no hurry. Line?! It's a multitude of people ten deep at a counter manned by a few ordinary-looking, worried officials. Take a closer look. These are not your usual harried bureaucrats. They meander from place to place, joking among themselves, some in their graceful *longyi* (sarongs). No hurry. You have time to notice the cobwebs in the corners. You have time to become part of this amazing blend of races. No hurry. If you could only breathe.

After immigration you search for your bag in the pile of luggage dumped on the concrete outside the terminal. "Get a sticker for your handbag," says a customs official. "Is this the right counter?" yells a confused tourist. "Those are my shoes on the outside and my underwear's packed inside," another foreigner informs the inspector. (There are no lockers, but Thai Air will store your excess bags if you flew in on their carrier.)

After spending perhaps two hours at the airport, you are accosted by taxi drivers the moment you come out. Taxis?! Before you is a vehicular geriatrics ward. Rows of vintage cars held together with wires and prayers wait for another wheezing ride down to Tourist Burma in the center of the city. (Figure Ks30 and a maximum of four passengers.) Before you've gone one kilometer you could have sold your whiskey and cigarettes. (Agree on a bottom price with the other passengers before you get in.) You rattle by a university with swarms of students in *longyi*. The women wear *thanaka* on their faces, a cooling cosmetic made

from aromatic sandalwood. Along the hedge-lined boulevards are some trees cropped like gum drops. Each red stoplight is a purgatory of exhaust fumes. Shwedagon Pagoda appears briefly like a chimera of gold in the late afternoon light. Turn the final corner and Sule Pagoda rises from the middle of the main avenue. The driver risks a swerve to the sidewalk and you've made it to Tourist Burma.

_____Getting Around

Be kind to yourself: use the internal transportation system as little as possible. Planes are a problem, trains a hassle, and buses and jeeps are time-consuming torture.

By Air: Given BAC's safety record, perhaps chances should be sold instead of tickets. Don't bother to schedule your flights outside of Burma. Even if you have booked a reserved seat, it won't be honored unless purchased or confirmed in Rangoon. Book all your flights in Rangoon. Even then there are no guarantees. An individual traveler holding a ticket and standing first at the BAC check-in counter can be bumped by a package tour. Schedules are pure fantasies, and all too often, flights are cancelled without warning. "Sometime today, probably. I can give a more definite schedule when the plane arrives," says the BAC official. (You pay a twenty-five percent service charge if you change your mind, and that must be done at least twenty-four hours in advance.) On the other hand, during off-tourist season (February-June, September-October), it is sometimes possible to buy your ticket at the airport while the plane's propellers are turning for takeoff. BAC provides free bus rides to the airport at inconveniently early times.

By Train: The Burmese are proud of their new express train between Rangoon and Mandalay. It zooms along at speeds faster than you can walk. Tourist Burma and the station master at Shwenyaung hold reserved seats for foreigners. They give no refunds and charge an additional fifty percent if you change your train reservation, (illness or death notwithstanding). Trains are tolerably comfortable, reasonably priced, and relatively reliable. On the local trains you will have plenty of time to get to know the people (and products) of the country, to munch on window-vendors' delicacies, and to study the terrain passing slowly by your open window.

By Bus and Jeep: Most of these land vehicles are miracles of mechanical longevity. Oil drums are pounded into shapes to replace the rusted out parts of WW II army trucks kept running with cannibalized portions of defunct vehicles. They carry Herculean loads of passengers, produce, gifts, and groceries along roads tar-surfaced by shovel and bucket. Comfort isn't a priority.

A Frantic and Frustrating Schedule: Arrive 1400; book night train to Mandalay and all flights. Leave 1800; arrive Mandalay 0700. Tour and trade. Leave 1200; arrive Maymyo 1500. Return the following morning for 1200 flight to Pagan. Tour Pagan Monday. Take Tuesday 0400 bus to Taunggyi; arrive 1400 or 1500. Stay in Shwenyaung and haggle for the eleven-kilometer ride to Yaungwe on Inle Lake. Stay at Inle Inn in Yaunghwe. Meander for minutes at the morning floating market Ywama; spend rest of the day at Phaungdaw U Pagoda in the middle of the lake. Spend night there free. (Sleep on floor with feet pointing away from the center Buddhas.) Catch early boat to Yaunghwe and jeep-car to airport in Heho, one hour away. At 1000 Thursday fly to Rangoon, leave bag at airport, tour Shwedagon and fly out. Breathe!

——*History*

The Rises and Falls of the Burmans: The borders of Burma, the second largest country in SE Asia, have never existed as they're shown on the map. States and vassal-states have ebbed and flowed in constant flux. Even today boundaries remain as alive with movement as the periphery of an amoeba.

Before the Burmans arrived the land was farmed by Mon people. They built ships of teak that could last up to a century and sailed them filled to the gunwales with cargos of rice, teak, cotton, velvet, ivory, rhino horns, silver, gold, precious gems—to India, Java, Arabia, China. The Pyu had grabbed part of the irrigated lands of the north by the time the Burmans arrived in the second century. These newcomers nibbled at the borders of the Mon Empire while totally devouring the Pyu. (Little is known about this vanished race; their only legacy is a few stones etched in a long-forgotten script.)

The Burman kingdom, meanwhile, expanded like cancer. In 1057 their king, Anawrahta of Pagan, attacked the Mon capital in Thaton. For the next two centuries the land belonged to the Burmans. In the late 1200s Kublai Khan sent emissaries to Pagan. The emissaries were beheaded for not removing their shoes before the king. The Khan's army descended on Pagan in 1287. The survivors fled and the houses rotted away, leaving Pagan an empty city of stone. The land was split between the Mon in Pegu and the Shan (a race from China related to the Thai), in Ava near Mandalay. Sandwiched between these two powers and vassal to both, the Burmans held on to their tiny kingdom in Toungoo for a couple of centuries, waiting for their chance.

Eventually, the Burman holdings swelled; the Mon capital of Pegu was taken by them in the middle of the sixteenth century. Under King Bayinnaung, the Burman forces spilled over into the plains of Thailand to Chiang Mai and all the way south to Ayuthia (1569). But within fifty years the Thai came back and delivered a humiliating defeat to the Burmans of Pegu. The heads of Pegu fled to Ava. Their remoteness allowed the Mon of Arakan to occupy the southwest state of Burma and to grow unchecked. The Mon retook Pegu and chased the Burmans out of their capital of Ava.

The Burman King Alaungpaya began his comeback from the small city of Shwebo, eighty kilometers north of Mandalay. By 1757 he had totally obliterated Pegu. His son, Bodawpaya, conquered the Kingdom of Arakan. The Mon have never recovered. Some say they have been absorbed into the Burman race like the Pyu. Others suggest they hide beneath the veneer of Burmese culture waiting for a chance to rise again.

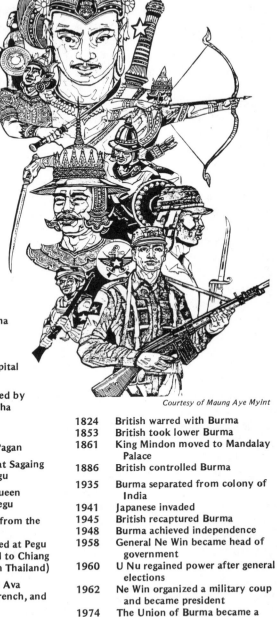

Courtesy of Maung Aye Myint

HISTORY OF BURMA

563-483 B.C.	Siddhartha Gautama Buddha lived
3rd Cent. B.C.	First Mon capital rose in Thaton
1st Cent. B.C.	Pyu established capital at Sri Ksetra
1057	Capital at Pagan established by Burman King Anawrahtha
1084-1167	Pagan's golden age
1287	Kublai Khan conquered Pagan
1315	Shan set up their capital at Sagaing
1369	Mon capital moved to Pegu
1453-1492	King Dhammazedi and Queen Shinsawbu reigned in Pegu
1519	Portuguese opened trade from the southern coast
1541	Burman Empire established at Pegu
1569	Burman Empire extended to Chiang Mai and Ayuthia (now in Thailand)
1635	Burman capital moved to Ava
17th Cent.	Trade with the British, French, and Dutch grew
1752	Mon conquered Ava and Pegu
1755	Burmans pushed north to Shwebo
1776	Burmans annihilated Ayuthia
1785	Burmans built capital at Amarapura
1824	British warred with Burma
1853	British took lower Burma
1861	King Mindon moved to Mandalay Palace
1886	British controlled Burma
1935	Burma separated from colony of India
1941	Japanese invaded
1945	British recaptured Burma
1948	Burma achieved independence
1958	General Ne Win became head of government
1960	U Nu regained power after general elections
1962	Ne Win organized a military coup and became president
1974	The Union of Burma became a socialist republic
1976	Attempted military coup snuffed
1981	Ne Win retired from presidency
1981-	San Yu, president of Burma

British Era: The Arakanese fled from the Burman forces into British India. For the Ava court borders were practical, but unspoken, limits to their powers. These diminished in direct proportion to the distance from the court. The Burmans pursued the rebels. The British had to draw a line somewhere. Diplomacy was stalemated when the ambassador from England refused to take off his shoes before the Asian King on the Lion Throne. By 1824, with troops finally freed from the Napoleonic Wars, the British won a brief conflict to take the lower part of Burma. Another short war in 1852 cost Burma its rich central plains. King Mindon was able to hold his diminished country together, but his successors, Thibaw and his queen, alienated the English by granting the French permission to build a railroad from Vientiane. The British feared the loss of the rich teak forests in the north. They were provided an excuse to interfere by the brutal and well-publicized massacre of all potential heirs to the throne. The British marched into Mandalay after two weeks and converted the lavish wooden palace into Fort Dufferin. King Thibaw and his queen were exiled and the British ruled from their offices in Dehli.

Not surprisingly, the Burmans did not adapt to the concept of rice farming for profit, and in the cities they proved to be less than efficient bureaucrats. The British found it difficult to teach them the concept of "hours" and impossible to communicate the idea of "minutes." Instead the Europeans chose as officials members of the Karen tribe who readily converted to Christianity. (The Karen mythology of a promised savior along with some amazing coincidences between their language and Hebrew led early missionaries to believe the Karen were one of the ten lost tribes of Israel.) To fill vacancies in Burma's officialdom, the British also imported ever-ready Indians who had learned English and the system.

WW II: Over the years, through a process of loans and foreclosures, the Burmans had lost control of their land. A group of "Thirty Comrades" led the dissatisfied to aid Japan in its takeover in December 1941. But the soldiers of the Rising Sun were harsher masters than the British had ever been. The "Thirty Comrades" secretly switched sides to help the underground movement's anti-Japanese activities.

Meanwhile, Burma became one of the main stages on which played the macabre drama of world war. The Flying Tigers of Chennault painted shark mouths on the noses of their planes, and on their wings they painted a Japanese rising sun for each enemy shot down. They bagged as many as fourteen-hundred Japanese aircraft. Merrill's Marauders fought five major and thirty minor conflicts, losing 2394 men out of the original 2830. Vinegar Joe Stillwell led a 182-km retreat through the jungle without losing a man. Wingate's "Chindits" wedded modern weaponry with ancient jungle tactics to create guerilla warfare. The Ledo Road cost allies "a man a mile" to build, and planes flying "the hump" over the Himalayas to supply Chinese troops lost a thousand men on the "aluminum plated" mountains. The war devastated the country; forty years later some of the rice fields are still not usable.

Independence: Aung San, leader of the "Thirty Comrades," petitioned Great Britain for a government separate from India. Instead, the British, nursing their own war wounds, were anxious to rid themselves of their war-devastated colonies and granted independence. Elections were held in April 1947 and Aung San was given the reins of government. But on June 19 he was assassinated and the short-

lived Union of Burma began to crumble. For two years, from 1958 to 1960, General Ne Win took control of the ineffective government of his comrade, U Nu. Then in 1962, Ne Win took control for two decades. Although he stepped down from his role as president in 1981, he is still in control of a country without stable borders.

Symbol of Burma

_____Government

The Union of Burma's existence is a minor miracle. The Karen, Shan, and other minority tribes had all made separate treaties with the British in the 1800s. During the negotiations for independence in the late 1940s, the separateness of these nations was understated. Each group was given its own state but they were tied together in a federation. The Karen were relegated to their traditional mountainous province. However, during British times, many Karen had moved to the plains and felt they deserved a greater share of its wealth. They revolted. At one time they controlled part of Rangoon, but the government fought back. (The government has been fighting back ever since; up to fifty percent of the country's land is yet to be pacified.)

Meanwhile in China, under the Kuomintang (KMT), Chiang Kai-Shek was defeated. Some Chinese irregulars, cut off from the main battalions in Taiwan, escaped into north Burma. From there they launched raids against Communist China. Burma couldn't collect taxes in the area. Worse, although the KMT never actually raised opium, they took charge of the trade routes and helped make it available in Rangoon. The KMT, supplied with guns by air via Taiwan from the United States, fought Burma as well as China. The Burmese asked the United States to stop supplying the arms. When the request was ignored, General Ne Win stopped all foreign aid and closed the country to outsiders. (The present seven-day visa is a relaxation of this policy.)

Each year the General appoints more military men to fill civilian posts; the Burmese "green revolution" means drab-olive uniforms in the National Cabinet. He initiated and continues to ad lib "the Burmese Way to Socialism" with lightning quick alterations in policy. Once, so the rumor goes, Ne Win was told by his astrologer that there would be a sudden shift to the right in Burma. The president, therefore, ordered all cars to drive on the right side of the road to fulfill the prophesy, without any change in his policies.

The custom of tipping is a current imported fad among government employees such as ticket sellers.

Economy

Rice is Burma's major export. Rice keeps its population of approximately thirty-two million from starving. Golden hills of rice on barges—thirteen million tons of it annually—flow down the Irrawaddy from the central plains. Ironically, inside Burma the grain is rationed. The government controls the buying and selling and only five kilograms of poor quality rice are sold to a household each month. Besides rice and teak (Burma has eighty percent of the world's teak), there are few other commodities in Burma that find places in the world market. Agriculture accounts for ninety percent of their export.

The government has nationalized the banks, oil refineries, the hydroelectric plant of Baluchaung (one of the largest in SE Asia), hotels, transportation, schools, even weaving and woodcarving. In addition, they have severely restricted imports in an attempt to stem the cash flow out of the country. The result is one of the most active black markets in the world, accounting for eighty percent of the nation's commerce. Cards of birth-control pills are sold by vendors on the sidewalks of Rangoon. There are flowered towels and cork thermoses from China, eau de cologne, "Kiss me quick" caps, fashion label underwear, silks from India, used books, 1978 Japanese picture calendars, transistors to pick up the BBC (Burma's only Broadcast Company), punk-rock cassettes, 1957 Chevy bumpers. A whole catalogue of products is available. But not quite everything. A jeep will have a brand new carburetor but no air cleaner. Cameras are sold back to the market when rare batteries give out. Prescription glasses are at best only close to the correct strength. And western whiskey will bring as much as three times the Bangkok retail price. A constant flow of goods is mule-packed into the country via the opium trails from northern Thailand, floated in on ships calling at Rangoon (customs officials seem surprisingly myopic), or carried deep in the pockets of travelers.

Language

The English called the Burmese script "bubble writing." With the exception of only a few characters, all the letters are composed of circles and segments of circles, an adaptation of the square Pali script brought from Ceylon along with

Buddhism. One theory suggests the rounded forms developed because the letters, instead of being carved on rock, were written by stylus on palm leaves. Though the written language originated to the south of Burma, the spoken language probably began to the north. It seems to be related only to the Himalayan Sikkim language. There's little language problem for the traveler; almost everywhere someone speaks English, although you may not always realize it's English they're speaking. Not until 1981 did then President Ne Win reverse his policy and order English to be taught once more in the schools. His decision came after his own daughter was refused admittance into a medical school in London.

CAPSULE VOCABULARY

Hello   *Min ga la ba*
excuse me   *jeezu pyu ywi*
good-bye   *tda da*
please   *jeezu pyau ba*
thank you   *jeezu tim ba day*
you're welcome   *jeezu ba day*
yes (polite)   *hoh kay*
yes (female)   *shin*
yes (male)   *kamyah*
no   *mohobu*
Where are you going?   *Beydt wa ma lay*
Where?   *beh ma lay*
It doesn't matter   *keit sa ma hyi ba bu*
How much?   *pey lau lay*
beautiful   *hlay day*
expensive   *zeem ya hay*
discount   *sho hze*
a little bit   *ne ne*
delicious   *yata shi lay*

slow   *pee byee*
fast   *myen myah*
right   *nga peh*
left   *bey peh*
water   *yea*
tea   *la bet yea*

1   *tit*   Ɔ
2   *nit*   J
3   *thone*   ၃
4   *lay*   ၄
5   *ngar*   ၅
6   *chak*   ၆
7   *kun nit*   ၇
8   *shit*   ∩
9   *ko*   ၉
10   *ta sair*   ၁၀

Note: "ky" is always pronounced "ch"; "th" sounds more like "t"; and "kt" sometimes comes out as "dj" or "z."

_Religion

Imagine a world coexisting with our own, where fairies live nine million years, where palm trees bear gems and fabulous garments, where pavements are crystal and palaces have columns of gold and walls of jewels, where the sound of quiet is a blissful melody and the air smells of fragrant flowers. This is the abode of the *dewa* (demigods), and *nat* (spirits). In this six-level heaven sumptuous feasts appear at a thought and young maidens grow on trees to satisfy carnal desires. Creatures of these realms are beyond humanity but not yet Buddha. Therefore, they are still caught in the cycle of birth-death-rebirth, although they

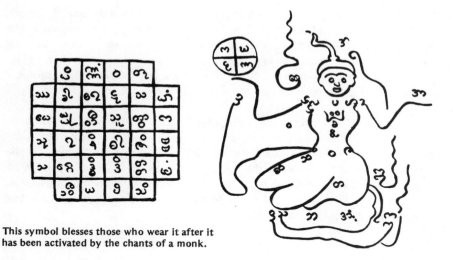

This symbol blesses those who wear it after it
has been activated by the chants of a monk.

have a nine-million-year breather between the phases. The Lord Buddha was said
to have been a *nat* in one of his many former lives (which included a term as a
white elephant, a tortoise, and a crane). The *nat* worship Buddha and earn merit
by helping man. Like Roman Catholic saints, they intercede in human affairs. In
this way, an ancient faith in animistic spirits has been amalgamated with Theravada Buddhism and is practiced by eighty-five percent of the Burmese. People
appease these often mischievous poltergeists—not all *nat* are good—by offerings
and special celebrations. A little more than a century ago, humans were sacrificed
to protect the gates of the palace from evil spirits—this, by the same Buddhists
who literally wouldn't kill a fly for fear of the negative effect on their karma.
The Burmese consult mediums, *weikza*, through whom these spirits are believed
to speak. They have a super-star pantheon of thirty-seven *nat* whose ranks now
include a little girl, a jovial drunkard, and a white horse.

___Events

In any other place the lights would appear anemic, but on the dark streets
of Burmese villages and cities, the florescent glow creates a surrealistic carnival.
There are stalls selling small, heavy logs of *thanaka* to be ground into the yellow
cosmetic paste applied to women's faces. Black market men's shirts hang behind
a mat of folded handkerchiefs. The next vendor sells alphabet posters to capital-
ize on the resurgence of English study. A Ferris wheel is turned by the weight of
riders as they climb to the top and hang on for the descent. Around the pagoda,
the center of all the activity, the sound of chanting can be heard and the rhythmic
voice of a monk at a microphone fills the air. Outside the pagoda, people sitting

in the street watch a black-and-white picture show (of the home-movie genre), about their leader shaking hands. Not far away the high-pitched singing of the *pwe* calls you to watch the acrobatic double-jointedness and grace of dancing Burmese women. The carnival ends at dawn. Except for Independence Day (January 4), Union Day (February 12), and Resistance Day (March 27), all Burmese holidays are religious festivals that coincide with new or full moons.

Thingyan: (late May to early April, often April 11). Moving from the old to the new year was a delicate occurrence in Burma. It took a council of full-time astrologers to ascertain the exact date of each year when King Thagyamin, the supreme *nat*, would descend to the center of this planet (i.e., Burma), and bring fulfillment of dreams in a water jug. Today the young, the majority in Burma, celebrate three to four days of water blessing by drenching "the part of your dress that clings most uncomfortably to you."

Kason: (April/May). Each new moon is a Buddha Day and the occasion for various temple festivals. But the full moon of Kason at the dramatic time just before monsoons begin, is the most universally celebrated Buddhist holiday. It marks the date when Gautama Buddha was born, subsequently enlightened, and years later ascended into Nirvana.

Waso: (June/July). On the full moon, the Buddhist lent begins. Members of the Sangha, brotherhood of monks, retreat into the monastery to study the words of Buddha and to meditate. Nine- to twelve-year-old boys are also allowed into the monastery, the first step on the road to Buddhahood. (At one time the rite of passage occurred at age fourteen, but this interfered with the exam period in British-run schools.) At a boy's *shin-pyu*, he becomes a "human" for the first time in his life. If he comes from a wealthy family he wears a bejeweled garment and is treated like Prince Gautama. The festivities surrounding him are designed to tempt him back to the world. Like the Prince, his worldly pleasures end when his hair is cut off and he is handed a plain crimson or saffron robe and an alms bowl.

Waso is everybody's last chance for celebrating before lent. Many families will fast and for the following three months there will be no festivals. For the sons and daughters of the devout, even romance must wait until the end of lent.

Thadingyut: (September/October). Buddha ascended into *Tavatimsa*, one of the six *nat* heavens, to preach a sermon to his mother, Maya. On his return, his path was lit by the glow of his own radiance. Light, therefore, is the most important symbol in this festival marking the end of lent. Pagodas are illuminated even more than usual. Little oil lamps are fastened to bamboo floats and sent drifting down the Irrawaddy like clusters of stars. In former times even the air was bright. Large balloons burst with fire, igniting fire crackers and occasionally the village below.

_Money: Five Paths to Burmese Kyat

Legal: Exchange your money at the government rate of approximately seven *kyats* (read chăt and abbreviated Ks), to one U.S. dollar. Check the amounts carefully: Some travelers have lost money at the airport exchange counter by hiding their calculators so they can sell them in the black market, instead of using them to check the rate. The amount you've exchanged will be recorded on your Currency Declaration Form. During your week's visit, each hotel room tariff and the cost of every train and plane ride should be recorded on this form. However, not all hotel managers remember to fill out your currency form, and some train station masters simply forget about the formality. Travelers who cash as little as ten dollars must watch their balance carefully, because the customs official will closely scrutinize their form at departure.

Aung San, leader of the independence movement

Whiskey and Cigarettes: Either the government unofficially sanctions the trade of these items on the black market or they believe all foreigners are alcoholics and nicotine addicts. Almost everyone coming into Rangoon carries along a duty-free bottle of Johnny Walker—the brand the English colonists preferred—and a carton of 555 cigarettes or their equivalent. At Sule Pagoda in front of the government-run Tourist Burma Office, Burmese merchants anxiously wait to buy. (You'll get an exchange rate of Ks17 to the U.S. dollar. In Maymyo and Inle Lake the rate is even better, especially for whiskey.)

The Diplomatic Store: You can shop here, but the locals can't. Buy cigarettes here and trade them on the black market for about Ks17 to the dollar. The trick is not to declare all your foreign currency when you enter the country. Then, even if you spend your hidden dollars at the Diplomatic Store, it will appear you are leaving with the same amount (minus the amount on your Currency Declaration Form). Of course, this trick is illegal.

Equally Illegal: Some travelers have failed to declare their cosmetics, perfume (a half litre can be imported legally, undeclared), transistors, calculators, camera lens and flash, prescription glasses, high quality ball-point pens, watches, and tennis shoes. In exchange for these items they receive good value in bartered goods. Customs charges up to 150 percent in tax on any item you "lose" during the week.

Embarrassingly Illegal: Many countries limit the amount of currency you can take out; Burma forbids you to bring any of their money in. The government rate of exchange is unrealistic. You can get more than two and a half times as much for your dollars at the exchange shops near the General Post Office in Bangkok. The penalty for smuggling in Burmese currency is severe.

___Visa

Seven days. Unless you apply for an extension to study Buddhism at the meditation center in Rangoon, you're not likely to receive a longer permit. (For some unknown reason, however, New Zealanders have asked for and received diplomatic visas of one month from the embassy in Bangkok.) The Burmese Embassy at 132 N. Sathorn Road in Bangkok will process your papers in twenty-four hours provided you have three pictures, a plane ticket out of Burma, and U.S. $5.00 or ฿100 Thai currency for the fee. Other embassies, including those in Kathmandu, Delhi, K.L., Manila, Dacca and Singapore, take two weeks to issue a visa.

___Conduct

Aneiksa, dokbka, anatta (change, suffering, no-self). These three words form a refrain that sums up the entire teachings of Buddha, the books of which fill three baskets called the *Tripitaka.* The Burmese realize the present life is one of many existences and know that change is inevitable. Their plans tend to be vague, the execution of them ineffective and open-ended. But they are rarely discouraged; they cheerfully accept failure and are incurable optimists.

Generally, the Burmese are willing to accept the strangeness of foreigners who have not yet left the ranks of animals to walk the path of Buddha. But even a rich woman from France had to argue for the privilege of wearing her panty hose up the steps of Shwedagon. Repeatedly, signs at temples read "No Foot-wearing Permitted." Even if the temple is under construction, dirty with bat guano, or hasn't been used in six centuries, footwear is out. For this slight sign of respect you'll receive innumerable heart-felt smiles and the world will be given to you with the right hand while the left touches the right elbow. It's worth it.

Rangoon: A Living Ruin

Street Scene: In the last century British engineers built a beautiful city of stately, sturdy structures centered around the Sule Pagoda. To capture the cooling breezes, they placed the wide streets in the same directions as the prevailing winds of the two separate monsoons. Rangoon has aged into a village of three million. Four-story buildings, green with moss, are not yet humbled by a single skyscraper. "Woody" buses made in America in the 1920s, like the telephone booths of the same era, are crammed with an uncountable number of people. Men in plaid *longyi* hang above the puffs of oil smoke on the buses' running boards. Three-wheeled *thombey* putter along like go-carts, and drivers pedal sidecars with their passengers sitting back to back beside them. People swarm the uprooted sidewalks, the crumbling blocks teetering beneath their feet. Merchants, waiting like scavengers, try to keep their trade alive with the carry-on packages from tourists: "Something to sell?" "Change money?" Fortune sellers spread their cloths on the sidewalks next to buildings. And the woman with the filtered water (full of amoebas), keeps slow time by pounding her plastic cup to attract customers.

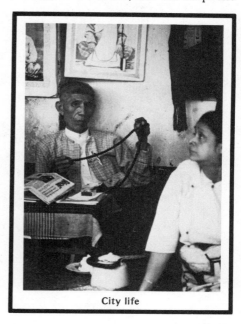

City life

Getting Around: Bus 10 rambles on a circular route past Shwedagon, Kyauk Htat Gyi (read chauk to gee), and Nga Htat Gyi Pagodas, Inya Lake and the Karaweik Restaurant, the jetty for the ferry to Syriam, Botataung Pagoda, the Strand Hotel, and Bogyoke Market. It's more than just a ride; it's a Burmese experience. Three-wheeled *thombey* or toy Mazda trucks (the only motor vehicles made in Burma at a factory in Prome), can be hired as taxis. They are less crowded and much more comfortable than buses and guarantee a front seat view as your driver weaves through traffic like a soccer player. Taxis charge Ks20 per hour after considerable bargaining. Bicycles can be rented for Ks2 an hour or Ks15 a day. Ask a Burmese friend to bargain for you.

——*Shwedagon*

The Pegu Mountain Range reaches from the Himalayas far south into the central alluvial plains. On the summit of the last spur of the Pegu Range, the *Paya* (Great Pagoda), overlooks Rangoon. The *Paya* is SE Asia's most sacred

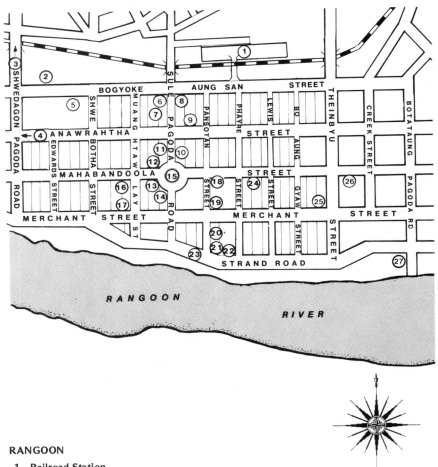

RANGOON

1. Railroad Station
2. Bogyoke Market
3. Bus 10 to Shwedagon
4. To Indian and Chinese Markets
5. Kyaik Htiyo Bus Station
6. Peoples Pastry Shop
7. Bus to Pegu
8. Dagon Hotel
9. Shwe Eng Si Restaurant
10. Bus for Kyauk Htat Gyi
11. Diplomatic Shop
12. Yatha Tea Shop
13. Tourist Burma
14. Garden Guest House
15. Sule Pagoda
16. Narawath Arakanese Restaurant
17. Bus 9 to Airport
18. Mahabandoola Park
19. Bank
20. Museum
21. Post Office
22. Strand Hotel
23. Bus 10 to Htinbonseik, Syriam ferry
24. Nilarwin Yogurt Shop
25. Minn Minn Restaurant
26. YMCA
27. Botataung Pagoda

Black Indian statues guard the Chidawya Tazaung (Pavilion) on the platform of Shwedagon. It's a wonder the great pagoda needs no other guard. The bud on top of the bell alone is plated with 850 kilograms of gold. From the terraces to the seven-tiered metal umbrella there are 6326 diamonds, rubies, jade, and sapphires. Humility seems appropriate.

Chidawya Tazaung

Shwedagon Pagoda, Rangoon

Shwedagon Pagoda, Rangoon

Buddhist monument. In a chamber hidden deep inside are buried not only relics of Gautama Buddha, but also of the three Buddhas that preceeded him. Kings and queens have given their weight in gold and jewels to decorate the pagoda. Boulders of alabaster, floated down the Irrawaddy River, have been carved into hundreds of sitting, standing, and reclining Buddha images. Other giant Buddhas are built of brick and covered with plaster. Countless pavilions cluster about the pagoda. Small spires have been constructed to adorn the places the pious choose to meditate. Pavilions are elaborately scalloped and carved with tin and teak. On the platform, worshippers say *ah mhya* (come and share), three times, and those that hear answer *sadu* (well done), three times. Vibrant!

Legend: After the first three Buddhas had left in succession a staff, a water-filter, and a piece of a garment, a monstrous scorpion came to dwell on the hill. He was so large he ate an elephant a day. He built a palisade out of the ivory. Seven foreign ships, attracted by the gleaming white, came to investigate and carried off the tusks. The scorpion gave chase and the ships were forced to squeeze between the claws of a gigantic crab. They made it but the scorpion didn't. The crab died of indigestion and the sacred hill was safe.

About the same time two brothers, Dove and Plenty, left from a nearby town to take rice to India where there was an extreme food shortage. (Some things never change.) A *nat*, their mother from a former existence, directed them to the spot where Gautama was meditating. They arrived just at the moment of enlightenment and presented him with rice. The Buddha gave them eight of his hairs in a golden casket and instructed them to put them on a hill with the gifts left by the other Buddhas. They were to recognize the spot by a tree balanced on the peak with neither branches nor roots touching the ground. After years of searching, and having four of the sacred hairs stolen, they dejectedly returned home. Somebody suggested they ask old *nat* Sule for advice. He was so senile they had to prop his eyelids open with tree trunks for him to see what they wanted. He pointed out the hill to the brothers. Before they buried the casket they opened it and discovered eight hairs—the four stolen ones had been miraculously returned. It rained knee-deep with jewels. The other relics were discovered in the small one-meter high pagoda made of meteorite rock (now displayed at Botataung Pagoda). The hairs and relics were covered by a pagoda, then by another, and then another. A series of seven pagodas, from gold to silver, tin, copper, lead, marble, and finally to iron preceded the present brick one to reach a height of almost one hundred meters. The land where the pagoda's shadow fell was consecrated as holy ground forever.

Myth History: Queen Shinsawbu, the Mon monarch of Pegu (1453-1472), gave her weight in gold to cover the entire *Paya*, from *hti* (top) to platform. She gazed at the shrine from her bed before she last closed her eyes. Her son-in-law, Dhammazedi, lavished four times his weight in gold on the pagoda. He also gave a bronze bell weighing 180,000 *viss* (about 50 tons).

De Brito, a Portuguese adventurer, had carved out his own empire in Syriam across the Irrawaddy from Rangoon. He tried to take this bell, forged for peace, to cast it into cannons. It sank into the waters of the Irrawaddy. Sinbyushin, King of Ava, raised the pagoda to its present height in 1774. His son, Singu, gave a bell of 55,555 *viss* (only 16 tons).

In 1853, after the "Second Burmese War," the British decided the bell would make a fine trophy and carried it off. They dropped it in the river. And all the king's army and his engineers failed to make it reappear. With the bell lost for good in the Irrawaddy, some locals asked if the British would mind if they were to try to raise the bell again. The English scoffed, "Sure, give it a try if you like." And they did. They attached countless tubes of bamboo to float the big bell to the surface.

The British converted this sacred temple of Buddha, in whose name no war was ever fought, into an arsenal. They closed up the west gate, taking out the whole stairway. They cleared a path for a new west entrance and built a tram to the north going past the arsenal. Over the years nature participated in the pagoda's destruction with eight earthquakes. In 1931, fire spread up the staricase of the reopened western entrance and burnt to charcoal every piece of teak, leaving a blackened semicircle around the northern side.

Enter from the South: When you finally take your eyes off those gaudy *chinthe* (lion-like giant sentinels), you'll notice the sign "Footwearing Prohibited." So, it's bare feet on a gritty terra-cotta floor and then on an even dirtier cave-like stairway. At the top of the first long flight of stairs is where the pagoda moat and drawbridge once were. On the stairway arcade to the sacred shrine, vendors sell little purple dolls, owls, puppet horses, alms bowls, *thanaka* and the mortar and pestle with which to grind it, red and black lacquer pages from the Buddhist scripture, altars, hosts of golden Buddhas, drums, cymbals, flutes, bells with clappers shaped like bodhi leaves, handmade tweezers, old clothes, irons that use hot coal, incense, candles, patches of gold leaf, small paper prayer umbrellas, flowers, . . .

Once on the platform, you look up to where your eyes start seeing lashes. From its one-hundred-meter-high perch at the top, a seventy-six carat diamond throws light back at the sun. You can't see it. To represent their detachment for things of this world, Buddhists placed thousands of their most precious gems where no one sees them, giving beauty back to the universe. And yes, that's real gold, tons of it.

Flowing Clockwise: No Buddha-respecting person would go counterclockwise. Heavy with gold and silver gilt, the ornate Konagama Adoration Hall (*A*) is flanked by the Mercury planet post, one of eight posts equally spaced around the base, one for each day of the week (Wednesday has been split in two). One person pours water over the animal figure that represents the day on which he was born and touches the earth, while another chants a carny-song-prayer. You pass pagoda after pagoda and the differences among them disappear. It becomes

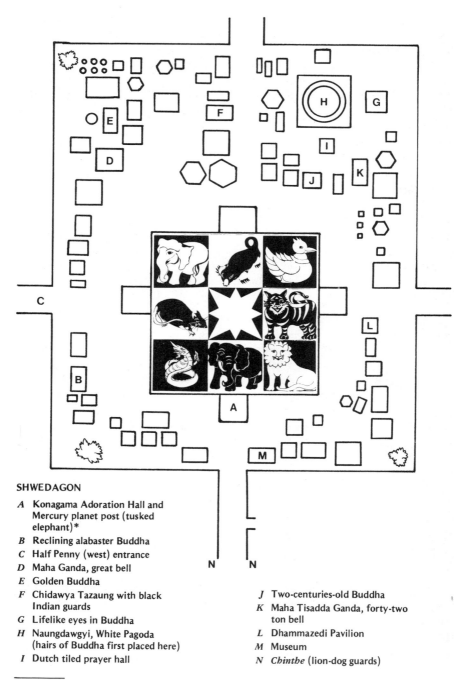

SHWEDAGON

A Konagama Adoration Hall and Mercury planet post (tusked elephant)*

B Reclining alabaster Buddha

C Half Penny (west) entrance

D Maha Ganda, great bell

E Golden Buddha

F Chidawya Tazaung with black Indian guards

G Lifelike eyes in Buddha

H Naungdawgyi, White Pagoda (hairs of Buddha first placed here)

I Dutch tiled prayer hall

J Two-centuries-old Buddha

K Maha Tisadda Ganda, forty-two ton bell

L Dhammazedi Pavilion

M Museum

N *Chinthe* (lion-dog guards)

*See page 192 for a description of the days of the week and their characteristics.

hard to tell that each elfin character is unique. In a glass case to the southwest is the aged, hobbit-like Sule *nat*.

Not far away are small rounded prayer stones. A devout meditates for stronger willpower. To test the success of his meditation, he lifts a prayer stone to see if it feels light or heavy. (If the latter, it's back to the beads.) Farther north a long slender alabaster Buddha (*B*) reclines in a *tazaung* (a pavilion for prayer). The west entrance (*C*) is deserted by comparison to the others—a ghostly place with dull red corinthian columns. Vegetable gardens grow on the slopes alongside the Half Penny entrance, so named because it was built from the minuscule donations of the poor.

To the northwest hangs Maha Ganda, (the great sweet voice) (*D*), the bell that made the British blush. A large golden Buddha (*E*) sits in the adjacent pavilion. The covered colonnade is decorated with painted wood-sculpted friezes. Black Indians dressed in diaper-like dhoti guard the gates of a pavilion to the north (*F*).

The last pavilion (*G*), hidden away in the northeast corner, is rarely visited. Few take the time to notice even the main Buddha much less the one to his left in the corner. This humble figure has "eyes that see": Unlike the normal Burmese statue with black painted pupils, his are deep and sparkling. The locals believe with a mellow certainty that these eyes are a miracle.

The second largest pagoda (*H*) on the platform was built to temporarily house the relics before the main *paya* was finished. The chamber to the south (*I*) is floored with Dutch-windmill tiles. The second figure from the center Buddha has two different-sized eyes. It represents Izza-Gawn, the fabled monk who overcame his blindness through faith. (Unfortunately his servant, who helped with the transplant, fetched one eye from a goat and the other from a bullock.) The two-centuries-old Buddha (*J*) is rumored to conceal a secret tunnel into the central relic chamber underneath the large pagoda. The large bell to the east (*K*), cast in 1841, weighs forty-two tons. The east entrance leads down to a nowhere road with several side paths through teak rabbit-warrens of monasteries; a great place to get lost. Dhammazedi pavilion (*L*) has carvings that tell the story of Dove and Plenty, merchants extraordinaire. After this overwhelming pandemonium of pagodas, escape to the quiet of the Bodhi tree and absorb the glowing white face of the Buddha or the green and gold plains stretching to the Irrawaddy.

____Around Royal Lake

Kyauk Htat Gyi: Out beyond the sidewalks of Rangoon, where birds can be heard above the chaos of traffic, lies a seventy-meter-long Buddha. The Burmese claim this Buddha is the world's longest human figure. Its glassy life-like eyes, almost 1.5 meters across, are ringed by eyelashes 1.5 centimeters thick. Although huge, the figure is sensitive to the human form, with attention given to details such as the thickness of the folded robe and the restful way the feet are turned. Down behind the reclining giant, crimson-robed monks lounge at the windows of their teak monastery.

Kyauk Htat Gyi

Largest Buddha figure in the world

Nga Htat Gyi: Across the road and up a long L-shaped stairway is a giant sitting Buddha. Plaster serpents crawl out from a moat that surrounds the Buddha. He looks uncharacteristically concerned. A rock crystal larger than a human head rests on a dilapidated table in front of him. The covered platform is big—there's enough room for the passengers of twenty Rangoon buses to meditate in solitude. It feels even more spacious because of the mirrored colonnade and fashioned balustrade that overlooks the thatched roofs of houses down the hill. A painting on the wall shows the flag of Japan as if in a dream. Romance novels are sold along the steps, side-by-side with garlic, onions, and flowers. Children attempt a "hello," falter and giggle off. Monks with alms bowls humbly pass—if they can resist the worldly temptation to stare. Out on the street a woman offers one spoonful of her rationed rice to each monk in a too-long line. Maybe that's why the Buddha looks worried.

Karaweik Restaurant: Unless you get stuck with extra *kyats*—something that often happens to those who underestimate the needs of the black market—don't eat here; it's expensive. Instead, plan a late afternoon beer at the restaurant before relaxing on the shore. Here you can see the orange of sunset joined by the distant Shwedagon golden spire echoed in the surface of Royal Lake. The restaurant is a 1970's reproduction of the double-hulled barge of the Ava king. The stacked roof lines are alive with filigree. Except for its color, the sculpted concrete is an excellent imitation of woodcarving. Rarely has stucco and cement appeared so elegant.

Classical Dance: In the evenings at 2000, classical Burmese dancers perform in this neo-classical Burmese setting for modern tourist prices. As an alternative, go to the National Dancing School on Shwedagon Pagoda Road and watch the kids laugh at you when you try to bend your fingers back. When they finally get around to dancing, their movements are elbows-in Burmese beauty. Besides happening upon a *pwe* at a temple festival, you might also catch a dance performance at Jubilee Hall.

The Burmese Oscar award

___Downtown Pagodas

Sule Pagoda: This temple was built to honor the *nat* who helped Dove and Plenty find the sacred hill for Shwedagon. Its geometric spire, forty-eight meters high, towers over all other buildings in the heart of Rangoon. Around the circular periphery of this traffic island, photographers dive under the black cloths of their ancient cameras to take professional photos, and merchants stop foreigners to encourage them to take a capitalistic counter-culture trip to the Diplomatic Store. Inside the temple, circular tubes of colored neon lights flash expanding halos behind the heads of the main Buddhas.

Botataung Pagoda: You are allowed to enter into the inner chambers of the *chedi*, a series of triangular rooms with mosaics of mirrors flickering on walls and ceilings. Walk a zigzag circular path and stare deep into the walls at your fragmented reflection. After three slow circumambulations, the lights continue to dance even after you close your eyes. It could alter your mind. That's the idea.

Nat at Sule Pagoda, Rangoon

___Other Sights

National Museum: Located on Phayre Street between Merchant and Maha-bandoola Streets, the museum's collection consists mostly of regalia from the last dynasty at the Ava court in Mandalay (1857-1885). The impressive eight-meter-high Lion Throne of King Thibaw was at the Calcutta Museum during WW II, and thus escaped destruction from incendiary bombs dropped on Mandalay Palace.

Mai La Mu Pagoda: The primary and pastel colors of the rounded, plastic-looking sculptures could compete with a corner of Disneyland. But the stories represented are from Buddha's former lives called "the Jataka scenes." Stop at U Myint Swe whose sign displays his degrees: BA, RL II. This "expert astrologer and scientific palmist" will read your palm by the "Cairo System" if you cross his palm with Ks20; "OK, Ks15. Special deal." His room is a menagerie of amulets, young coconut sprouts to ward off evil *nat*, metal plates inscribed in each corner, and altars with banana offerings in front.

The temple receives its name from the mother of King Okkalapa, mythical founder of Rangoon. It's located in the Okkalapa suburb about twenty minutes by *thombey* from the city center. Tip the driver and he'll wait while you have a simple meal at an open-air stall or have a mystic look at your future: "You will be joyous in your life, but avoid long journeys this year."

___Shopping

Thein Gyu, The Indian Market: It's India with the volume turned down. There's very little advertisement or hustle here. You dive into shadow from the bright city street and are swallowed by the merchants' cubicles. Teak cabinets stacked nearly three meters high with goods tower above you on both sides of library-like aisles. Burlap bags of beans, grains, tangerines, oranges, tangelos, limes, avocados, palm oil, and bananas are offered in a heap in one section. Powdered, raw-leaf, granular, corn or prepackaged spices are in another part. Using balance scales some vendors weigh out leaf tea by the *tecal* and the *viss*. There's coffee, cocoa, chicory and various mixtures of these. Cigars, with degrees of quality from the natural exploding kind to ones with deluxe corn-husk filters in toilet-paper-roll-like packages, are found not far from stacks of colored crepe paper. Notebooks with dancing Burmese beauties and big-eyed, mod-dressed girls are in vertical files on the raised platforms of several stalls. There are odd-sized envelopes, some seventy-five centimeters long, some with cliché sentiments—love, joy, peace, don't hate—printed in English on the outside. There are slate pencils and small hand blackboards "for the children's lessons, sir." Strips of lace and silks are surrounded by women buying for some home tailoring. Men's sarongs are sold in more sedate stalls in a separate area.

The market can't be confined inside. On sidewalks you'll see termite mountains of *thanaka* paste. The women vendors love to be asked by a foreign woman for a test of this cosmetic. They might finish off the beauty treatment by fixing *thazin* in her hair. These flowers sprout from a rooted bulb and will stay alive in her hair for two weeks.

Bogyoke Market: (read Bo kyo ji). Broad lanes separate stalls of fabric, antiques, and housewares in this comprehensive bazaar for Burmese crafts. There are sequined chickens, dance costumes with glittering accessories, government-school paintings on black velvet, weavings from the Shan states, black lacquerware from Pagan, teak carvings from Mandalay, and delicate sculpted ivory. It's a place to browse or to spend the *kyat* left at the end of the week. Prices once stated ring through eternity like a precept of Buddhism. There's little luck bargaining.

Rangoon street vendor

___Stay

Dagon Hotel: A young Al Capone would look natural walking up the steep steps to the second-floor, saloon-like cafe and then going through the curtains and up to the next floor. But instead of a gangster, an attendant dressed in a starched white uniform waits for you. He and the nameless others that haunt the desk keep a clean place (by Burmese standards). They won't tolerate anyone who acts without the proper decorum. Make jokes about the hotel and they quote ridiculously expensive prices to get rid of the disrespectful. Normally, you'll get the straight prices for the fat rectangular rooms with sinks that sometimes work and beds covered by clouds of mosquito netting. Towels are provided. The lobby on each floor leads out to a balcony from which you can see the gold-blazing spires of both Sule and Shwedagon Pagodas.

Garden Guest House: On several floors the halls have been partitioned with painted plywood. Dorm beds squeak in the large central lobby on each floor. The manager is considerate of travelers' money-form problems. The showers work and mosquito nets are in place. Travelers gather around the table and chairs or lean out the open windows to watch the quasi-legal whiskey and cigarettes being sold and bought.

YMCA: Moldy-gray gloom hangs on the walls, but the floors are clean. There are dorm beds without mattress, softer sleeping singles, and deluxe rooms. It's aged institutional.

Strand Hotel: Like the enamel on their bathtubs, the charm of this poorman's colonial hotel is wearing thin. The higher up you go the more tolerable the deterioration.

The Sikh Temple: Men are welcome to stay free for up to seven days, if they respect proscriptions against alcohol and women on the premises.

___Food

Burmese Food: The waiters scurry about when you walk into the Minn Minn at 434 Merchant Street. The older waiter with the dusty English takes your order for curry—tea, a plate of raw vegetables, sour soup, and a mound of rice. The meat dishes aren't large (they rarely are in Burma even by Asian standards), but the waiters are attentive and bring more curry sauce at no extra charge. At the end of the meal, they serve you tea and *jaggery* sweets.

Arakanese Food: The Narawath Restaurant is hard to find; it's about thirty meters south of Mahabandoola Street at 84 30th Street and has an inconspicuous blue and yellow sign written in Burmese. But it's worth the search, especially if you enjoy spicy eating. (Arakan is between the central plains and India and the food grows hotter as you move west.) The owners moved to Rangoon about five years ago and appear to keep the recipes true. Try *wathani*, succulent pork that melts in your mouth. Ask for a lean piece; Arakanese like theirs fatty. Or sit back and let it come: soup, salad, dahl, curry, insidious green-fire-they-can't-be-good-for-you condiments. This intimate place with only six tables is likely to be alive with the free-belly laughter of Arakanese who hover around it.

Chinese Food: The Palace Restaurant is near the Pagan Bookstore at 84 37th Street, just north of Merchant Street. It has a separate room for each table and its menu is extensive, high-protein, and delicious. You'll find cheaper Chinese noodles and see big brass pots of *kow suey*, delicious fried noodles, at Kyioh (read Chi oh), on Latter Street. (Latter Street is named after the English lieutenant who discovered a secret passage into Shwedagon that allowed the British to overrun the temple.)

Indian Food: A proprietor on Anawrahta Street will order his cook to dip deep into his big stainless-steel streetside kettle for yellow briyani rice. And for *lassi* go to Nilarwin and order the sweet yogurt drink. In season they add real strawberries. Sit on stools at terra-cotta topped tables near a mirror where the young male workers constantly preen. Their yogurt is fresh and kept in a chest refrigerator.

Snacks: Yatha Tea Shop is just west of Sule Pagoda. Plates of tempting sweet cakes are brought to your table. The firm-willed have been known to resist for minutes. For novelty, you can try *faluda*, an icy milk-syrup drink, but you're safer staying with hot or bottled drinks. The airy lobby of the Strand Hotel is a proper, decadent place to watch a Mandalay beer bottle sweat.

___Services

Tourist Burma: It's set up at the center of town to help tourists spend their money. All trains and planes must be booked out of Rangoon and air flights out of Burma should be reconfirmed here or at the Thai Air office next door. The tourist counter people are generally friendly and helpful with suggestions, and will gladly watch your pack until they close at 2000. (The train station also has a baggage room.) Tourist Burma quits selling train tickets for the night express to Mandalay at 1600. The money exchange counter is open 1930-0800.

Meditation: Think about it. You're guaranteed at least a two-week visa extension if you're willing to undergo "sitting practice" and walking meditation for twenty hours a day. See the Mhasi Meditation Center, found fittingly at 16 Hermitage Road, or the International Meditation Center at 31 Inya Myaing Road. The latter is university affiliated. It's tough.

Pagan Bookstore: The selection at 100 37th Street is small, but if you want any books about Burma other than the grim government publications sold at the Diplomatic Store, you'll have to search among these shelves of recovered books. (Some even have missing pages photocopied and inserted.) The really good books are so rare the owner will only let you read them at his place. He'll never sell them. In Burma they're irreplacable. Bring books for trade—recent novels, science texts, English dictionaries. If you don't, he'll close.

Syriam and Kyauktan: Across the Rangoon River

Getting There: Rangoon isn't the only Burma and the easiest trip out to rural life begins at the Htinbonseik Jetty—take Bus 12 from any bus stop on Bogyoke Aung San Street. A ferry pulls out into the Pazundaung Creek at 0530 and 1300, (the last boat returns at 1800), bound for Syriam across the Irrawaddy. Leaning at the railing during the forty-five-minute trip (there are no seats), you can watch a modest number of vessels: tramp coastal steamers, wooden barges, and craft with bandaged sails. Shwedagon grows smaller as Kyaik Khauk Pagoda grows nearer. On board, a gypsy woman coaxes her two infants to dance while she suckles a baby and sings. Then a sad-eyed child begs you for a few *pyas*. When you reach the wooden dock on the other side, look for a horse cart to jiggle you up the hill. The large pagoda at the top is trimmed in velvet moss and the view is a sweeping panorama of hazy plains beside the river.

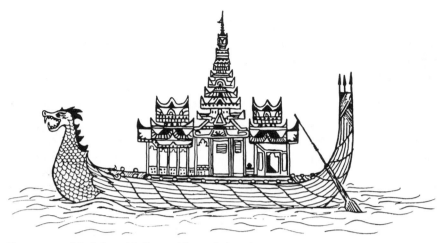

Sixty men paddled the gold gilt royal barge designed to represent
the *karaweik* bird, the sacred mount of the Hindu god Vishnu.

Ye Le Paya, Mid-River Pagoda: The island in Mohwon Kya River, a five-minute rowboat ride from Kyauktan, is built solid with pavilions and pagodas. Buy some food to attract the fish; monsters a meter long and weighing thirty kilograms inhabit the safe, sacred waters around the temple. At a country market along the gravel lane of Kyauktan a woman squats, chats, and smokes a giant corn-husk wrapped cheroot (cigar). Behind her are crudely glazed cups.

The jolting trip from Syriam to Kyauktan takes fifty minutes on a truck with hurt-hard benches. It doesn't depart until the last seat is twice taken. Try for a place up front in the cab, or hang on at the back for the view, or be prepared to deal with close inquisitive stares.

DE BRITO, THE PORTUGUESE KING OF LOWER BURMA

De Brito came east as a cabin boy and found his way into the Arakan court. King Razagyi, ruler of all the Mon after his victory over Pegu, appointed the foreigner to manage customs and taxes at Syriam, a port busy with trade near the mouth of Burma's main river. The tax man wasn't popular and he soon found it necessary to build a fortification. After expediently marrying the viceroy's daughter in Goa, De Brito returned to Syriam with men and artillery. In 1599 he used his personal army of mercenaries to pillage Pegu of sacred Buddhist treasures. For thirteen years he sent his gunships out to coerce all grain barges to his port, his kingdom. But in Burma, karma is a certainty. In 1633 twelve thousand Burmans beseiged the city and surged in when the four hundred foreign defenders had fired all their powder. Most of the survivors were taken as slaves to various small northern villages near Shwebo. But De Brito was judged a demon, impaled, and left to die a slow death. Today, the few ruins left from this historical footnote are located in the grounds of an oil refinery. The only way in is with a Tourist Burma tour.

Pegu: Two Birds and a Stone

History: The Mon are gone, scattered by the Burman army. "Taliang," the name they used for themselves when they ruled the silted flatlands of Burma, has become the Burmese word meaning "trampled under foot." Some historical anthropologists, citing the similarities in the names, claim the Mon came from Telingana, India (not far from Madras), in the early centuries A.D. They settled in the Gulf of Martaban where the Sittang River meets the Andaman Sea. Their kingdom flourished in the vast delta land and they constructed systems of irrigation in the north where the southwestern monsoons fail to bring water. Their capital in Thaton, near present-day Moulmein, was sacked by Anawrahtha of Pagan in 1057. However, the Mon again grew strong after Kublai Khan annihilated Pagan in 1287, and they moved their capital to Pegu in 1365.

Dhammazedi (1472-1492), perhaps the mightiest king of Pegu, saw a schism in Buddhism eroding his power and brought monks from Ceylon to revitalize the faith. A frenetic period of construction followed. Pegu became a fabulous cityport famed among European sailors for its magnificence. The Golden Days of the Hamsawaddy Dynasty continued for 200 years, fed by the wealth of rice and teak floated down the Sittang.

In 1541 the Burman Dynasty of Toungoo maneuvered into the position of power, supplanting the Mon monarch's control of Pegu. King Bayinnaung (1550-1581) extended his kingdom all the way to Chiang Mai and twice sacked Ayuthia, the heart of Siam. The wars were costly despite the treasures carried off. Meanwhile, the Sittang River was silting in, robbing the king's coffers of trade revenue. The Burmans retreated to Toungoo. In an attempt to quell a rebellion, King Anaukhpetlun plundered Pegu, finishing off the Portuguese in Syriam at the same time. Then the Thai attacked with such vengeance even the paddy farmers felt the horror of their scorching hatred. In 1635 King Thalun moved north to Ava for protection.

The Mon rose once more in 1740 to take Pegu for their own, only to be ravished less than two decades later. Pegu was demolished, its temples destroyed, and its people were either enslaved or escaped as refugees to Thailand. Today, Pegu yawns beside the sluggish Sittang, afloat only with bamboo rafts.

Getting There: The hole-in-the-wall bus station on Maung Htaw Lay Street in Rangoon is marked by a faded sign showing two *hamsa* birds, one on top of the other. A bus leaves every hour between 0600 and 1830. If you arrive late, you'll have to take a wooden stool in the aisle. The two-hour, eighty-kilometer ride takes you past the British War Cemetery with the patterned foreign graves of 27,000 allied soldiers. Occasionally the flat distance is interrupted by hills that rise so abruptly they appear man-made. Pagodas crown the tops.

The last bus returns at 1630. Reserve your return trip when you arrive in Pegu. Taxis will take you there and back for Ks200, a fair price if you intend to go out of Pegu to visit the giant Buddhas of Kyaik Pun. The express train doesn't stop here and the other trains stop everywhere.

Shwemawdaw Pagoda: You can't avoid the comparison to Shwedagon when you first gaze at the huge handbell-shaped tower aspiring to heaven in gold magnificence. Inside, two hairs of Buddha lie on a diamond-studded slab of creamy marble, covered with a lid embedded with emeralds, placed inside a gold pagoda, surrounded by images of Gautama, and buried beneath a mountain of brick. Earthquakes jolted the pagoda twice, before completely crumbling it in 1930. A brick portion of the toppled spire rests at the base, a small spire balanced atop it

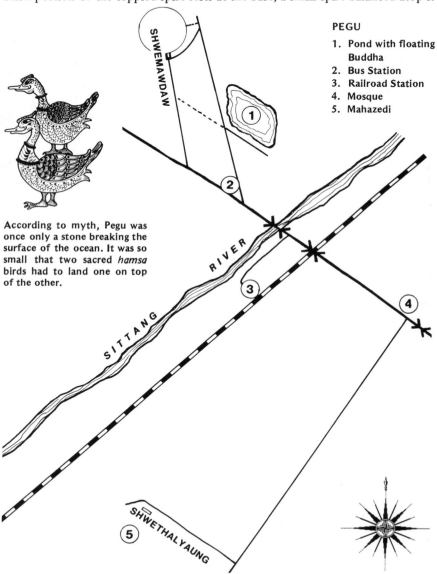

PEGU

1. Pond with floating Buddha
2. Bus Station
3. Railroad Station
4. Mosque
5. Mahazedi

According to myth, Pegu was once only a stone breaking the surface of the ocean. It was so small that two sacred *hamsa* birds had to land one on top of the other.

like the precarious perch of Kyaik-tiyo Pagoda on the mountain's edge near Moulmein.
With the last reconstruction in 1952, Shwemawdaw grew taller than Shwedagon. And
when the diamond-laden golden *hti* was
placed on top in 1954, it reached out 114
meters into the sky.

Climb Shwemawdaw's *zaungdan* (the
staircase). Buddhas sit composed in the open
mouths of the two monstrous salmon-colored
chinthe, crested lions set out as sentinels at
the west side approach. You could sit on one
of the lion's toes. Like covered stairways to
pagodas throughout the country, the arcade
is an ascending bazaar.

Chinthe

Near Shwemawdaw: On the rise east of the pagoda are the remains of walls
of the ancient city. Nearby, the ruin of the Shwehinthgone Chedi (stupa), marks
the spots where the two *hamsa* are said to have landed.

Shwethalyuang, Giant Reclining Buddha: He
slept forgotten underneath jungle growth for a century and a quarter after the sacking of Pegu in 1757.
Then a British engineer needed a bed for his railroad tracks and discovered a mound full of bricks.
"Full of what?" cried the monks. The monks
searched their records, gave their pagodas a recount,
and discovered they had misplaced Shwethalyuang,
a fifty-five-meter-long reclining image of Buddha
built in 994. Today, Buddha's long, slender torso lies
in an Erector-Set shed much like a richly-appointed
airplane hanger. Buddha doesn't care; he reclines
on his pile of mirrored pillows with an enigmatic
smile on his face. At the other end of the echoing
pavilion, spirals of inlaid glass represent the master's
toe prints. Behind lies a lake and the distant Maha-
chedi, a pagoda restored in the 1980s after four
centuries in ruin.

Buddha's revered footprint

To and From Shwethalyuang: Take a bus running from downtown Pegu
past the front of the pavilion, or ride the three kilometers in style on a hired
horse cart. Consider walking back to town—past silver and goldsmiths' shops,
pottery for sale on the ground beside the road, a shop specializing in scissors and
knives, a blacksmith, and a maker of wooden shoes. Find the obscure pond behind a moss-laden wall and spend a quiet moment.

Shwegugyi and Kyaik Pun: Queen Shinsawbu (1453-1472) had been widowed twice before she wedded herself and her country to the king in Ava. But she wasn't happy with the marriage and enlisted two loyal monks, versed in the science of supernatural incantations, to help her escape. On the flight south on the Irrawaddy, the monks magically changed the boat's colors several times. Twenty-three years later the queen wished to pass on her throne to one of these monks and set out symbols of royalty for one of their alms bowls. One monk, Dhammazedi, got there first, The other, Dhamapala, demurred—he was downright disappointed—but died in a duel of occult power.

Dhammazedi didn't feel marrying Shinsawbu's daughter was enough to secure the throne for himself. He first brought in authoritative monks from Ceylon to clean the land of scattered religious abuses. He built or improved countless pagodas, among them Shwegugyi and Kyaik Pun. Even sceptics of his devotion took notice when the earthquake toppled Shwemawdaw pagoda in 1492, the year of his death.

Shwegugyi Pagoda: A copy of the Bodhgaya temple in India, an unusually straight style for Burma, Shwegugyi is located in an area of ruins five kilometers south of town. Small reliefs at the base represent various animal-headed men, grotesque mercenaries in the army of Mara that attacked the Buddha. They lost.

Kyaik Pun: Massive thirty-three-meter-high sitting Buddhas dominate your eye. Four sisters helped on the construction, each on her own side. They vowed chastity as a gift to make the images more sacred. One married. Three statues remain standing.

Mandalay: Last Days of the Lion Throne

The predominant street sound in Burma's second largest city comes from the pounding hooves of cart-pulling ponies. The wide streets are dirt—extending all the way to the wooden buildings on either side. There's room for benches, some trees, and a line of bicycles and sidecars along the edges of the movement of pedestrians, peddlers, and bullock carts. A lane in the center grudgingly widens to allow rusty buses and bouncing jeeps to pass. Motor vehicles are an afterthought. In 1981 this attitude cost Mandalay thousands of homes. Because of a sharp rise in gasoline prices, the whole fleet of four fire trucks was caught without fuel when fire struck. Temporary shacks built for the homeless on the slopes of Mandalay Hill have only their orderly arrangement and the fading newness of the woven bamboo to differentiate them from other residential areas.

___History

The recent fire was a minor tragedy in the city's short history. Mandalay was founded in 1858 when King Mindon ordered construction of his palace. Walls, almost two kilometers on each side, were built to mark the boundaries of

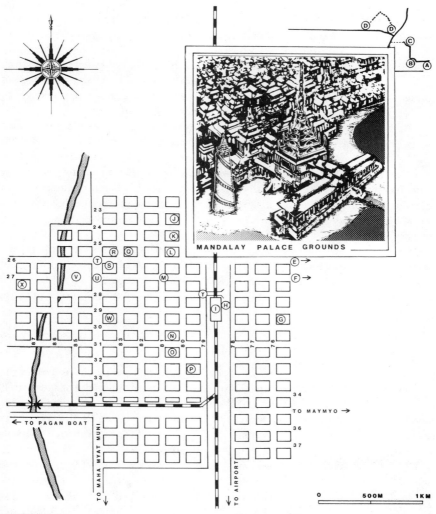

MANDALAY PALACE GROUNDS

MANDALAY

A Shwenandaw Kyaung (monastery)
B Atumashi Kyaung
C Kuthdaw Pagoda
D Kyau-taugyi Pagoda–Mandalay Hill
E Mandalay Hotel; Tourist Burma Office
F Tunhla Hotel (Myamardalar)
G General Hospital
H Jeeps to Maymyo
I Train Station
J Post Office
K Museum and Library
L Telecom and Telegraph

M Bus to Inle Lake
N Man Shwe Myu Hotel
O Man San Dar Win Guest House
P Shwe Wah Restaurant
Q Mann Restaurant
R Nylon Ice Cream Bar
S Man Thiri Restaurant
T Clocktower
U Bus/Truck to Sagaing, Amarapura, Ava (#8)
V Zegyo Market
W Hong Kong Restaurant
X Eindawya Pagoda
Y Overpass

this sacred place of power. It was built three kilometers from the river so that foreign steamers wouldn't "disturb the royal repose." The palace was in the heart of a planned city inhabited by the peasants of Amarapura who had been forced to relocate by the king's soldiers. *Pyathat* (multi-tiered towers), rose from each corner and above the gates at the center of each side. Underneath each of these a child was buried alive to become *nat-thein*, a spirit strong enough to protect the interior from the malevolent beings pressing in.

It was a copy of Asoka's palace but, instead of gemstones set into marble as in the Indian royal residence, Mindon's was made of crafted teak pavilions embedded with glass and overlaid with gold. The Lion's Room, tallest (seventy-eight meters) and most magnificent of all, stood in the very center. The outer halls had nails that were set with points up to prevent the barefoot subjects from moving with unseemly—and dangerous—haste so near the monarch. Inside the Lion's Room was the Lion Throne, a two-story-high staired pedestal of gold-covered teak.

Mindon moved into his palace in 1860. Twenty-five years later, the British marched in, cleared away some of the women's quarters for barracks, converted the hall of audience into a Tamil mission chapel for their Indian soldiers, and exiled Thibaw and his queen to Calcutta. In 1945, in a battle to retake the city, British bombs turned the palace to ashes.

Transport

Mandalay Express: The inside of the Rangoon railroad station is dark in the twilight as you make your way to the train. A last minute purchase of soda water, and at 1845 the train pulls away. As a man walks through the train passing out comic books in Burmese, you search around for a way to enjoy the rest of the evening. It won't be easy. It's thirteen long hours on the road to Mandalay. The seats are immediately uncomfortable, a twangy voice blares over the speakers, and the lights glare at you with stark fluorescence. Don't complain to the Burman across the aisle; he's relishing the luxury of windows and clean toilets that work, water to wash, and locked doors that keep the aisle from becoming a market full of people and products. By the time you're in the country, the outside dark is interrupted only by the passing of Christmas-tree-lit pagodas. Lucky foreigners find a claustrophobic spot on the floor underneath the seats to lie flat, with the rhythm of the tracks bobbing their fitful sleep. (Bring a newspaper to cover the floor.) Dull sermons are short in comparison to each quarter hour that passes.

Water served to train passengers

Finally, the sun gives its reassuring light to the flat countryside, and now you can see a few large wooden houses, barely alive with waking peasants. A woman, arms folded to the morning cool, stops to watch the train; toddlers play in the dirt behind her. Farther on, two bullocks in front of a cart nose the edge of the tracks and wait for you to pass. Men start walking slowly to the day's work in their fields. Inside the train, a man collects his rented books, women straighten their hair and apply cherry red lipstick, and people rise from the floor. At 0745, the train pulls past a sign reading "Charitable Cow Center" and into Mandalay station.

Other Transportation to Mandalay: The plane from Rangoon leaves at 0750; it costs extra if you're stuck on a jet (the choice is not yours); and it takes up to three hours, depending on whether or not it stops at Heho. From the airport, buses or horse carts will take you the six and a half kilometers north to the city. Planes also fly daily from Pagan and Heho. A bus leaves Pagan at 0430 from Tourist Burma's office and arrives at Mandalay at 1400.

Getting Around: The city stretches out along the west and south sides of the palace—meaning long walks along hot, dusty streets. *Tonga* (pony carts), have little doors at the back to allow you to enter the steep-slanting, canvas-covered cabs. The lanterns on their sides dance along the dark streets at night. Bikes with sidecars are pedaled around the city, often taking convoluted courses because their routes are restricted. Antiquated buses are the place to meet the folks. Take Bus 10 from 79th Street to the airport, Bus 2 to Maha Myat Muni and eventually to the airport, Buses 1, 6, and 10 to Maha Myat Muni, blue Bus 8 to the Mingun ferry jetty, and Bus 4 to Mandalay Hill. Buses 1 and 5 start at the clocktower near the market and take you past the Mandalay Hotel to Mandalay Hill. Jeeps, the only private vehicles, can be rented for across town, to the airport, and for six hours of sightseeing from the Mandalay Hotel.

Sights

Northeast of the Palace Moat: King Mindon died in his sleeping pavilion and his successor, Thibaw, decided he needed a new, ghost-free place to sleep. He had the pavilion dismantled and transferred the boards to their present site for his private meditation chamber. The inlaid glass and carving of the pavilion, the only remains of the Mandalay Palace, have since become the Shwenandaw Kyaung Monastery.

Shwenandaw Kyaung, Mandalay

Atumashi Kyaung, Mandalay

Walking west from the monastery you pass the remains of Atumashi Kyaung, the multi-terraced building ravished by fire in 1892. There are staircases leading to nowhere, still guarded by demons sculpted to defend the vanished interior that once was rich with purple curtains and velvet carpets. Just to the north, Kuthdaw Pagoda is surrounded by rows of white plastered huts like mausoleums. Sheltered inside each hut are two stones. Each stone is etched with one page of the 1458-page *Tripitaka*, the "three baskets" of notes from Buddha's teaching. Children play hide-and-seek among the files of buildings. At the center pagoda, the coin operated puppet-danceomatic plays a calliope tune while people lounge on the cool stone floor.

Going west towards the stairway to Mandalay Hill, you pass the main hall of Kyau-taugyi Pagoda. This chamber of mirrors surrounds the giant sitting Buddha, smooth-hewn from a single boulder of marble. This slab was floated down the river from the Sagyin quarry. To move it from the jetty, three kilometers away, took thirteen days and 10,000 men. At the foot of one of its two southern staircases, Mandalay Hill has *chinthe* with permanent curls in their manes. Tin roofs cover the steps all the way up the 236-meter-high hill. School boys in uniform beg for pens; nuns offer you a chance to earn merit by donating a few *kyat*; photographers with cardboard reflectors pose tourists by cutouts of cars; and men sell sweet frozen water sticks. At the summit you gaze across the terrain to the distant haze that collects at the base of the Shan Mountains. The palace below is green with tree tops.

Maha Myat Muni Pagoda: The people of Mandalay call it simply *payagyi*, the great pagoda. A 3.8-meter-high image has, perhaps, the actual features of Gautama Buddha. According to legend it was cast in huge sections of brass during Buddha's visit to an Arakan kingdom. Although this kingdom probably didn't exist until six centuries after the master's death, worshippers aren't deterred. So many pilgrims have attached small squares of gold leaf to the body of the image, it has literally grown fat with wealth.

In the antechamber to the northwest of the main hall are six bronze figures that several times have become spoils of war. Originally, they were crafted by Khmer artists to the glory of Angkor Wat in Kampuchea. The Thai carried them off to their capital in Ayuthia. Then the Mon took them to Pegu and later to Mrauk U (Myokaung, Arakan). Finally, Bodawpaya's raiders returned with them to Amarapura in 1784. One of the figures is a three-headed elephant (mount of the Hindu god Indra). The others are three horse-like lions and two warriors. The latter are believed to have healing powers for those who touch the parts of the statues that correspond to their illnesses. Judging from the shiny stomach with the belly button practically gone, even the Burmese have trouble with their spicy food.

During festivals, the corridors leading to the shrine are filled with the faithful. But even on normal days these halls are rarely quiet. The entrance is an arcade of crafts for sale: papier-mâché *nat* dolls, laquerware in black and amber, curtains of Buddha-beads, *ka ma wa* (palm-leaf pages of Pali writing of the master's words), ivory bone carvings of miniature Buddhas and combs, marionettes, white silk umbrellas, paper parasols, solid color sarongs with bold borders trimmed with gold thread woven in the Kachin States. Off in the side alleys you'll find Burmese carving wood images or pounding metal into *hti* for the country's temples. Furniture, like the honored pedestals for temple offerings, is constructed here to be shipped throughout Burma. Shelters for Buddha statues stand sanded and ready for lacquer. The products of one cubicle lie in different stages—from raw material to dust-covered piles of finished items that look as though they'd always been there. It's a factory for temple paraphernalia.

When you come out of the cool east colonnade, you're struck by the warm sun. You get an idea why the eighteenth-century monarch Bodawpaya had a covered brick road built from his palace to this entrance. Only a few cobbled portions remain of this six-kilometer royal road.

Eindawya Pagoda: Enter the meter-wide alley near the west end of Zegyo Market—where 27th Road should be—and squeeze past people walking in the opposite direction until you come to a main road. A cow grazes by the side. A woman washes her child at the public water faucet. Ox-cart wheels squeal slowly along the dirt path. Men, backs curved by their loads, gain on the cart. Vivid colors catch the eye when you turn into the pagoda. On either side of the approach, women sew on turn-of-the-century treadle machines. The deep-burgandy bags and vests hang for sale beside crimson and saffron robes. Women sitting on platforms chat through red, betel-stained smiles or joke innocently with casual monks. Not-so-saintly novices scramble to get in camera range. The pagoda conceals a clouded translucent Buddha carried back to Burma in 1839 from Bodhgaya, the site where Gautama became enlightened.

Zegyo Night Market: The young woman scratches a match to flame (no mean trick with Burmese matches), and a candle is lit to shine on the four or five black market items she has collected on a tray. A man pumps his lantern until it exhales light on his exhibition of rare Raleigh bicycle parts laid out on the gravel. A board on a box is the table for a few plastic toys illuminated by a single smoking oil lamp.

After sundown, 84th Street between 26th and 28th becomes a market, a social event. Young people stroll down the lanes between meter-wide stores of goods. The teenage girl adjusts the plastic comb adorning her hair. A woman at a cart sells Lucky Strike, Benson and Hedges, and, of course, *Dooya* (the Burmese brand in the green package). And in the shadows of an alley, a crew-cut vendor opens a tiny brass vial of opium oil.

Working Water Buffaloes: These animals are living tractors, working with cumbersome precision to maneuver logs from the river onto trucks. They're no match for elephants, but they beat a hundred strained backs. You see them slogging logs at the end of Road C; take a *tonga*.

___Practicalities

Stay: When you get off the Mandalay express, you'll be funneled through gates to a narrow room. There Tourist Burma will process you like an inductee about to be assigned to his barracks. You have four choices and are asked to decide on one, sight unseen. You pay here; it will be recorded. (If you go to the hotel first, you'll be sent back to the station.)

At Man Shwe Myu Hotel, on 31st Street east of 81st, a member of the Chinese family will welcome you as you enter this two-story structure. You'll receive tea, maybe cookies, and a room where you can rest until later in the day when other guests get around to checking out. (No official time is set.) Use one of the three splash-baths and liberal toilet facilities. The rooms are arranged for two, with mosquito nets over cots, and are cleaned down to the permanent finger marks on the walls. A family meditation room with Buddha, mats, and family photographs is on the second floor. The hotel will store your bags, and when you leave, the manager will give you a small owl for *your* good luck and his card for *his* prosperity.

Man San Dar Win Guest House is across the street and, for the same price, has gregarious managers who aren't much help when you bargain with sidecar drivers. They serve free Chinese tea in the lobby, a hangout for many travelers. Room 18, farthest from the bath, is on the corner and has two windows opening onto a pond out back. The mosquitos compete with the bedbugs for food.

The Tunhla Hotel is located in a quieter neighborhood on the east end of 27th Road. This hotel is a mellow place with lawn and swimming pool (more like a green water reservoir). The government nationalized it and changed the name to Myamardalar, but few locals know it by that name. The distance from town draws sidecar and *tonga* drivers to congregate outside the gates. They have a penchant for doubling prices and ignoring attempts at bargaining.

Mandalay Hotel, Burma's tourist-class hotel across from the south moat of the palace, looks like a cleaned up barracks. The staff is burnt out from fielding complaints by dissatisfied tenants who have paid Ks50 for their air-conditioned double.

Note: Anyone who has problems balancing his Currency Declaration Form might consider other alternatives: Sleep the night on the deck of the Pagan boat that leaves the next morning; or, take a jeep directly from the train station to Maymyo.

Food: Shwe Wah Restaurant on 80th Street near 32nd Road serves delicious chicken and walnut or duck in a succulent black bean sauce for Ks8. Sit near the front to watch the life gathering around the public faucet on the street. The Mann Restaurant on 83rd Street between 25th and 26th Roads, and the Hong Kong on 29th Street between 83rd and 84th also have tasty Chinese food. Both serve plenty of fresh vegetables from Maymyo: cauliflower, peas, cabbage, untranslatable greens, . . .

Attempt some *durian* ice cream, and sit beneath posters belonging in a parlor of the thirties at the Nylon Ice Cream Bar on 83rd Street across from the Mann. Both the tea shops that are conveniently situated on the corners near the cheap hotels serve *nanpya* (sweet flat bread, fried until it bubbles), and other inexpensive snacks. The government-subsidized Man Thiri Restaurant east of the clocktower has the cheapest beer in Mandalay. Pineapple, pears, pomelos, mangos, and strawberries share the same July-to-October season. Buy them along 79th Street.

Paranoia Corner: Burmese gems are legend. Miners were once sent down into the earth wearing locked wire meshed masks at the ruby mines of Mogok to the north of Mandalay. Today, this city remains the outlet for rubies, jade, sapphires, and silica. Rumor has it that underpaid Tourist Burma employees recommend pedicab drivers who "secretly" suggest a trip to Rocky's shop where some of the world's most expensive glass is unloaded on the naive. And Rocky's not the only one. Travelers with their karma crooked have invested in gems only to have them change to melted sand during their plane flight out of the country. Unless you're a gemologist, don't buy gems in Burma!

From Mandalay: Rebook your plane or purchase your train tickets at the Tourist Burma office in the Mandalay Hotel (open 0800-1600). Sleeping car berths to Rangoon are available if you request them three days in advance.

Deserted Cities Near Mandalay

Under each corner of the royal city, four jugs filled to a rounded brim with oil were buried. The Brahman priests checked them once each seven years and from their condition deduced the physical and spiritual state of the palace, and thereby the entire kingdom. If the jugs were intact the palace—the center of the universe—was deemed powerful enough to resist evil cosmic forces. When a few jars broke, it was time to move to a new capital with a new palace and a new world center (an ancient method of urban renewal).

For the people living around the palace this was bad news. Fifty-two of them would be buried alive around the new city to become protective spirits for the monarch—a practice of the court astrologers who happened to be Hindu

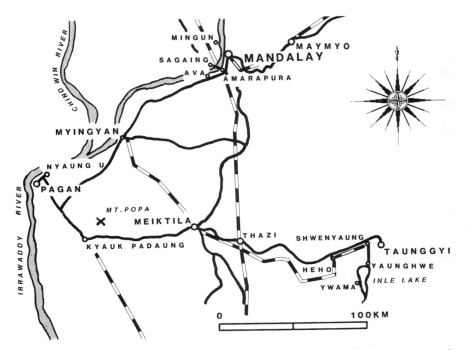

Brahmin priests, not Buddhists. Those selected for sacrifice had to be pure of body: boys without tattoos and girls without pierced ears. People would hide in their homes to avoid being selected by the king's officials. The officials would throw celebrations to lure people out.

The first capital in the north after the Pagan era was the Shan city of Sagaing around the turn of the fourteenth century, but by 1364 it had moved to Ava. The Burmans started in Shwebo in 1760, but in four years they moved to Ava. Nineteen years later, Amarapura was built on the urging of the cracked pots. This palace was abandoned in 1823 in favor of Ava once more. An earthquake caused the jars to break in 1838 and it was back to Amarapura. The last move to Mandalay occurred in 1860. Maybe that's why pierced ears and tattoos were so popular.

Mingun: After his prayers, the Burmese Buddhist pours water over a *nat* statue with long wet hair, hammers a bell, and touches the ground so that the spirits of water, air, and earth are called into harmony with the pilgrim's strengthened willpower. The bell has the added advantage of calling others to reconfirm their commitment to the path. The larger the bell, the farther the sound carries. The bell at Mingun weighs eighty-seven tons and is the world's largest uncracked bell. It was cast by pouring molten metal in a large hole. Bands clashed and people gathered for the great ceremony. Women were so caught up in the energy of its creation that they cast their gold jewelry into the pit to the glory of Buddha. Today, the 3.7-meter-high bell hangs on a thick steel I-beam, ready for you to call up the powers.

Next to the bell towers perhaps the world's largest pile of bricks. Although Mingun was never a capital, King Bodawpaya chose it to be the site of his 150-meter-high pagoda. They scrapped the project when he died. While you stand in the shadow of the unfinished pagoda, a small girl earns merit by carrying a warm glass of tea to you from her home a hundred meters away. Take off your shoes if you intend to climb via the gully-sized crack on the right caused by the 1838 earthquake. On the other side of the bell, Hsinbyume Pagoda is white with cake frosting decorations. Smooth alabaster statues of Buddha sit on the terrace at the top.

To get to Mingun, take a ferry from the jetty at the end of B road. They leave several times in the morning, beginning at 0600. The trip takes an hour. As you make your way upstream, you pass houses built on the assumption that floods are not a disaster but a necessity. Get off at the second dock and walk through the infirmary. A man asking for donations rings a gong to call the world to testify to your merit. Catch the boat for the thirty-minute return ride from the downstream dock, past the five-meter-high model of the great unfinished Pondawpaya Pagoda.

Amarapura: Take Bus 8 (which goes through Amarapura on its way to Ava), from the corner of 84th and 27th or the Sagaing truck-bus between 84th and 85th. Get off at the roadside cooling platforms and walk a hundred meters across the rice paddies to the village. You'll hear the weaving shuttle thudding as you enter the cluster of thatched homes. The streets are ankle deep in dirt, except where they're eroded ruts. You take to a ditch to let an ox cart pass. You're a stranger here and the focus of all the eyes looking up from their tiring work. Peek into the dark loom-filled rooms beneath the stilted houses. Here they make formal *longyi*, called *acheithtameins*, that are longer than ordinary sarongs. Nearby you'll hear the working of metal as Buddhas are cast in bronze.

Someone will point you to the Patodawgyi Pagoda in the village. Spider nets robe a stucco Buddha resting among the crumbling stone and overgrown with flowers and plants green from the moisture of the nearby river. A walk along the top of the five terraces of the main pagoda will reveal vistas of rice plains and the Irrawaddy River. It's like a symbol of the Buddhist doctrine of change and detachment: Built to perfection, it's now allowed to fade slowly, quietly back into the ground. To the south is Lake Taungthaman, a wet season body of water. A man picks his way among the missing planks of U Bein Bridge, a one-kilometer span of teak lumber salvaged from the great palace of Ava when the court moved two centuries ago.

Ava: All that remain of the walls that once outlined a giant *chinthe* is the former north gate. Where once stood the magnificent palace, the leaning Nanmyin Watchtower, ironically built to prevent ruin, stands alone. But for a century Ava was the only name Europeans knew in Burma. Its magnificence spread out in the form of pagodas rising over the countryside. The Maha Aungmye Bonzan monastery, not far from the palace, was built in 1818 by the married queen for her favorite abbot. (There was a great deal of whispering about those two.) With its flamboyance of eaves and angles, the plaster imitates Burmese woodcraft. Walk through the rice paddies toward any of the many pagodas rising above the green pedestal of trees.

You climb into a Zaya Mann truck-bus heading for Sagaing, get off before it crosses the Ava Bridge, and follow the dusty road to the Myitnge River where a ferry waits. On the other side of the river, you hire a *tonga* to the ruins. It's a poetic way to enter; "Ava" means "lake's entrance." When the rivers flood, the reason for the name is obvious.

Sagaing: There's majesty in the way the hills rise from the Irrawaddy, each crowned and necklaced with pearly-white pagodas like the fabled city of a child's dream. Paths meant only for the feet of pilgrims lace the slopes and knot near cooling platforms before branching off toward the next intersection. *Pongyi* in robes that borrow color from the dawn hug their black lacquer bowls to their stomachs as they return to one of the 600 monasteries here.

Sagaing! The name echoes the clash of cymbals, which along with the tintinabulation of wind chimes, the round sound of gongs and large bells, and the earth-touching reverberation of chanting, ornament the air as the pagodas do the land. Even for those from the tranquil towns of Burma, Sagaing is considered a retreat, a place to meditate. It's a fitting site for a *shin-pyu* ceremony, when a son takes his first steps down the "Eight Paths" of the master. Sagaing! Divine!

Ten kilometers to the west, the round sensuous form of Kaunghmudaw Pagoda rises forty-six meters over the legendary Tooth of Kandy. King Bayinnaung heard that the Buddha's tooth had been pillaged from Jaffna in Ceylon (1560) and offered to buy it for a king's ransom. This chance to own the most sacred of all Buddhist relics slipped through his fingers when the Portuguese viceroy, fearing purgatory or worse at the hands of the Inquisition, publically pulverized it and scattered it on the ocean. Or so it seemed—he sold the real one to the king of Colombo who became broker for the gold inlaid human ivory. The tooth eventually found its way to the reliquary inside this huge, inverted alms bowl.

On the eve of Thadingyut on October's full moon, the reservoirs at the top of the 812 pillars are filled with oil to illuminate the pagoda. The village smiths in Ywataung, on the road between Sagaing and this hemispherical pagoda, follow their forefathers in fashioning silver.

Take a *tonga* to the foot of the hill and wind your way up along walls of monasteries to any of the several

Manussiha, twin lion adapted from design by Maung Kyaw

summits. U Min Kyaukse Pagoda is one of the most spectacular, a spired castle with stairways spiraling outside the four corner turrets. Your gaze roams across the wide river to Mandalay Hill in the north, the Shan Mountains to the east, and Amarapura to the south before resting on the pinnacle of a nearby hill.

You get on the Sagaing truck-bus in Mandalay at the corner of 29th and 83rd. The road bed, raised above the rice paddies, bypasses Amarapura before turning across the humped series of girders of the Ava Bridge, the only bridge to span the Irrawaddy. On your way back, you amble down past the tea shops and through a school (and the clamor of children crazy from the event of your arrival), to the river. You bargain with hands and fingers for an hour-long voyage across the river south to Amarapura. The gems on the tops of the pagodas catch the sun and throw its blinding light across the water to you. (In poorer places they substitute a soda bottle that also acts as a lightning insulator.) You get off the boat where rafts of teak are moored to the river's edge. When you climb up the bank and walk through Amarapura to catch the bus back to Mandalay, the whole village comes out to watch.

Maymyo: Yorkshire Pudding and Pine

Some say the British couldn't live without rain and that's why they came to Maymyo. Although the sun shines occasionally in this village 1075-meters high in the hills of the Shan Plateau, most travelers come to these mountains instead for the cool fresh air and the morning mist among the pines, oaks, poplars, and chestnuts.

For warmth in the evenings, they gather around the fireplace at Candacraig. This authentic replica of an old Scottish manor stands inside a white picket gate at the end of a horseshoe driveway. It was built at the turn of the century as a holiday retreat for British employees of the Bombay Trading Company. It has since been converted into a hotel and hasn't seen a new coat of paint in years. It's a scene for an Agatha Christie mystery. Ask for room 126 with its huge private bath, several heavy bureaus with enough space to handle trunks of clothes, a mildewed nook with windows in one of the turrets, and its own fireplace.

Downstairs in the dining hall, Burmese waiters in white coats with gold buttons serve "a bit stodgy" Yorkshire pudding, succulent roast beef, a spread of ghee on hot bread, and, in season, glazed strawberries for dessert. (Strawberries are in season in March and April, the same time as lychee and raspberries; pears ripen in August.) In the morning, the strawberry preserves on the breakfast table are fattening just to look at; you might as well eat them.

The Town and Around: The sign reads "Local Made Foreign Liquor." One taste of it will explain why the merchants are so anxious for your whiskey. They'll also settle for your calculator, camera lens, gold coins "for their collection." "What's your last price?" they ask, before you've had time to think of your first.

Candacraig

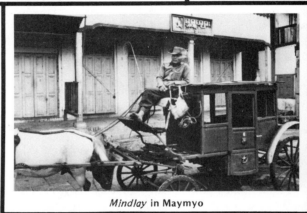

Mindlay in Maymyo

There's a heavy helping of Indians as well as Nepali in the population, families of Gurkha soldiers formerly serving in the British army. Today, the town is the home of Burma's "West Point" military academy.

In the market you'll find nests of tobacco and baskets of chrysanthemums. Buy some wood for your night's fire and carry it back in a *mindlay*. These horse-drawn closed carriages would have been at home in nineteenth-century England. The driver jumps down, squabbles a little over the price, and swings the door open for you to enter. He waits until you're seated before securing the door and climbing back to the driver's perch. Take a *mindlay* to the waterfall, forty-five minutes away, or walk the three kilometers to the botanical gardens past road-side rhododendrons. The lakes were dug by Turkish prisoners taken in the Crimean War.

Getting There: The driver cranks up the jeep and the two-and-a-half-hour journey begins. You leave either from the south corner of 29th and 83rd or di-rectly from the train station after getting off the morning express. A jeep leaves when full (about every half hour between 0730 and 1500). They'll wait for an hour instead of heading off with nine passengers, an unlucky number. If they can't find another person, they'll bring along a rock so that "Mr. Stone" will fool the malevolent forces. The climb offers views of the plains from hairpin curves. Roadside stalls sell sweet, sticky *pun* cherries for a *kyat*. The train, leaving at 0500, takes five hours to climb the hill via a zigzag series of switchbacks.

Pagan: A Plain of Ruins

The wind blows across the wasteland, picks up some tumble brush, and carries it against the side of the crumbled bricks of a ruin. Deep gulleys have been dug into the earth by water, in a hurry to leave this doomed kingdom, rushing down to the Irrawaddy. Once trees covered the fertile land. Then the Burmans came and absorbed the Pyu who were already farming the flood plains. More land was cleared. The population expanded as fast as the trees could be cut. With more rice to feed his army than his predecessors had dared to hope for, King Anawrahtha of Pagan began to envy the society of the Mon. He longed to have his city become as great as Thaton. So in 1057 he took Thaton—literally. Everything that might hold a key to the Buddhist society was put on top of pachyderms or floated on barges back to Pagan. It took thirty elephants just to carry off the copies of the sacred scriptures. Almost the whole city of Thaton, including King Manuha and 30,000 wise men, artisans, stone masons, and monks, were taken as slaves.

Anawrahtha set about reproducing Thaton, structure for structure, on the plains of the Upper Irrawaddy. Logs were burned to fire the bricks and thousands of buildings grew. Using the lumber from the constantly expanding border clearings to fuel the furnaces, the construction continued for more than two centuries. Because of the logging, the winds of draught gradually became more intense, but the kings found it necessary to build and build. More and more temples were constructed to maintain the respect of the 500,000 Buddhist subjects. But as the city grew in magnificence, the land became progressively less fertile, and more farmers were forced to the borders.

Kublai Khan's emissaries rode into a Burman capital that bragged of 13,000 religious monuments in masonry, in addition to a rich palace and countless homes and monasteries of teak. They rode out with their bodies separated from their

Wi Tong Dre, goddess of the earth, adapted from eleventh-century fresco in Pagan temple.

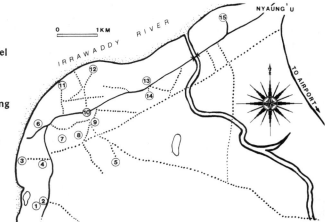

PAGAN

1. Nanpaya
2. Manuha
3. Thiripyitsaya Hotel
4. Mingalazedi
5. Dhammayang
6. Gawdawpalin
7. Nathlau Ng-Kyaung
8. Thatbyinnyu
9. Ananda
10. Sarabha Gateway
11. Irra Inn
12. Leya
13. Kubyaukgyi
14. Htilominlo
15. Shwezigon

heads, King Narathihapate's answer to the Khan's demand of tribute. The Khan's army approached Pagan in 1278 with "a host of twenty-six million men," as the Burman chronicler recorded. (This may be inaccurate. Marco Polo wrote that the attack force consisted only of "a valiant captain and an army composed mostly of jesters.") Burman spear-slingers on the backs of elephants filed confidently out to do battle. They were routed. The king desperately tried to strengthen his fortifications, tearing down 6000 temples for their bricks. A prophecy foretelling Pagan's doom was discovered in one of these temples, and the king, his court, their servants and friends fled. The Khan's army marched into an empty city in the middle of a dying land.

Almost eight centuries have passed since then. Goats graze in the outer chambers of some of the 2000 buildings left standing. The furrows of a parched, plowed field swerve abruptly around a rust-colored stupa and the wind urges the thorny, dead bush from its temporary rest.

_Transportation

By River: The boats that ply the route between Mandalay and Pagan are dim reminders of the river steamers that once carried more than 2000 passengers at a time. Except for numbers, however, little has changed. As they always have, passengers heading back to their village board with babies, baskets, and betel nut. The boat anticipates the dawn, leaving at about 0500. It pulls away from the jetty at the end of A Road (35th) in Mandalay to begin the twenty-four-hour float down the river. Cabin class is in an airless common sheltered area; bring your own sleeping mat for the deck.

During the rainy season, when the Irrawaddy swells to touch its distant banks, the boat docks at an occasional hamlet. Vendors with trays on their heads come down to sell food. But in the dry months from February through April, sandbars threaten to ground a boat for days. The river shrinks far from the villages and you're forced to settle for tea from the kettle and curry from the pot kept hot at the back of the boat.

After long hours of bobbing, you turn a bend in the river. The sun, rising behind the ruins of Pagan, spreads a bronze sheen on the water. The boat docks at Nyaung U, a seven-kilometer *tonga* ride from Pagan village.

By Land: From Rangoon take the express train to Thazi, then catch a jeep to Meiktila, thirty minutes to the west. Transfer to a bus bound for Kyauk Padaung, another three hours west, then change again for the two-hour ride to Pagan. If you're coming from Inle Lake, consider stopping for the night at Meiktila. From Mandalay catch the bus to Pagan scheduled to leave 29th Road between 82nd and 83rd at 0330. Check to make sure of the time. The route through the desert plains weighs heavy on the eyes and you arrive dazed at 1400.

By Air: Daily flights from Rangoon to Nyaung U leave at approximately 1500 and follow the Irrawaddy for an hour and a half. Sit on the left side for the view. From Mandalay the plane takes only thirty minutes after it finally leaves. Although officially scheduled as a morning flight, it has yet to depart before 1200, and may not leave until 1600. From the right side, you'll see the white pagodas of Sagaing and Ava at take-off and the expanse of desert, dotted with ruins, when you land. BAC runs free bus service to Pagan village.

Ananda and Thatbyinnyu

Getting Around: A walk to a remote site on the periphery of the dead city offers a million perspectives in the ever-changing parade of pagodas. Many pagodas have gaping wounds left by treasure-seeking vandals over the centuries. The walk takes you on dusty paths, under scorching sun, and possibly on top of needle thorns that pierce cheap sandals. *Tonga* provide the only alternative. Often the driver speaks English and will act as a guide as well. If you let him know the places you'd like to see, he'll get the keys to open those buildings locked to vandals. Or tell him to take you to his favorite place away from tourists and touts.

___Sights

Ananda: If you choose only one temple in Pagan, it has to be this one. Serene, standing Buddhas, lit by sunlight through slits in the roof, face out from the four-sided center of a catacomb. The floor plan forms a perfect Greek cross. On the west porch is the only statue of a Pagan king in all of Pagan. Kyanzittha is shown humbly kneeling before Buddha—not the normal posture for a monarch. The figure nearby represents Shin Arahan, the Mon monk from Thaton who converted Anawrahtha to Theravada Buddhism. As religious leader of Pagan, Shin Arahan crowned the three kings who followed Anawrahtha. The temple holds a colorful festival in January.

Htilominlo: The walls scrape your shoulders as you tunnel up the steps to the top terrace. You've arrived early to see the rising sun turn the rust-colored earth to cinnabar and tinge the white spire of Ananda Temple with rose.

Shwezigon Pagoda: The early morning light is a strobe as you walk through the series of shadows in the colonnade. Flashes of sunlight riot off the three-terraced pagoda, a reliquary covered with tarnished gold for a few of Buddha's bones. Green plaques at the base depict the stories of the former lives of the master. Carved wood graces the eaves and *nat* play in the surrounding pavilions. The temple festival on the November-December full moon is dedicated to the thirty-seven *nat* of the Burmese pantheon.

Thatbyinnyu: Two massive cubes of brick, stacked one on top of the other, reach a height of sixty meters. This is Pagan's tallest structure and the most popular spot to view the sunset spreading fire on the Irrawaddy. Wait until the tourists leave and then enjoy the descent in the company of the quiet spirits of twilight.

Gawdawpalin: The earthquake of 1975 rent the base as if it were cardboard and toppled the sixty-meter-high spire. Reparations have been financed in a large part by the Rockefeller Foundation. A museum of statuary protected from vandals sits across the *tonga* path.

Manuha Temple: When the captured Thaton monarch was granted permission to build his own place of worship, his architects designed a visual metaphor of his imprisonment. The Buddha statues, despite the claustrophobic closeness of the walls and ceiling, are at peace; they have escaped the temporal trap of life-death-rebirth.

Nanpaya Temple: Built early in the eleventh century by Hindu worshippers, this former house of worship was ironically converted into Manuha's prison. It was his compromises with the Hindu Brahmins in Thaton that caused the strict Buddhist monk, Shin Arahan, to flee to the forest of Pagan. The monk eventually converted Anawrahtha, who then conquered Thaton and gained ownership of sacred Buddhist scriptures. Inside are four pillars of solid stone etched with design. A monk who speaks English is often here to welcome visitors.

Dhammayang Temple: This moss-gray mass of brick stands aloof from the other large temples, an unfinished memory of a wicked king who smothered his father and murdered his Indian wife. During the temple's construction, he

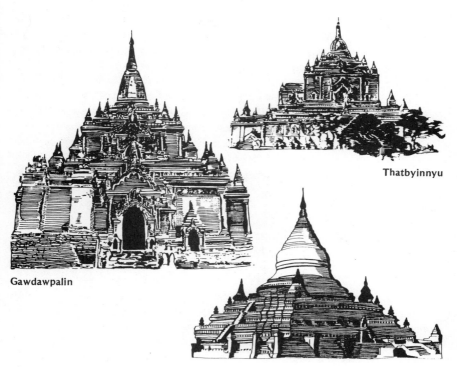

Thatbyinnyu

Gawdawpalin

Mingalazedi

threatened a horrible death to any of his masons who left so much as a crack the size of a needle in the brickwork. The king wanted perfection; he needed the merit. One day eight Brahmins were granted audience with the king. In the middle of an incantation they drew their blades and stabbed the king, avenging the death of the Indian princess. Then they took each others' lives to avoid spilling the blood of the blameless guards who had rushed in. Today, in the solitude of the upper terraces, you can feel the emotions of past centuries.

Kubyaukgyi Temple: The Myazedi Stone, etched with the same passages in Mon, Burmese, Pali and Pyu, is found here. Just as the Rosetta stone helped to break the ancient Egyptian hieroglyphic code, the dust-covered Myazedi Stone proved to be the cipher for the previously forgotten Pyu script. In 1911, seven centuries after it ceased to be written, the Pyu script was deciphered. But the sound of their tongue has disappeared with the Pyu race.

Mingalazedi: The last of Pagan's pagodas was commissioned by King Narathihapate, an over-proud monarch with a fertile imagination. He had a stone at the base inscribed with the claim that he ate 300 dishes of curry daily and enjoyed the company of 3000 concubines. During construction, a rumor circulated that when the spire was finished Pagan would be doomed. The king gave his workers a few years off. Eventually, however, the delay caused him to lose face. He ordered the pagoda completed and lost his kingdom to Kublai Khan.

Cave Temples: Dark subterranean hermitages were dug for monks so they could meditate far from the distractions of the frenetic capital. In Kyanzittha Cave near Shwezigon, the arches that separate the rooms form frames for a receding series of doorways. The frescoes were painted in the eleventh, twelfth, and thirteenth centuries. A few were sketched by Mongol invaders—an example of thirteenth-century graffiti. Kyaukku Temple stands alone on the slopes above the Irrawaddy, three kilometers upstream from Nyuang U. The labyrinth of tunnels, lavished with carved reliefs, lead from a central pillar of brick. The underground portions date from the eleventh century; the buildings above ground were constructed a century later.

Charm or tattoo, often seen on Buddha's forehead

Beside the River: The bulging Bupaya Pagoda, perhaps the first of Pagan's temples, was built in the second century. Its whitewashed surface has helped eighteen centuries of riverboat pilots navigate past treacherous sandbars. The monastery of Leya is a little more than a kilometer upstream. To get there from Pagan village, first pass through the Sarabha Gateway guarded by two *nat*, Handsome and Golden Face. Then walk to the right of the long rounded hill, the remains of the ninth-century city wall. The monastery itself isn't old or large, but its carved-wood construction provides a living memory of the Pagan of the past, when palaces, homes and most monasteries were made of magnificently ornate teak. Today, the sonorous chanting of monks in meditation blends with the breezes across the timeless Irrawaddy.

Lacquerware: The Mon settlement of Myinkaba, two kilometers south of the old city wall, grew up around the temple-prison of the exiled King Manuha. Here the Mon practiced crafts that their barbarian conquerors were unable to imitate, creating exquisite pieces from turned wood, woven bamboo, and even carefully wound horsehair. The craftsmanship continues. In one piece, courtly figures in bright orange jump out from a receding black background. A chicken preens his gold, orange, and green plumage. A priceless cup made from horsehair is so pliable that one side of its lip can touch the other side without cracking its shiny surface. The multi-stepped process is slow; top quality work begun by one generation is completed by the next. The village has a school and museum where you can see the craft in its many stages.

In Pagan village there are numerous outlets for the country's finest lacquerware. Even if you don't intend to buy, stop at the Daw Nu Nutin shop located by the turnoff to Gawdawpalin Pagoda. You'll be treated to cigars, tea, candy, and even brandy, while they show you their collection of new and antique wares. (If you arrive by *tonga*, the driver gets a ten percent commission.)

___Practicalities

Stay: Rooms at the Burma Guest House across from the Tourist Burma office are comfortable. Mosquito nets hang above the beds. The walls, like those of a Burmese home, are made of woven bamboo framed with wood. The windows at the back open onto a view of Ananda Pagoda. There's time here for a free cup of Chinese tea and a conversation in English with the family. The nearby Aung The Ha Ya Lodge and the Moe Moe Inn at the only corner in Pagan village are the alternatives for inexpensive lodging at government-controlled prices.

To find a room with a fan you'll have to go either to the Cooperative Hotel or the Irra Inn. The Coop is a utilitarian concrete building within a minute's walk of Gawdawpalin Pagoda. The Indian manager is concerned for your comfort: He yells at his help for them to clean your room then asks, "Is there anything else *I*

Smoking cheroot

can do for you?" The Irra Inn stands majestically on a knoll; an expanse of dried lawn slopes down toward the wide river. The lobby/dining area could double as a basketball court—both in size and lack of concern for aesthetics. The rooms with attached bath and dramatic view are upstairs suites. The inexpensive rooms in back are reminiscent of moldy monk cells in cave temples, but the fans work. (Keep your bags locked securely.)

Only the swank Thiripyitsaya Hotel has air-conditioned rooms. Only here will your lodging expenses be recorded on your form. The price is beyond the budget of those concerned enough to ask.

Food: Pagan is a great place for a fast—the food is an epicurean nightmare. The sweet-sour pork at Zoe Zoe's Restaurant approaches palatability, if you can endure the surly Chinese cook. Bide your time by inspecting the fake gems for sale. The lacquerware at the Nation Restaurant near the city gate is more interesting for browsing. There, you sit at a once-white linen covered table, a large stain in front of you. The waitress deftly whisks off the cloth and repositions it so the stain faces an empty seat. Service is their specialty; cooking isn't. Even service suffers at the Cooperative. Order everything twice. The toast comes without even the normal yellow lard spread; the jam is merely a sticky cosmetic.

Most lodging houses have their own small restaurants. Moe Moe's has become a popular meeting place for travelers. Try their fresh lime juice. Drink cold beer while you enjoy the excellent lacquer panels that decorate the bar at the Thiripyitsaya Hotel. Or pull your chair onto the terrace for a view of the sunset across the Irrawaddy River.

From Pagan: Tourist Burma has a bus to Thazi that leaves at 0400 and takes four hours. You arrive at Thazi in time to catch the morning express on its run from Mandalay to Rangoon. It's scheduled to pass through the station at 0900. Unfortunately, this means a lot of daytime travel because the train doesn't arrive in Rangoon until 1800. Surprisingly, it's cheaper to bus first to Mandalay and then catch the evening express to Rangoon, but this is even more time-consuming. Boats upriver to Mandalay take at least two days.

Planes leave for Rangoon late in the afternoon and take only an hour and a half. Unfortunately, Tourist Burma requires you to use their bus service to the airport and it leaves around noon. This means hours of waiting at the airport. (The Tourist Burma director can be cajoled into stopping at a few temples on the way for quick five-minute glimpses.)

The last alternative is slowest of all: Take a *tonga* to Nyaung U and catch the bus bound for Kyauk Padaung, a three-hour ride. Change to the bus to Meiktila for a two-hour ride. Catch a jeep for the thirty-minute trip from there to Thazi. Tickets for the overnight express from Thazi to Rangoon are always available to foreigners. However, there's no guarantee of a seat, so plan to sleep the night on the floor. This route opens up possibilities for overnight stops at Mount Popa and Meiktila.

_____Vicinity of Pagan

Mount Popa: It shouldn't be here. This 1518-meter-high monolith juts out of the barren plains like a massive, misplaced pillar. It rose from beneath the earth's crust in a violent volcanic eruption in 442 B.C. to become the dwelling place of the gods. What else could it be? The volcanic soil flowered into a mountain-top garden (*popa* means flower in Sanskrit), high above a parched land where peasants toil to coax out a poor crop. Its power was real in the minds of the people; for 700 years, from the fourth to the eleventh century, every king had to make a pilgrimage here to consult the spirits before his reign could begin. Even today the mountain is considered the earthly font of power for the mystical world of *nat.* A shrine to the Mahagiri *Nat*, Handsome and Golden Face, stands halfway up the steep path to the summit. During the month of Nayon (May to June), it's busy with pilgrims. You can stay overnight at the old monastery at the base of this Burman Mount Olympus. To get there, hire a jeep from Pagan or stop en route between Nyaung U and Thazi.

Meiktila: They've seen a few strangers here before. Travelers have spent hours here waiting for their bus to overload enough to leave. Some foreigners may have even ventured into town from the lakeside bus terminal. When they did, they met as many smiles as they did faces. Most foreigners, however, feel satisfied to sit in the shade of the giant old tree that spreads its branches down the banks to almost touch the lake. Across the mirrored surface, a pagoda on its own peninsula reaches out to the air and into the water. You might wish to spend the night at the Myuma Hotel. Take off your shoes before you go upstairs to the plywood cell. Just ask anyone for directions; they're all interested in where you're going. It's a thirty-minute jeep ride from Thazi.

Meiktila Lake

Inle Lake: They Walk on Water

The Intha people glide across the lake by standing on one leg at the prow of their slender wooden boats, while, with the other leg wound around the oar, they push themselves along as though riding a floating scooter. From this standing position they can navigate through the thick underwater growth of Inle Lake, which is only three meters at its deepest. They can also spot the movement of fish that they catch with conical, bamboo net-cages. If they trap an eel, catfish, or perhaps a meter-long lake carp, they use a spear to stab it.

The 70,000 "sons of the lake" (as their adopted name translates), have had to make many adaptations in the two centuries since they moved from their former home near Tavoy along the Andaman Sea. Caught between the recurring wars of revenge fought by the Thai and Burmans, they migrated north in the 1700s to the Shan Plateau. Here they discovered Inle Lake, a beautiful refuge nestled in the cleavage between two mountain ranges.

They built their villages on stilts above the water. Because solid ground was scarce in this swampy plain, they designed *kyunpaw*. These floating gardens are built by lashing tuberous plants together and filling the six-meter-long troughs with rich loam scooped from the lake bottom. The buoyant fields are towed into position and anchored there, thus reversing the normal irrigation process by bringing the soil to the water. The gardens are tended by women from their boats and grow peas, beans, eggplant, cabbage, cucumbers, and cauliflower.

___*Getting There*

By Land from Rangoon: The Mandalay Express from Rangoon arrives in Thazi at 0500. You walk bleary-eyed out of the station and through the dark streets of the sleeping city to the bus terminal. You wait for a few hours at this shack with a few WW II army trucks and a jeep out front. Then the sky begins to lighten and, at some unknown signal, people pile into the waiting vehicles. The jeep heads straight across the plain. The driver, greedy for the one lane of asphalt, forces everyone—pedestrians with bundles on their heads, bicycles, ox carts—into the grooved dust beside the road. By the time the road reaches the hills and starts to twist like Burmese script, the twenty passengers are squirming for new uncomfortable positions. The road passes through several settlements with neat geometrically-woven bamboo homes, varying in pattern from one hut to the next. You'll pass jungle-covered hills and valleys while the pain in your leg, pinned beneath a gunnysack, turns to numbness.

At the halfway mark, you stop for a delicious Burmese meal. The extra helpings of lentil soup, rice, and curried meat stop coming to your table only when you've quit eating. Once back in the jeep, the road bounces you up to conifer country, where broad perspectives of hills step up to the horizon. By the time the pain, exhaust smoke, dust, and heat have become intolerable, you begin the winding descent into the Inle Valley. You cross the flat expanse toward Shwenyaung. (Here horse carts and a rare taxi wait for passengers going eleven kilometers south to Yaunghwe on the shore of Inle Lake.) Your jeep continues for forty-five minutes to Taunggyi at the top of the hills on the other side of the valley. Barring likely breakdown, you arrive from Thazi after five hours of travel. (A train leaves Thazi in the morning daily and reaches the Shwenyaung railhead ten hours and many open-window markets later.)

By Land from Mandalay: The bus leaves at 0430 from 27th Street near Zegyo market and arrives in Taunggyi between 1430 and 1630. Datsuns take about eight hours for the same trip and offer the relative comfort of a cushioned seat, euphoria if you've ridden a Burmese over-the-bumps bus.

By Air: Planes land daily at the Heho airstrip from Rangoon and Mandalay if weather permits. BAC offers transport the thirty-five kilometers to Yaunghwe and the forty-three kilometers to Taunggyi.

___*Yaunghwe*

The tangle of reeds and water hyacinth sinks away from either side of the tarred way leading south from Shwenyaung. Large white birds garnish the limbs of trees, a temple decays in the sun, wide-horned water buffalo saunter by the roadside, and waterpaths line the fields along the way. Yaunghwe, oldest of the Intha settlements, rests at road's end. In an open-front shop, a barber mows a bald swath on a boy's head. Women pound their family's clothes in a shaded canal and titter under your stare. A little girl offers you an unblossomed flower.

| Inle Market | Temple statue, Yaunghwe |

The Market: Before the sun throws shadows, tribespeople come to spread their mats and fill the permanent tin shelters with vegetables, sarongs, Shan handbags, pottery, and dried white fish. Food steams in the pots of numerous stalls. Delicacies like *we ta chin* (sticky rice mixed with pig's blood and steamed in a banana-leaf wrapper), *me chin* (the same with buffalo blood), or *nga ta miney* (fish and rice served cold), are sold for a couple *kyat*. *Kinbon kyaw* (a fiery patty of onion, ginger, curry, tomato, rice flour, and pork), is deep fried in peanut oil.

Colors of clothes mark the different tribespeople. Danu and Shan are in khaki and brown. The Pa-o are in black or dark blue with orange trim and wear bright-colored dish towels on their heads. Taungyo women with red stained lips and teeth glide by, their short black dresses sequined with shells, their legs heavy with copper rings. Home town Intha men clad in plaid sarongs and women in bright flower prints add to the earthy rainbow. The market shifts from day to day to Taunggyi, Yaunghwe, Shwenyaung, Heho, and Kalaw with a return every sixth day.

Stay: The Inle Inn is past the bridge, about 500 meters left of the town's main intersection. It is set back from the dusty street, protected by a hedge, and offers clean rooms with cement floors. The woven bamboo walls are held together with bottle-cap headed nails. The separate showers and restrooms are kept tidy. Ask a member of the mellow Indian family managing the place for an extra blanket during the cold season.

Many of the monasteries allow visitors to sleep on their floors. The terrace around the Phaungdaw U Pagoda is cold and hard, but free.

Food: Even when there's no market the early moring stalls here serve tea and fried bread. The one nearest the gate may put a charcoal-filled bucket under your table to warm you until the sun peeks over the trees. A block west of the main street is the aptly named Friendship Restaurant. It serves a large plate of fried rice, Chinese tea, soup, and fruit. It has an English menu, a stereo, and is the only place in town that serves beer.

___Sights

Nanthes Island: You walk along the canal leading south from Yaunghwe and at the path's end you see the large sitting Buddha of Kyauthwe Temple dominating the horizon. You happen across a boat just pushing off and are offered a ten-minute ride along the reed-lined channel to the temple. The narrow footpath leads past the unsheltered statue to a small village of crude houses. To the right, in a slightly more substantial wooden shed, women deftly twist tobacco leaves around chopped *kadaya* leaves, a tobacco substitute, to make cigars wrapped in bundles like sticks of dynamite. A grandmother presents you with a pocketful. The path leads east about two kilometers to the main road back to Yaunghwe.

Lighting up

Along the way men slush mud from the water to fertilize their paddies. A stubborn ox begrudgingly makes room for you to pass. Old men and women, retired from the field, carry heavy bundles of firewood back to the village.

At the main road you turn right, away from Yaunghwe, and take a gravel driveway into a small sugarcane community of two houses. The over-sweet smell of boiling cane juice fills the air. You sit on a shaded bench next to the ox tread that runs the cane press. Someone offers you a stalk, its end sticky brown with congealing syrup like an all-day sucker. You offer cigars and they disappear. On your way down the gravel road, two children scamper to catch up with you to hand you a ball of sugar candy.

Across the Lake: People gather early at the gate, a wooden bridge over the canal about 200 meters west of the Friendship Cafe, to wait for the ten-passenger ferry that runs to the Phaungdaw U Pagoda. A rower straddles two boats and paddles beneath you, picking up another boat on her way. After all passengers pile in and sit on the matted floor, the antiquated Johnson outboard coughs to a start and you putter off down the canal street. Along the water lane, houses give way to reeds held in check by a bamboo fence. Purple hyacinth creep into the boat lane. A small boy leads his docile water buffalo through neck deep water, holding the rope while he stands to row his boat. Blue flashes from the fence as a kingfisher takes flight. The water lane opens onto the broad lake, a smoked mirror in the morning mist. Fishermen stand on their boats.

By the time you reach Ywama, the water market is breaking up and the women with mushroom-like *khamout* (hats) on their heads are rowing home with their bartered produce. The main streets and alleys of this Venice-like village are all *chaung*, waterways.

Phaungdaw U Pagoda: Twenty kilometers south of Yaunghwe, about halfway across the long lake (foreigners aren't allowed any farther south), the Phaungdaw U Pagoda stands out of the water. It's a stately structure with cool, black marble floors. Steps lead up to the large central hall. A sign written in Burmese, Chinese, Japanese, and English says, "Ladies are prohibited from the center dais." Here rest five figures, rounded with so much gold leaf they look more like golden snowmen than the Buddhas they were sculpted to represent more than eight centuries ago. Out back, Shan handbags embroidered with *chinthe* or with "Inle Lake" woven across the top are among *longyi*, shirts and wrap-around trousers, betel nut scissors, bronze opium weights, and what-nots.

A half-minute boat ride away, the weaving center offers free tea and cigars and fixed prices. Outside, children with flowers for sale sing Frère Jacque. You're not the first foreigner here. A Burmese hat may make you look like Bob Hope on the "Road to Rangoon," but will protect you from the blazing sun on the hot ride back to Yaunghwe.

Nanthes Island

Intha-powered waterbus

Buddhist novice

Inle Lake, where the people work
and worship on the water.

Tours: Tourist Burma runs a service from the office at the Taunggyi Strand Hotel and back, plus a boat for ten passengers. They also run a boat from Yaungwe. These trips will be recorded on your form. Pyisonn, a graceful Burmese who speaks excellent English, runs a six-hour private tour for about half as much. He stops at the 135-year-old island monastery of Ngaphe Chaung where he spent a brief time as a monk. On a different ride, he'll take you for forty-five minutes to the sulfur springs that seep into the two-meter deep west side of the lake.

Events: Each year for seventeen days around the September-October full moon, the five figures are taken from Phaungdaw U Pagoda and floated aboard a golden barge with a *karaweik* bird at its prow to the ten major Intha settlements. The water procession is reminiscent of the ceremony surrounding royalty in ancient times when a king would travel on water escorted by his entire retinue. Today, leg rowers compete in races across the lake. Occasionally this festival entices Paduang tribespeople to make a rare trip north across the lake to "civilization."

PADAUNG WOMEN—THE BRASS RING WEARERS

At five years of age, the first few brass rings are wound around her neck by the medicine man. Later others will be twisted on her arms and legs as well, and she will waddle under almost twenty kilograms of metal jewelry. What appears to be a "giraffe neck" is actually the result of collapsed shoulders and deformed rib cage caused by the constant strain. Those who remove the rings to become modern women have trouble holding their heads up. Their muscles have atrophied.

About seven thousand of the Padaung live on the southern section of Inle Lake. Foreigners aren't permitted in this area because of the Moebye Dam, Burma's largest hydroelectric project. The Padaung call themselves Kayah, a sub-group of the Karen tribe. They are Buddhist, but they practice many animistic rituals. The rings that identify the tribal women protect them from tiger bites.

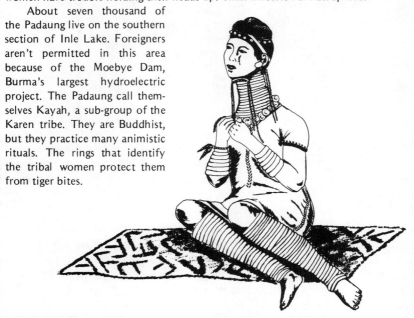

___Taunggyi

Clouds darken designs on the wide plain as you ride up the hill to this cool country city at 1800 meters. The jeep stops near the top and those hanging onto the outside jump off and disappear up a path. The jeep climbs up the hill past a checkpoint where military men are on the lookout for vehicles violating the passenger load limit. At the next turn the lost passengers jump back on.

The town wakes with the chime of church bells loud in the cool air. At the once-a-week market you find tofu stained custard yellow with tumeric, large bouquets of flowers, and baskets of fresh strawberries. Near the market are cross-country buses and jeeps. If you don't board the vehicles here, your chances for a ride are small. On the dry pine and eucalyptus covered hills above the city are pagodas with commanding perspectives of the land. These are often off limits because of fire hazards.

Taunggyi baby crib

Stay: The May You Hotel near the market has cubicles with mosquito nets but no showers. The Sanpya Lodging House up the road toward the Taunggyi Strand Hotel has cubicles with showers but no nets. The first has a restaurant with over-priced food. The latter has no restaurant, but serves free milk tea in the morning with complimentary Burmese-English newspapers.

Kamaladevi Restaurant: You ask the portly waiter of this hovel on main street, "Do you have milk tea?" He answers no and later brings it to your table at no charge. A picture of the owners, husband and wife, from younger days when they migrated from Madras hangs on the wall. You ask, "Why did you move to Burma?" He answers, "1928." You try again, "Why?" Happy to finally understand you, he replies, "Wife? Yes, yes, that's my wife."

___To Thazi by Train

The station master issues you a special *torris* ticket from his throne inside the Shwenyaung station. When the time wanders around the vicinity of ten o'clock, the warmed-up engine jerks your car and the echo chains through the other four cars to the caboose. You're off like a jackrabbit with a hernia. The car moves through the flats, picking up momentum for the climb out of the valley. The train snakes up the hill and coils around in a complete spiral, bridging over the tracks below. Salesmen are busy from the beginning. Bottles of the "finests" booze—cherry wine, Two Monkey brandy, Paduang rum, clear, blinding alcohol— are carried in baskets down the aisle. You've got to want to be drunk; you don't drink these for the taste.

At every hint of a town the train grinds metal to a stop. An instant market passes beneath your open window on the heads of women. Children with earthen jugs offer water. Wood for cosmetics, spice, or medicine are carried on trays. An energetic merchant whittles a piece of aromatic *payoud* (sarsaparilla) root for a potential customer. "It's for headaches and toothaches," your neighbor informs you. Oranges and unripe avocados, soybeans, sunflower seeds, *aloo* (potato cutlets with onion inside), potato chips without salt, hard-boiled chicken eggs and speckled ones the size of quails' eggs, betel nut, cherry blossoms, bouquets of mountain flowers that dwarf the saleswomen: all these dance before you in the bazaar beneath your window.

The train continues to climb through the jagged mountains. The slopes are frequently shaven to become fields so steep the foothold of the farmer looks precarious. Erosion is swift. The dull half-sleep induced by the monotonous clatter of tracks is broken by a salesman's panhandling. Standing on the seat's edge, he projects his fifteen-minute spiel about a cooking spice that smells like sweetened baby urine. Rock cliffs move by slowly enough for you to study cracks. Thick bamboo jungles and sensuously curved tree trunks pass by.

A temple appears above the town to the right and twenty minutes later you arrive with the town and temple on your left. Clouds shade the train and then, darkness of an airless tunnel, sunlight, another tunnel. Then the tracks waltz down the mountainside in a series of switchbacks. At the next station the aisles completely fill with people and packages. You hear a clamor on the roof and at the next wide turn find the top of the train full of peasant passengers.

The night comes before the train arrives on the central plains, and the rectangles of light from the train windows pour over the ground. A whistle from the darkness and someone on the roof shines his flashlight to find a boy on a bullock cart waving and smiling. You pull into Thazi at 1930, only an hour and a half late. There is plenty of time to catch the night express to Rangoon that arrives in Thazi at 2030. Get your ticket at the station from the master in his office for the national lines.

A TRAVELER AND THE AIRPORT TRUCK

He should have known better than to catch the city bus to the airport, especially after yesterday's fiasco. He had been in a mob of men as they squeezed to get on the bus, when he saw a woman slip into the back door. He followed her and grabbed the first empty spot to sit down only to discover he was surrounded by women, their heads covered with shawls. A wire mesh separated the front of the bus from the back, and all the men were on the other side. They looked angry, as if he had walked into their harem. He got off.

So on the last of his seven days, when he decided to go by bus to the airport, he made sure he asked the number. When he saw Bus 9, he asked again. He wasn't sure he read the Burmese number correctly. Then he climbed up the back of the troop truck, ducked under the tarpaulin, and sat on a smooth wood bench. Each time another passenger entered on his side, he had to slide deeper into the hot darkness, until finally he was breathing in the exhaust coming up the clouded chamber between the truck bed and the cab. As he groped to the back of the truck for air, the other passengers stared and were too startled to make way, so he had to stumble over their knees, onto toes, and into baskets of vegetables.

Perfect! He could drink the wind while he watched the earth colors of modern Rangoon fly by. All those other travelers were taking thirty-*kyat* taxis and he was going to make it out there for *pyas* (pennies). He laughed at his freedom.

The truck passed a university. Fifteen students rushed on at a stop. Fifteen more got on when the truck slowed down for a corner. Before long he was standing on one foot, with a foot on top of his. He was hanging on with one hand to the bar solid with clenched fists. Two men were using his belt as their handhold. It started to rain . . . hard. The tires ripped through puddles. He was soaked. He thought of the taxi again and his decision not to take one. The truck swerved and gallons of water gushed off the tarpaulin and onto the head of the man next to him. They both laughed.

He finally got the bus to stop about a half kilometer beyond the airport turn-off. It had taken much longer than he had anticipated and he still had two and a half kilometers to the airport, with the rain and a backpack weighing him down and only twenty minutes to get there. "It's hopeless," he thought. "Might as well enjoy the rain." He slowed down. A car pulled over and a Burmese man signalled for him to hop in.

He made it in time even though he was delayed while he explained to customs how he had managed to eat all week for only the three *kyat* left on his Currency Declaration Form. The plane was late. Just as he had been doing for a week, he had to wait for transportation. After he discovered the shower in the men's room, he cleaned up and went upstairs for a civilized cup of tea. The waiter was sincerely friendly to him. He sat back with a bummed *Dooya* cigarette and relaxed. He felt an itch on his leg from cane mites in the chair. BURMA!

Burma bus

Thailand

*Say "hello" to Buddha. You see his image
everywhere. The gold symbolizing his enlightenment
beams off the glazed tiles and glass embedded naga-serpent
gables of temple roofs. The gold is intensified in the yellow
dawn when marigold monks with blessing bowls form
lines of saffron. There's a tranquil gold in the
peasant-farmer's straw-amber paddy fields.
Say "hello" to Buddha. The serenity of his being
smiles on you from countless statues in the country's
countless wat (temples). He smiles on you from almost
every amulet worn by almost every Thai. He smiles on
you through the people you meet. If you absorb the
culture, he will smile on you from a mirror.*

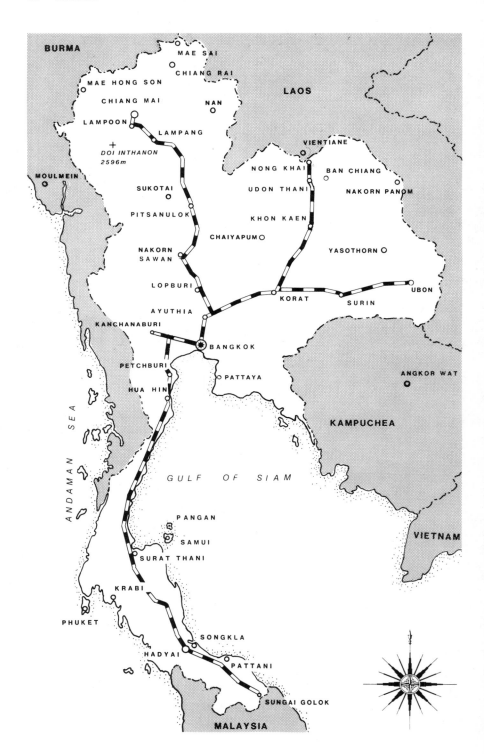

____Religion

Buddhism: The monk looks humbly at the ground as the village woman fills his black lacquer alms-bowl with his morning meal of rice. She says, *"Kup koon ka"* (thank you), for the opportunity to gain merit; kindness creates good karma that will return as blessings in this life or the next. In front of a radiant Buddha statue, a man lights incense and tapers to honor, not worship, the Lord Buddha. He meditates for inner strength, he doesn't pray for divine intervention in his problems.

In theory, the Thai brand of Theravada Buddhism is a back-to-basics belief, more a tolerant, eclectic philosophy than a religion. As such, it's been able to keep up with changes. Buddhism is alive. You frequently see new temples under construction, the artisan-villager painstakingly placing each square of mirrored glass in a mosaic column. One of the functions of the Supreme Patriarch of the *Sangha* (a Buddhist College of Cardinals who keep the religion pure), is to anoint Thai Air passenger jets before their maiden flights. Almost universally, each male will spend at least three months, and usually a full year, with a shorn head as a novice in one of Thailand's two-thousand monasteries. About ninety-four percent of the population is at least nominally Theravada Buddhist. Outside a *wat* gallery lined with hundreds of statues of the master, a tourist turns to his Thai guide: "It seems Buddha has had quite an effect on Thailand."

Animism: About eighty percent of the people are farmers, uneducated peasants who have maintained simple superstitions and beliefs in spirits. Evidence of this is everywhere. A child in Kanchanaburi will wear an amulet containing bits of dried human fetus. A businessman in Bangkok waits for an auspicious hour to open shop. A sneeze is considered a deeply spiritual event—as it was once in western cultures. A marriage occurs only in an even-numbered month, for the couple is two and the spirits will not be mocked. A funeral is held in an odd-numbered month for the same reason. Amulets are available at gates to temples. Pre-Buddhist *Phi* (spirit) houses stand in an auspicious corner outside even the most modern hotels. Murder defendants plead not guilty—"The demons made me do it." Palmistry classes are packed, and sidewalk seers snare Thai with astrological charts, cosmological maps, and phrenological skulls. And apothecaries do a booming business in love potions.

____History

The people lived in boats that either floated on the surface of the water or sat above it on stilts. A vast network of canals meshed the rich rice plains along the Chao Phraya River. The people floated teak logs down this river, aged the wood for a century, and fitted hand-hewn boards together with such precision that there was no need of pitch or paint even in their rice barges. Someone, somehow, somewhere dropped copper ore in a tin furnace and the Bronze Age was born. These people have been called the Dong-son culture, named after the site in Vietnam where the first evidence of them was discovered. But the oldest Bronze Age artifacts in the world have been found in northeast Thailand.

Migration of Nations: In the first century, the Mon came from Burma, following the valleys between the mountain ranges. They were Hindu-Buddhists who grew strong wherever one of their clans settled in a valley. Kingdoms blossomed, merged, and were absorbed. Some Mon clans settled land farther to the east to become the powerful Funan Kingdom. Funan was overrun by Khmer who came from the north. Some say the Khmer were a Spartacus-like band of slaves escaped from Genghis Khan. Some say they built Angkor Wat, SE Asia's marvel of art and architecture. Others say they only occupied Angkor Wat by chasing the Funan-Mon out of Kampuchea (just as the Vietnamese are doing to the Khmer Rouge today).

Into this cauldron of cultures, barbarian tribes of Thai entered from the north, forced through the bottleneck mountain passes by pressure from expanding clans in China. Wave upon wave of these hardy mountain people came looking to the plains for the fabulous promise of unlimited food. Chiang Mai, Sukotai, Lopburi, Ayuthia, . . . in all fifteen Thai cities were once capitals of city-states. Ayuthia, founded in the middle 1300s, was the greatest and longest lasting of these. This dynasty endured for more than four hundred years during which thirty-three kings ruled. Then in 1767, they were annihilated by a Burman-Mon army invading from Pegu.

Chakri Dynasty: General Taksin, an insane Thai fighter, rallied his troops from his hide-out cave in southern Thailand and within a few years he was king of all Thailand. His insanity, which had been an asset in war, was dangerous in peace. His top general eased the reins of power from the insane king's hands, ordered him executed and, in the late 1700s founded the Chakri Dynasty. This dynasty has led the people of Siam to the present.

Settling in Bangkok, the Chakri rule extended all the way south to Singapore and east to present-day Kampuchea. Vassal kings sent solid silver or gold trees, sometimes several meters tall, as symbols of homage to the Chakri Court. A Cambodian king was even crowned at the palace in Bangkok.

The Europeans were strong rivals for power in the Gulf of Siam. However, King Mongkut, Rama IV, and his son Chulalongkorn, Rama V, skillfully played the English against the French, and Thailand was the only country between Persia and China to remain free from colonial rule. But this was not without cost. Near the turn of this century, the British annexed several provinces to the south, and the French, in a series of takeovers, gained control of Laos. In 1932, a bloodless coup changed the country into a constitutional monarchy.

During WW II, the Japanese were able to take control of Thailand only after five fierce hours of resistance—once again the practical Thai yielded without breaking. An active guerilla movement and an ambassador who refused to deliver the declaration of war to United States officials softened post-war treatment by the Allies, and Thailand became the first former allied-enemy to be admitted into the United Nations.

HISTORY OF THAILAND

3000 B.C. Bronze Age civilization began in northeastern Thailand

563-483 B.C. Siddhartha Gautama Buddha

6th Cent. Funan Kingdom flourished in southeastern Kampuchea

7th Cent. Khmer overran Funan in mid-7th century

10th to 11th Cent. Thai crossed the Mekong River; capital cities were established in Chiang Saen and Payao

1113-1150 Khmer built Angkor Wat

1253 Khan's army destroyed Nanchao

1258 Sukotai gained independence from Angkor; the Camelot days of Siam

1300 Sukotai King Ramkamhaeng (1278-1318) made his first trip to China to pay tribute to emperor

1350 King Rama Tibodi started Ayuthia

16th Cent. Mon forces from Pegu, Burma, captured Chiang Mai and destroyed Ayuthia

17th Cent. Ayuthia destroyed Pegu

1688 French suspected of plotting to overtake government of King Narai; Siam closed doors to Europeans

1767 Burman army devastated Ayuthia; the city was deserted

1770s King Taksin reunited kingdom

1782 Taksin went insane; Rama I started the Chakri Dynasty

1785 Capital moved to Bangkok

1809 Rama II crowned second Chakri king; arts blossomed

1851 Rama IV, King Mongkut opened doors to Europeans

1868 Rama V, Chulalongkorn, who abolished slavery, began his forty-two year reign

1932 Absolute monarchy ended on June 24 in a bloodless coup during the reign of Rama VII (1925-1935)

1940-1945 Thailand joined co-prosperity sphere with Japan

1946 Rama VIII assassinated; King Bhumibol ascended to the throne as the Chakri Rama IX

Government: A Thai king is thought by peasants to be a reincarnation of god. Thus, when some military force takes control, it's judicious of them to pay homage to the monarch, even though the usurpers keep control of the real power.

King Bhumibol, Rama IX of the Chakri Dynasty, is Thailand's figurehead and unifying image despite the rapid change-overs that have resulted in various military juntas holding political power.

It's been said that consensus among more than two Thai is an impossibility. Thus, the coup d'etat has developed into a political art form. In the three years after WW II, there were nine different governments. One faction, perhaps ten to fifteen VIPs of the top two percent echelon, tries to outmaneuver another faction. Sometimes the events become a ridiculous melodrama as

King Bhumibol, Rama IX

when the Thai air force bombed the Thai navy. The prime minister, aboard to accept a ship as a gift from the United States, was kidnapped by the army and taken to another ship. He escaped the bombing by jumping overboard and swimming to shore.

Sometimes the uprising is bloody, as during the student revolt in 1973 and the military's brutal resurgence in 1976. In 1980, the coup was a medieval drama. The king sided with General Prem, the present leader of the country. Without royal support, the rebels soon capitulated. Typical of Thai politics, these revolutionaries were freed within a few months. At news inverviews, they justified the coup attempt and promised to try again with greater finesse. Little of this matters at the lower strata. The petty government officials remain underpaid and are forced to augment their incomes by accepting the "white envelope," a euphemism for the traditional bribe money.

Customs and Conduct

Three concepts outline Thai behaviour: *kwan sanuk*, *mai pen rai*, and "face." *Kwan sanuk* means to derive a sense of pleasure from what you're doing. A good job doesn't necessarily have to pay well, but it must be fun. City bus drivers behave like stunt men, zooming around corners with no hands on the wheels. A shopkeeper will spend days bargaining and have more relish for the barter game than for any potential financial gain.

Mai pen rai translates approximately as "never mind." Since whatever happens is what one deserves by his accumulated karma, the inevitable result of a person's action is neither tragic nor changeable. It's merely accepted. Anger is considered an immoral failure to accept responsibility for your actions, while at the same time creating more negative forces. The Thai make every effort not to increase their bad karma. Some of their military search-and-destroy missions have turned into ludicrous noise-making expeditions: They shoot into the air to scare the enemy into hiding and thus avoid the adverse spiritual effects of killing. On the other hand, when bad karma must be faced, Thai have little with which to hold back raw violence. Many young men carry guns and will use them when a smile doesn't work and they're forced into a face-saving situation.

The Thai is honestly concerned that everyone around him should be happy, or at least not appear to have bad karma. In greeting he says *sawatdee* (good fortune to you), and accompanies it with a *wai*, the Thai gift of respect made by placing the hands together, elbows down, and then slightly bowing the head. The higher the hands are raised, the more respectful. To show their concern for you, they will ask what seem to be personal questions: "Where are you going?" "Are you married?" "How old are you?" "How much money do you make?" "Have you had a bath today?" Gift giving is common, almost epidemic. Presents are offered with the right hand while touching the right elbow with the left hand.

Thai avoid offending each other. The head is considered sacred, the foot just the opposite. It's extremely rude to pat a child on the head. It's equally uncouth to point the bottom of your foot at anyone. Most Thai try to keep their feet pointed to the floor or avoid crossing their legs at all. Shoes are removed when entering a home. When a man touches a woman in public, she loses face and appears to other Thai as a prostitute.

Because of their tolerant nature, Thai will rarely object to the strange antics of a *farang* (foreigner). However, some behavior is not tolerated. One tourist was rude all night to an owner of a restaurant, and no one said a thing to him. But finally, he threw his crumpled Thai *baht* note on the ground. He was then im-

mediately tackled and beaten by every male Thai in the place. His offense was disrespect to the image of the king on the bill. In the most backward area of the northeast, the king is considered nothing less than sacred. Even in Bangkok, people will stop in mid-street to show respect for the monarch during the morning national anthem—a tune strangely like a German military march and blasted over speakers along busy streets. Small wonder that the movie "The King and I" portraying King Mongkut as an arrogant despot, was banned in Thailand.

Religion is another area of taboos. A few years ago, two *farang* were imprisoned when they stirred up the righteous indignation of the Thai populous by posing for a photograph while sitting on the head of a

The *wai* salutation

Buddha statue. Feet must never so much as *point* toward the Buddha, much less tread upon his holy head. (In temples, people sit on their feet.) Shoes must be removed when entering the main chapel of a *wat* and shorts aren't considered proper temple attire. Shoes are acceptable in the temple grounds, but Thai wear shorts only for peasant work. Inside temples, speak softly. If you wear a Buddha amulet—not advisable unless you're a Buddhist—never enter a brothel or walk under a clothes line. Monks are given a great deal of respect as representatives of Lord Buddha. Women are never to sit next to them, and a monk should always be seated at a higher level, even if it's only the symbolic thickness of a seating cloth. Behavior codes are breaking down. If you unintentionally offend someone, smile, apologize, and *wai. Mai pen rai.*

___Food

Delicious pain! Spicy, sour, slightly sweet Thai cuisine uses sensational combinations of seasonings: garlic, ginger, basil, cardamom, bits of red and green chilies, sprigs of lemon grass, and a liberal amount of coriander leaf. Splashes of *nam plah*, a salty soy sauce substitute made from fermented fish, and *nam prik*, bottled fire; join the excitement. *Dtaang guah*, cucumbers usually fried in coconut oil, are served with the meal to put out the flames. The Thai use the backs of their metal forks to heap food onto large, thin, tin spoons. Chopsticks are impractical for the predominately soft noodles, soups, and saucy dishes.

Main Meal: Rice, *kow*, is served plain (*kow plow*) as a foundation for a sauce dish, or fried (*kow pat*) with the meal. For eight to fifteen *baht*, fried rice (*kow pat*) is served with beef, *neua*, (*kow pat neua*), pork, *moo*, prawns, *gung*, or fish, *plah*. At the more expensive stalls, the fried rice is often topped with a fried egg, *kai tawt* (*tawt* means deep-fried). Locals call this dish the Mount Meru of fried rice. *Mas-man* is curry cooked in a peanut sauce with potatoes added. *Aroi mahk* (delicious)! Chicken fried with ginger, *gai pat gin*, is superb.

Soups and Noodles: For an inexpensive breakfast, try *kao tom*, a gruel-like rice soup with scattered bits of prawns, pork, fish, or vegetables. Vegetable soup, *gang judd*, has a spicy curried flavor. On practically every corner and in the middle of almost every block stands a *kwey teow* stall, ready to quick boil a noodle soup for five *baht*. *Bah mee nam* is a yellow noodle soup. One of the most distinctively Thai flavors is *tohm yum*, a sour soup sprinkled with lemon grass and usually made with shrimp or fish.

You'll occasionally find *nom tien*, noodles with tasty gravy, for about ฿4. *Non sen nam meu*, noodles in a hot sauce, comes as cheap as ฿2 in the rural towns of the north. Although few foreigners develop a taste for it, the totally adventurous might spend ฿8 to try *yen too for*, a sweet red sauce with noodles, vegetables, and pig-organ-meat. *Mee krob* is fried noodles sprinkled with whatever the cook has on hand. *Pad Thai*, a savory vegetarian dish made by heaping raw vegetables on fried noodles and sprinkling on salt, sugar, and ground peanuts,

Mai kon and *gahcha* (pole and baskets) are common in Thailand.

can often be found at night stalls for about ฿10. For other vegetarian dishes, say *"Ahan chey dai mai?"* or, request that the meat be left out, *"Mai sai neua."*

Street Snacks: Deep-fried donut-like *pradanko* dipped in sweet tea makes a sinfully good breakfast. Deep-fried banana fritters, *gloo-ay tawt*, are sold everywhere, sometimes with peanuts sprinkled on the outside. Look for the woman squatting by her *mai kon* and *gahcha* (pole and baskets), and selling bamboo-joint cylinders of *kow lam*. (This is simply rice, sugarcane, sweetener, and coconut milk pressed together—sometimes with sweet beans added to give the chewy rice a purple color.) For other sweets try the many varieties of coconut jellies in molded designs, mung bean curries, *lunglun* (coconut cream favors), taro root custards, *khao tomphad* (paper-thin pancakes with coconut centers), *kanon kok* (creamy white half-moons of coconut), and ice cream dipped into rice and black beans.

Drinks: Hot Thai tea (*nam cha rawn*) has an orange color and a muted vanilla-like flavor, especially when mixed with liberal amounts of sweetened condensed milk. Cold tea (*nam cha yen*) tastes like an unusual milkshake. If you like your tea "brown"—without milk or sugar—order *cha dahm* and ask for a glass of *nam rawn* (hot water) to thin it.

Coffee (*gahfaa*) is unlike any other coffee you've ever tasted, super sweet and syrupy. *Oliang*, iced black coffee, is sold in sweating plastic bags by vendors beside your train car. To the unwary it appears to be a cola. Lemon juice (*nam mannow*) and orange juice (*nam som*) are alternatives. The Thai serve these with salt added to increase the sweetness. If you don't want salt, say *"mai sai guah."* For an unusual beverage, try *bia bia*, a green sludge said to cure stomach problems, fevers, blisters, and infections.

Amarit and Singha are the two slightly bitter beers available. Beer is so heavily taxed that often mixed drinks are a better deal. Mekong whiskey has a hint of rum with its slightly caramel flavor. It's wicked. *Nam kaang* is ice. *"Mai sia nam kaang"* if you don't want ice in your beer. And last, here are a few good words to know: *au ma eek neung gaa-oh*, "please one more glass."

_Events

Songkram Festival: Beginning on April 13, the middle of Thailand's hottest month, a three-day water war erupts each year. People go crazy drenching each other with buckets full of water. For artillery, hoses are hooked up to faucets. Patrols of trucks, the backs filled with licensed hydromaniacs, barrage anyone ignorant or unlucky enough to be riding in an open-backed minibus. Demure beauty queens on floats conceal squirt guns for sneak attacks.

Ostensibly, the festival celebrates Buddhist New Year. Young people show respect by sprinkling the palms of their elders with perfumed water while saying *Sawatdee Pimai* (Happy New Year). But the roots go back to a pre-Buddha, pre-Hindu belief in the *naga*-serpent. *Naga*-serpents lived high above in fabled Lake Anodat of the mystical Himalayas. Splashes of water spilling over the hills during their love-making season fertilized the world as rain. The festival is celebrated all over Thailand except in Bangkok where complaints from foreign residents caused it to be banned.

Coronation Day: The present king and queen of Thailand were made sacred when they ascended to the throne on May 5, 1946. Each May 5, the Thai honor that very important day.

Visakha Bucha: The holiest of Buddha days occurs in May. It celebrates the master's birth, enlightenment, and death. Although religious, it's far from austere. Drama and dance mesmerize you while exotic music carries you to a new reality. *Wat* courtyards throughout the land are transformed to surrealistic carnivals. Colored neon lights shine on children holding cardboard puppets, while nearby an array of food stalls sell sweet-flavored favors.

A celebration for *nen*, novice monks, entering the monastery

Buddhist Lent: In July, *Kao Phansa* signals the beginning of this period of spiritual recommitment. Monks return to their monasteries to meditate. In bacchanalian surroundings, novices emphasize their piety by abstinence. In Ubon, in the northeast corner of Thailand, the people hold a Candle Festival with tapers taller than a man. Then the light of gaiety dims and for three months the devout turn inside themselves. Only the sedate celebration of Queen Sirikit on August 12 interrupts these somber months, and the mornings see few saffron robes.

Kao Phansa in October marks the end of lent and the beginning of gaiety once more. The colorful cacophony of activity again surrounds the village *wat*. In Nakorn Panom in the northeast, wax candles parade down the streets and along the canals; and in Surat Thani in the south, native-made boats compete in a regatta.

Loi Krathong: (The floating leaf cup.) In November, banana-leaf boats carrying cargos of flowers, bob on the surface of *klong* (canals) and rivers. Burning incense and flaming candles look like a galaxy drifting on the water. People put all their energy into creating a work of beauty, even more awe inspiring for its transience.

The event was originally an animistic tribute to *Mae Khonka*, goddess of the waters. According to legend, a flawlessly-shaped maiden gave the king an exquisitely-fashioned ship. He doubted the propriety of a Buddhist monarch accepting such a non-Buddhist gift, but he wanted the vessel. Therefore, he reinterpreted the focus of the festival. Today, Buddhists believe the star-ships float over places in the beds of rivers and streams where Buddha left footprints.

King Bhumibol's Birthday: From December 3 through 5 the Thai reaffirm their allegiance to the ninth king of the two-century-old Chakri Dynasty. He was born on December 5 in Cambridge, Massachusetts, while his father was attending college. Each year the Royal Guard parades around the palace. And men inspired by the current hit song "I'm Vasectomized," undergo the seven-minute operation in temporary tents decorated with inflated blue condoms for the celebration.

Practicalities

Getting Around by Train: Thailand's 3765 kilometers of track emanate from Bangkok in three major lines: One goes north to Chiang Mai. Another goes northeast to Nong Khai on the Laotian border. The third goes south to Hadyai where it splits, one branch terminating in the border town of Sungai Golok on the east coast and the other going via Penang down the peninsula to Singapore. Make reservations at the Hua Lumpong Station no more than two weeks in advance. The ticket room is to the right as you enter. Grab a number and wait on the hardwood benches until the number cackles over the speaker in Thai. Just keep showing your number to the person next to you if you haven't learned Thai numbers yet. Always buy your tickets in advance—they cost twice as much if you buy them from the conductor on the train. To carry your bicycle on a train, add one and a half times the third-class fare.

Buses: Before an owner allows his vehicles on the road, he has a priest sprinkle them with holy water. And that's the extent of the safety precautions. Accidents are frequent, often caused by buses from competing companies racing at breakneck speed. This practice combined with robberies in the south make rail travel far safer. On the positive side, there's an excellent system of roads, and frequent bus service makes travel between towns easy. Buses are less crowded during the day than at night. The non-air-conditioned buses stop to pick up passengers anywhere along the road and will make impromptu, hurried rest stops on request. The prices are similar to train fares.

In and Around Town: Taxis rarely use their meters. *Songtao*, pickup trucks with passenger benches in the back, normally charge from ฿3 to ฿5. (In groups of three or more, fares are negotiable.) *Tuk tuk*, motorized tricycles with passenger compartments in the back, are slightly more expensive; and *samlor*, trishas powered by the bulging calves of the pedaler, are justifiably more costly.

Language: Pasa Thai (the Thai language) was originally polysyllabic, but through years of phonetic erosion, it has become monosyllabic. For instance, words like "match" are made by combining syllables for wood, strike, and fire. Five tones now replace the dropped portions of the word. Thus, *suay* spoken with an upswing at the end is a complimentary "beautiful"; but *suay* with a downswing means "bad luck to you." (The effects are vastly different.) Whereas a westerner is accustomed to listening for initial consonants in syllables to catch the word, Thai hear mostly vowels. Often the varying tones spell doom to the traveler trying to learn the language. Don't give up; just keep singing the sentence different ways. The locals laugh at your ridiculous accent, but their giggles also cover nervousness at not being able to speak English. And they're adaptable to foreign tongues; the king is said to speak Thai with an American accent. His wife speaks Vassar-ese.

So few people in rural areas know English that even a small Thai vocabulary is a priceless aid to travel. A *sawatdee* (hello) disarms a potentially dangerous situation, and a *tow rai* (how much) will bring prices plummeting to near local levels. *Robertson's Practical English-Thai Dictionary* is a handy pocket-size addition to the vocabulary in this book.

Money: The Thai *baht* (฿) hovers between ฿20 and ฿23 to a U.S. dollar. Be sure to break money down to ฿100, ฿20, and ฿10 denominations before heading for the back country. Mammoth ฿5 and ฿1 coins quickly weigh down your pockets and make you feel richer than you are. Thailand has no currency black market; money changers often give poorer rates than banks. Change money at American- or Thai-owned banks for the best rates. Some banks in Bangkok have walk-up exchange windows that are open to 2100.

Visas: A fifteen-day transit visa is given automatically to citizens of the United States, West Germany, Sweden, Denmark, Norway, and Hong Kong, and also to transit passengers from other countries as long as they have either a ticket out of Thailand or the money to buy one. This usually isn't checked unless you dress like a "hippie," whose characteristics, according to published official government guidelines, are: "people who wear just a singlet or waistcoat without underwear, those who wear shorts which are not respectable and people who wear any type of slippers or wooden sandals, except when they are part of national costume."

To extend this visa, a cash or bank guarantee of between ฿5,000 and ฿20,000 is required. In Bangkok only, it's possible to extend the fifteen-day pass to two

CAPSULE VOCABULARY

Kahp, literally "sir," is spoken at the end of sentences as a sign of respect. Only men use *kahp*. Women say *ka* except when they're being very informal. Men also use *ka* when they speak to someone of superior status such as a monk.

hello *sawatdee kahp/ka*
How are you? *Sabai dee reu?*
Fine. *Sabai dee.*
Excuse me. *Kaw toht.*
What? *Arai kahp/ka?*
What did you say? *Arai nah?*
Please. *Kaw roo nah*
slowly *cha cha*
speak *poodt*
again *eek*
say it again *poodt eek*
I don't understand *mai kow chai**
where? *tee nai?*
Where is _____? _____ *yoo tee nai?*
toilet *soo um*
when? *mee uh*
tomorrow *proong nee*
today *wahn nee*
no (not) *mai*
now *dee oh nee*
maybe *bahng tee (achah)*
how much *tow rai?*
1 *neung*
2 *sawng*
3 *sahm*
4 *see*
5 *hah*
6 *hohk*
7 *jet*
8 *baat*
9 *gow*
10 *sip*
11 *sip-et*
12 *sip sawng*
20 *yee sip*

21 *yee sip eht*
100 *neung roi*
250 *sawng roi hah sip*
1000 *neung pahn*
expensive *paang*
very *mahk*
very expensive *paang mahk*
OK *OK*
yes *chai*
good *dee*
Thank you. *Kawp koon kahp/ka.**
left *sai*
and *laa*
right *khwa*
and then *laa-oh gaw*
straight *dtrohng bpai*
near *glai***
tourist office *nahk tawng tee oh prai sanee*
good luck *chohk dee*
stop *yoot*
want *ow*
I don't want *mai ow**
post office *tee tahm gaan prai sanee*
train station *satani roht fai*
bus station *satani roht meh*
or *reu*
airport *sanambin*
wait *dee oh dee oh*
What is your name? *Koon cheu arai kahp/ka?**
friend *peu un*
beautiful *suay, ngahm*
can *dai*
can't *mai dai*
It doesn't matter. *mai pen rai*

*Koon is an informal you. *Tahn* is more formal. It's best, however, not to refer to "you" for the same reason you should avoid using I (*pohm*, male, *chahm*, female and informal male). Individual identity is less important than the group. The language reflects this tendency.

**glai also means far but it's a different tone when spoken.

months, but this is difficult. At Thai consulates outside the country, a two-month visa is obtainable for about ten dollars and a three-month one for fifteen dollars. Bring five photos and be prepared to take all day. The two-month or three-month visa is not renewable. If you wish to stay longer in Thailand, find a Thai friend to sponsor you, become a Buddhist monk (male option), or streak down to Penang or the friendlier Thai consulate in Kota Baru, Malaysia where it's three dollars, no questions asked, and here's your new two-month visa.

Bangkok: City of Angels

Bangkok's real name is the world's longest with 157 letters: Krungthepmahan-akhonbowornratanakosinmahintarayudyayamahadilokponoparatanarajthaniburi-romudomrajniwesmahasatarnamornpimarnavatarsatitsakattiyavisanukamphrasit. In an attempt to convey the grandeur of the more than two-hundred-year-old capital of the Chakri Dynasty, the official court namer decided to leave off none

of its glorious attributes. And the name stuck, although today it's abbreviated to simply Krung Thep. (Many Thai don't understand the word *Bangkok*, "What's a Bangkok?") Krung Thep means "City of Angels"—like California's L.A.

History: When King Rama I took control of the country from General Taksin on April 6, 1782, he moved his capital across the S-shaped Chao Phraya River to take advantage of the protection offered by the sea of mud to the east. He built his golden palace and, inside its walls, the richest temple in the land. A network of canals cut through the plains. And shanties, shipbuilders, shops, and finally, cement-grey apartment buildings grew up along these waterway *klong* (urban bayou).

Today: Krung Thep is sinking under the weight of heavy buildings. The older level of town is only 1.8 meters above sea level. The supporting underground water is being pumped out to supply the ever-increasing needs of the five million people living here. (The population is expected to double by 1995.) Nine out of every ten vehicles in Thailand rumbles down the roads of Bangkok in a chaos of traffic.

Inside this neon-modern, jet-age nexus are glimpses of the old Krung Thep. More than three hundred *wat* send gold stupa spires into the skyline. River taxis, ferries, barges, and bus-boats scuttle up, down, and across the Chao Phraya. And in the outskirts, you see simple wood houses set above the water in their front yards. The unshaded electric light bulb reveals the naked modesty inside a home: no furniture, a poster on the wall, a cooking fire, a color TV.

____Getting Around

In the Airport: There are five reasonably cheap ways of traveling the 28.8 kilometers from Don Muang Airport to downtown Bangkok. Near the exit lounge, the International Limousine Service will take you to your hotel door. For more than twice as much, a taxi will do the same. Air-conditioned Bus 10 goes to the Victory Monument and from there, Bus 201 goes to the T.A.T. (Tourist Authority of Thailand; open only during the day). The airport bus stop is past the parking lot by the highway. Bus 29 crawls into the city, the choking traffic fumes pouring in the open window and robbing the muggy air of oxygen. It heads past the northbound bus station, goes near the Siam Center, and then on south to the Hua Lumpong Railroad Station.

Or, you can start your adventure immediately. Skate past the taxi drivers with a *mai ow* (I don't want), and walk across the two overpasses to village Thailand. People smile at your smile. About three hundred meters to the left is a small railroad station where trains stop on their run into Hua Lumpong. At night you pass the fireflies—open, outdoor fires and sparks of light reflecting off the glass squares on temple roofs. The cool breeze blowing in the window brings whiffs of burning wood and coriander leaves from cooking. The light gets brighter as you enter the metro-machine. The popsicle colors of the neon-illuminated outdoor nightclub float past. A few minutes later you pull into Hua Lumpong Railroad Station, a beaux-art-industrial-revolution classic of iron and glass.

Districts of Bangkok: For ease in conceptualizing this vast metropolis, the city can be divided into six sections: (1) the old palace and surroundings, still the heart of the city; (2) Yaowarat/Chinatown, the crowded former financial center of Bangkok, a city more than half Chinese; (3) the government/military complex, characterized by broad lanes, parks, and ponderous Victorian office buildings; (4) the old tourist haven, centering on the Oriental Hotel and along Bangkok's first road, formerly an elephant path, now New Road; (5) the expanded air-conditioned tourist traps going up Silom Road and containing instant-sin lanes, such as the infamous Pat Pong; and (6) modern Bangkok starting around the Siam Center and spreading on and on and on out Sukumvit Road. *Soi* (lanes) are numbered consecutively, but even numbers are on one side and odd numbers on the other side. This can be confusing, especially way out in suburban Sukumvit where Soi 24 is opposite Soi 39.

Taxis and Tuk Tuk: Taxis are reasonably priced at ฿20 for short runs and ฿30 for crosstown trips such as from the G.P.O (General Post Office) to Siam Center. They're required by law to have meters, but the law doesn't say they must use them. You'll be forced to bargain before the trip, knocking off at least ฿10 from the asking price. There are many taxis so if you find the driver intransigent, try another. Few drivers speak English; have your hotel write out the address you wish to go to.

BOAT LANDINGS

A Thammasart University Tha Prannock
B Wat Po Tha Tien
C Tha Rachini
D Tha Wat Muang Kae
E Tha Oriental
F Thanon Tok boat landing

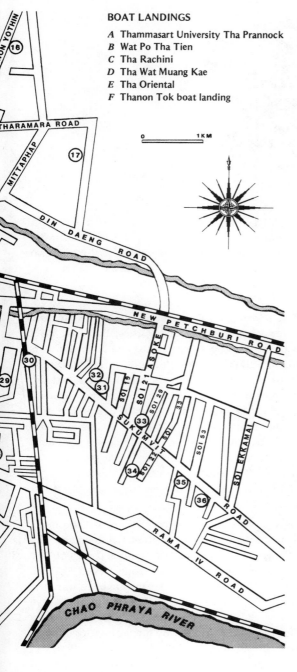

BANGKOK

1. Bangkok Noi Railroad Station
2. South Bus Terminal
3. Wat Arun
4. Wat Po
5. Grand Palace and Wat Pra Keo
6. Sanam Luong
7. Democratic Monument
8. Wat Suthat and Sao Ching-Cha (Giant Swing)
9. Golden Mount
10. Tourist Office (T.A.T.)
11. Wat Benjamabopit (Marble Temple)
12. Dusit Zoo
13. Chitlada Palace
14. Victory Monument
15. Weekend Market
16. North Bus Station
17. Kay Guest House
18. Hua Lumpong Railroad Station
19. Boy Scout Hostel
20. Jim Thompson House
21. Siam Center
22. Wat Pathumwan and pond
23. Indra Hotel
24. Pratunam Market
25. Thai-Daimaru
26. Erawan Shrine
27. Lumpini Park
28. Lumpini Boxing Stadium
29. U.S. Embassy
30. Phasuk Guest House and Atlanta Hotel
31. Danish Bakery and Asia Bookstore
32. India Embassy
33. Bharni Restaurant
34. Starlight Hotel
35. Post Office
36. East Bus Station
37. YMCA
38. Immigration
39. Sukol Bakery and Saladaing Phojana Restaurant
40. Snake Farm
41. Pat Pong district
42. Burma Embassy
43. General Post Office
44. Oriental and Swan Hotels
45. Bangkrak Market
46. King Taksin Statue
47. Wat Lao
48. Wat Bang Waek

A *tuk tuk*

Tuk tuk, third-generation rickshas with motors, have replaced the *samlor*, outlawed in 1957. *Tuk tuk* are open-air vehicles and the pollution and traffic heat are definitely not comfortable. The price for a short run for one or two passengers is ฿10. They won't make long trips because each has its own territory to cover.

Buses: For two *baht* buses will take you almost anywhere you want to go. Bus maps are available at the T.A.T. office on Ratchadamnoen Nok Road, and at bookstores and the main train station Advertisement Office. Bangkok buses have developed a permanent list to the left as passengers hang on outside like bats on a cave wall during the rush hours (0700 to 0900 and 1600 to 1900). During these times you'll be lucky to get a toehold on any of the major routes. Instead, take one of the air-conditioned buses listed in larger numbers on the bus map. You are hermetically sealed away from the overwhelming din of Bangkok traffic.

To read the bus map, remember that traffic is on the left. Bus numbers are on the sides of the streets that the bus travels on or in the middle if it goes both ways. Buses 1, 15, 25, and 76 have two routes; check to see if you want a red or green bus or be prepared to jump off. The unofficial truck-buses carry the same numbers as the city service. They travel the same routes for a cheaper, if less comfortable, ride with the ordinary people.

Water Transport: River boats provide a way to cool off while you move through the city. The routes are noted in dotted lines on the Bangkok maps. The express boats, *rua duan Chao Phraya*, run every fifteen minutes from 0600 to 1800. They leave from Thanon Tok and go past eighteen stops to Non Thaburi. There is rarely a place to sit at the public docks, and you may have to wave the boats down. To get off the express, tell or point out your destination to the conductor. To find six of the piers: take Bus 22 to its terminus at Thanon Tok Pier; walk left of the Oriental Hotel ignoring the hawkers who'll try to trick you onto an expensive tourist boat; walk down the first road left of the G.P.O. (there's an arch for Wat Muang Kae at the top of this path); walk left as you come out of the Grand Palace; walk west from Wat Po to the end of Thai Wang Road; take

Bus 6 to its terminus and walk to the end of Vasut Kaset, one block past a giant three-story Buddha at Wat Indravihan.

Ferries, *rua kham fak*, cross the river every three minutes for a half *baht* (fifty *satang*). Take a chance and hop aboard a *rua hang yao* ("long-tailed" boats with long propeller shafts slanting into the water at their sterns), to ride with the locals through the smaller *klong*. Ask the price before you go. Some long-tails hire out as taxis.

For pedestrians, jay-jogging is mandatory. But generally, movement on foot is slow; in the hot muggy climate you feel like a bubble of air in oil. At intersections a courteous driver will slow down before he hits you.

___Sights

Wat Arun: The temple of the dawn catches the morning light from the west bank of the Chao Phraya River. King Taksin intended Wat Arun to be the central monastery of his kingdom. When his general returned from Vientiane with the sacred Emerald Buddha, Taksin ordered it sheltered here. In 1785, that same general became Rama I and moved the Buddha and the capital across the river. However, his descendants kept building at Wat Arun. The result is an eighty-two meter Phra Prang tower, jagged with art and decorated with hundreds of embedded pieces of Chinese porcelain. Climb to the second terrace. Slender, banana-shaped boats scurry about on the river below, dodging green islands of floating hyacinth.

Wat Po: Fort-like walls surround the temple. There are sixteen gates but only two are open, one east and one west. An entry fee is charged at the east tourist entry. Inside, the eight hectares are crowded with chapels and more than ninety *chedi* (stupas). The largest four *chedi* are in their own courtyard, opposite a Hindu *linga*. The green one was built by Rama I. Rama III added the white and yellow. Rama IV constructed the blue one, the largest and most ornate, and then ended the competition by forbidding future construction of *chedi* here.

In another courtyard, the *bot* (main chapel) is surrounded by 394 Buddhas. At the entrance to the marble structure hang huge doors of teak inlaid with mother-of-pearl designs. A carved marble portion showing scenes from the Rama-kien (the Thai version of the Indian Ramayana), was carried here from the ruins of Ayuthia. In the interior, rich red and gold lacquer designs cover the ceiling and square pillars. People venerate the ashes of Rama I held in the high altar. Once a god, always a god.

As you meander in the maze of Wat Po, you run across walls inscribed with instructive pictures on everything from astrology to feudal military tactics. A mound of rock has statues that illustrate the torturous art of Thai massage. Rama III (1824-1851) wanted the *wat* to be a learning center with a library and visual aids to help his generally illiterate subjects. An x-ray hangs on one of these education mounds. It was brought here to help the spirits in making their diagnoses and magical cures.

Enormous grey-white stone statues guard the gates of Wat Po. These statues are said to be a Chinese artist's rendition of European "devils." Three other recurring figures are: Hok, dressed as a high-ranking courtier; Lok, wearing the clothes of a rich man and carrying a child; and Siew, an old man with fruit in one hand and a cane in the other. Respectively, they symbolize power, wealth, and health or longevity. The graceful gold-plated reclining Buddha (forty-nine meters long) in the west courtyard usurps the large hall. There's little room for your ego next to the Buddha.

Presumably Marco Polo was the model for this statue carved in China. It was brought along with a great many other granite statues as ship ballast in the hulls of the large seagoing rice barges on their way home to Thailand. Many of the sculptures were given to Rama III at a discount since they were scavenged from deserted monasteries in China's interior. Entire carved stone Chinese *Keng*, resting pavilions, were dismantled and reassembled in several of Bangkok's *wat*.

Grand Palace: This palace once housed Chakri kings and their courts until the mysterious murder of King Ananda in 1932. The formerly forbidden grounds are now open to the public (0830 to 1130 and 1300 to 1600). On Saturdays, Sundays, and Buddhist holidays everyone is allowed in free.

Enter the outer starch-white walls from the north and pass through the salmon-colored inner wall, once used to house royal white elephants. On the other side of this gate stands the elegant Chakri Mahaprasad Hall, a sturdy Victorian structure startlingly covered with a flamboyant Thai-style roof. It was designed by a British architect in 1868 for Rama V to celebrate the first 100 years of the Chakri Dynasty. Two years later electricity was installed. The hall is still used for banquets to welcome visiting heads of state.

To the right is the delicate Abhornpimok Pavilion. Rama IV ordered it made so it would be easier for him to move from his shoulder-high palanquin to the Throne Hall. The pavilion was reproduced at Bang Pa-In and again at the 1958 Brussel's World Fair as a representation of classical Thai architecture.

In the adjacent court to the west stands the simple Dusit Hall, Krung Thep's oldest royal residence. Since the death of Rama I, it's been used primarily for the lying-in-state of Thai kings. In the courtyard east of Mahaprasad stands Amarin Vinichai Hall. The upper boat-shaped throne is now used as an altar. In front, another throne is sheltered by a nine-tiered canopy, a symbol of royalty borrowed from the vanished Mon Kingdom. When the king receives an audience, he enters, hidden behind a curtain which is then theatrically parted with fanfare.

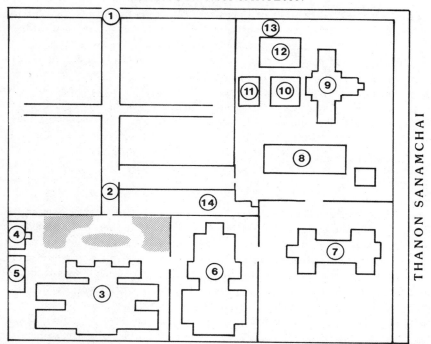

THANON NAPHRALAN

THANON SANAMCHAI

GRAND PALACE

1. Entrance
2. Inner gate
3. Chakri Mahaprasad Hall
4. Abhornpimok Pavilion
5. Dusit Hall

6. Amarin Vinichai Hall
7. Boromabiman Hall
8. The temple of the Emerald Buddha
9. Prasat Pra Debidorn Hall

10. Pra Mondop
11. Pra Sri Ratana Chedi
12. Model of Angkor Wat
13. Ramakien Mural begins
14. Thai Decoration and Coin Pavilion

Interior of Chakri Mahaprasad Hall

Wat Pra Keo: This worship chapel for kings is located in the northeast corner of the crenelated white walls of the palace. The heady richness of the courtyard is guarded by *Yaksha*. These giant saber-toothed, leering, green-faced demigods with three vertically stacked heads are so ugly they turn evil away.

The blue-tiled temple is the final haven of the famous Emerald Buddha, the most important icon in all of Buddhist Thailand. The air is hazy from burning joss sticks as the devout kneel to honor their Lord Buddha. The seventy-five-centimeter-high statue has been sitting dramatically lit in this dark hall since 1784. Its origins are unknown. Probably fashioned out of jasper (not emerald or jade), by some artisan of northern Thailand, it was discovered in Chiang Rai in 1434. It was moved to Lampang for 32 years, to Chiang Mai for 84 years, to Laos for 226 years, and finally brought to Thonburi by the future Rama I, who later moved it across the river to the statue's present home. The Buddha has an opulent wardrobe of three jeweled and golden costumes. The king alone is allowed to change Buddha's clothes, once for each season: summer, winter, rain. Only the king and queen are allowed to enter the central door of the temple, and even they must take off their shoes. No monks live at this sacred *wat*.

To the north stands Prasat Pra Debidorn Hall covered in mirrored mosaic and trimmed in gold. It was built under the command of King Mongkut to house the Emerald Buddha, but it proved too small for the ceremonies. In front stand mythical *kinaree* (half woman, half bird), their hands in a prayerful *wai* gesture. Behind this building, the *mondop* (a square building housing a Buddha), has

exquisite mother-of-pearl cabinets containing early Buddhist scriptures. Behind this, the gold pagoda, Pra Sri Ratana, contains some of the bones of Buddha. To the north of the *mondop* is a model of twelfth-century Angkor Wat fashioned for Rama IV who wished to survey his possession. (Kampuchea was then a vassal of Thailand.) North of this, on the wall of the gallery, is the beginning point of the Ramakien story which encircles the whole courtyard. You walk past the monkey general's exploits and the intriguing sections dealing with the everyday lives of ordinary people in the early eighteenth century.

To the left of the exit, the Royal Thai Decoration and Coin Pavilion, open daily except Sunday, displays fabulous gold-embossed teapots, incredible plumed crown-hats, an engraved

Inner palace gate in front of Chakri Mahaprasad Hall

cigarette case, bejeweled boxes, and examples of coins and gambling tokens used in Thailand over the centuries.

San Lakmuang: Standing diagonally across from the northeast corner of the palace, this small shrine contains a pillar-like *lingam* covered with flakes of gold and draped with ribbons and garlands brought as gifts to the city's spirit. (Stone *linga* are centers of worship and symbolize male-female union, oneness.)

Some supplicants promise to pay for *Lakorn Chatree*, dances given in honor of the gods. On Sundays and holidays, women in traditional pants costumes balance on one leg and weave their arms to the music in the chamber next to the *lingam*. Outside, vendors sell gold leaf and caged birds to be set free as donations to the spirits. (There are similar dancers on the corner of Ratchadamri and Sukumvit at the elaborate spirit house built to stop spirits harassing workers.)

Kinaree are mythological angels who flit between this plane of existence and a higher one. Manohra, a captured *kinaree*, put aside her wings and tail feathers to marry Prince Pra Suthon. Her beauty caused the lusting monarch in a neighboring kingdom to wage a war for her. Meanwhile Manohra was threatened with fire at the stake by her fickle father-in-law. She asked for her costume so she could dance her heavenly dance finale, after which she flew away.

Wat Benjamabopit (The Marble Temple): This temple is considered by many to be the pinnacle of Thai architecture. Built under the patronage of the fifth Chakri king, it is made of the finest Italian marble. Two vicious *singha* (lions) stand sentinel at the entrance of the *bot*. A drum donated by the non-Buddhist Karen tribe of northern Thailand is kept inside. You compare the diverse styles of the bronze Buddhas in the gallery which surrounds the immaculate marble-paved courtyard. Some are from as far away as Japan. On the south wall sits a gaunt figure representing the Buddha after forty days of fasting and self-torture before he decided there must be a better way to enlightenment. On the west wall stand two graceful, almost feminine, walking Buddhas of the Sukotai era.

A *klong* runs through the *wat* grounds, separating the worship area from the monks' quarters. Here the present king spent his days as a penniless novice. Early in the morning before most tourists come, monks cross the wrought iron bridge to chant in the chapel. The temple is on Si Ayuthia Road near Chitlada Palace of the King.

Walking Buddha of the Sukotai era

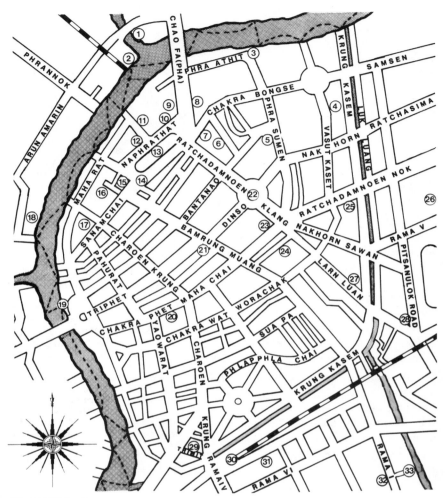

HEART OF BANGKOK

1. Royal Barge Shed
2. Bangkok Noi Railroad Station
3. Outer Palace Wall remnant
4. Wat Indravihan
5. Wat Bowonivet
6. Khaosan Road guest house area
7. Padung Cheep Store
8. National Gallery
9. National Theater
10. National Museum
11. Wat Thammasart
12. Wat Mahathat
13. Sanam Luong
14. San Lakmuang
15. Wat Pra Keo
16. Grand Palace
17. Wat Po
18. Wat Arun
19. Pak Klong Talaat (Vegetable Market)
20. Nakorn Kasem (Thieves Market)
21. Wat Suthat, Giant Swing
22. Democratic Monument
23. Wat Rachanada
24. Wat Sraket (Golden Mount)
25. Tourist Office (T.A.T.)
26. Wat Benjamabopit (Marble Temple)
27. Narayanaband Handicraft Store
28. Adventist Hospital
29. Wat Trimit
30. Hua Lumpong Railroad Station
31. Sri Hua Lumpong Hotel
32. Boy Scout Hostel
33. Jim Thompson House

___Museums, Gardens, and Parks

National Museum: The first buildings in this compound northwest of the Sanam Luong oval were constructed in 1782 as a palace for the second or "vice" king. It was his duty to ease transition from one monarch to the next; only one of them ever became a Chakri king. The museum is open from 0900 to 1600, Tuesday through Sunday. It has forty-seven sections containing a diversity of archeological, artistic, historic, anthropological, and cultural artifacts. Guide pamphlets are sold near the entrance.

The maze of rooms contains seventh-century B.C. pottery from Ban Chiang, royal palanquins, an all ivory howdah (a passenger pavilion built for riding on top of elephants), theatrical masks, marionettes, musical instruments, weapons of war (including a life-size model of a battle ready elephant), and a model train sent by Queen Victoria to the Thai monarch (he was amused). A large shed is parked full of royal funeral cars, the largest one is more than twelve meters high and weighs twenty tons. Without brakes, this car required a hundred men dragging their heels and pulling on ropes to bring it to a halt. The museum gives excellent tours in English at 0930: each Tuesday, the Thai culture tour; each Wednesday, the Buddhism tour; and each Thursday, the art tour.

The Jim Thompson House: At the end of Soi Kaseman 2, which branches off Rama I Road opposite the Boy Scout Hostel, is a collection of priceless antiques sheltered in a beautiful house beside the *klong*. The building was pieced together from several old homes brought in from the country by Jim Thompson. He made his wealth and fame by introducing Thai silk to the world. He mysteriously disappeared while on vacation in Malaysia's Cameron Highlands.

The Suan Pakkard Wang Palace: This Thai house on Si Ayuthia Road is generously surfaced with gilded woodcarvings outside and quality lacquer inside. There's a pleasant garden in the back.

Royal Barge Museum: On the bank of Bangkok Noi Canal, this large water-floored warehouse shelters ornate swan-necked boats for the king and his court. Years ago when a Chakri monarch traveled by water, he was accompanied by 10,000 men and 113 barges. During the bicentennial celebrations in 1982, Rama IX commanded a resplendent flotilla of fifty-one craft.

The Dusit Zoo: The zoo is located on Rama V Road across from Chitlada Palace. Shaded paths twist around a large pond where excursion boats may be rented. Sit and watch the animals from one of many food stalls scattered throughout the park.

An All-But-Forgotten Park: Walk a hundred meters east from one of the busiest areas of Bangkok near Siam Square past the Intercontinental Hotel to Wat Pathumwan, the Lotus Temple. Taxi drivers come here to have their vehicles blessed against accidents. A huge green pond covered with lotus pods is behind the temple. An island in the middle of the pond is covered with trees draped with a tapestry of vines. A portion of the balustrade of a forgotten pavilion can be glimpsed through the lush foliage. It was once used by Rama IV when he fled the heat of the city to the then-rural area. Around the pond are plank walks connecting houses on stilts. It's still country.

___Walks

Backwater Walk: This walk can take from two to four hours. Beginning at the T.A.T., you cross Ratchadamnoen Nok Road, turn left on the last lane before Ratchadamnoen Klang and follow Parinayok Road around to the oil-black *klong.* From the center of the first wooden bridge you see the reflection of the Golden Mount framed in the flame trees that line the canal. In the early evenings, waterside stalls sell cold, sweet drinks. From your table you gaze on the electric glow of the man-made mountain bright against the dark sky.

At the next bridge, you cross through a small market in a narrow alley. At Pra Sumen Road, you turn right for 600 meters to Wat Bowonivet. There are usually monks here willing to teach Buddhism in English. In the nineteenth century, King Mongkut presided here for four decades as head abbot before he became Rama IV. He totally reformed Buddhism in Thailand and initiated the revival-pure Dharmayut sect. He gave Reverend Caswell a room in which the American could preach Christianity to monks in exchange for teaching the Lord Abbot English, mathematics, geography, and astrology.

Today, many *farang* stay here, and some sermons are in English. On the walls inside, a mural shows a physician leaning over a patient and performing a cataract operation. In the background is a house with windowpanes, which were not found in Thailand when it was painted. In a different section, among traditional Thai angels, a righteous man points the way of virtue to a gathering of people dressed in western clothes, complete with top hats and tails. Behind them stands Mount Vernon. The murals were probably inspired by photographs sent to King Mongkut by Franklin Pierce, President of the United States.

Bus 15 passes in front of the *wat* on its route by the Golden Mount and the Grand Palace and the Siam Center.

The Walk to Wat Suthat: Past the Golden Mount to Wat Suthat, this walk may take from thirty minutes to three hours. From the T.A.T., go left and cross Ratchadamnoen Klang. Next to the Charlem Thai Cinema near Wat Rachanada, vendors sell, or rather "rent," amulets. (Thai then take the *bai huang,* literally away-with-worries, to a mystic monk to activate the power and pay as much again in donations.) They also sell gold and silver charm chains.

Across the road and the *klong* rises the Golden Mount (Phu Khao Thong). On top, Wat Sraket overlooks temple-filled Bangkok. This area was once a swamp. The king would come in his barge from the Grand Palace, via a *klong* that is now Ratchadamnoen Klang, to officiate boat races here. After two attempts to build a *wat* (both sank into the marsh), Rama IV decided to build a mountain. The Golden Mount is only seventy-nine meters high, but that's Himalayan in comparison to flat Bangkok.

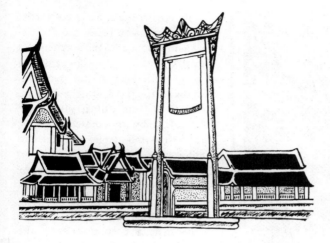

Giant Swing,
Sao Ching-Cha

As you go down the back way, an ice cream vendor offers an irresistible square of cold sweet on a bamboo stick. Walk south on the road parallel, but not adjacent, to Klong Ong Ang. Turn right on traffic-congested Bamrung Muang. The shops on each side display a variety of Buddhist monk's paraphernalia, all wrapped in translucent orange plastic: saffron robes, black lacquer bowls, oval monk fans, incense, pedestals, and the sparkling new Buddha images. Farther down the street towers the Chinese-gate-like frame for the Giant Swing (Sao Ching-Cha), at one time the central object in a Brahman festival. Acrobats would snatch in their teeth bags full of coins that were suspended at dangerous distances from the swing's arch. Many of them died.

Wat Suthat, across the street, took twenty-seven years to complete. The dark interior of the *bot*, Bangkok's tallest, is covered from floor to ceiling with some of Thailand's best classical frescoes. These were painted during the reign of Rama III. A jungle of leaves and animals is carved on the middle front door panels.

Walk to Wat Trimit and Chinatown: For this easy three-hour stroll, start at the railroad station and go diagonally southwest to Wat Trimit on Trimit Road. This temple contains a particularly valuable Buddha. More than two centuries ago, monks covered the sacred icon with plaster to hide it from the invading Burmans. In 1953 the image, believed to have had a bronze core, slipped from a crane during transport and crashed to the earth, cracking the covering. A torrential rain the same night widened the crack. Inside the plaster was a gleaming five and a half ton gold Buddha. The three-meter-high image sits in a small salmon-colored chapel.

From the *wat*, continue to Yaowarat Road. Here, many glowing red-painted shops, some more than a hundred years old, sell gold ingots and chains. Chinese apothecaries offer pickled snakes and embryo of doe. Fortune tellers trace futures on their patrons' palms. And all the while, the tumultuous roar of *tuk tuk* competes with blaring loudspeakers.

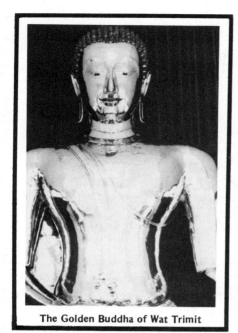

The Golden Buddha of Wat Trimit

To escape the motorized traffic, turn left until you reach the vehicle-free Sampeng Lane (also called Soi Wanit). On weekends you join a stream of people drifting past cramped cubicles that offer fake Ming porcelain, exotic food from China, silk by the bolt, velcro by the meter, buttons, zippers to match, denim material, and a tailor who makes jackets. A small Chinese clothing store sells *gangen par* (silk pants with a sarong-like wrap-around waist). This old market dates from when Rama I moved the Chinese to this district from the site of the Grand Palace. Occasional teak-carved lintels are reminders of past eras. In one large tailor shop, rotary fans cool the sedate surroundings, and Chinese chairs are set in straight rows against the walls. While you have your shoes repaired, you stop at a tea shop to munch on some fresh-from-the-fire chestnuts.

At the west end of the lane, the road jogs a few meters to the right to the Indian market of Pahurat Road. Here gold-coated jewelry is sold to wear with sarongs, wedding dresses, and Thai classical dance costumes. Fabrics from India and batiks from Malaysia are also on sale here. Turn left on Triphet Road and pass the art supply stores (Sanchai's is well stocked). The road ends at the busy Pak Klong Talaat vegetable market, where an incredible array of produce pyramids to the ceiling. The food steaming at the stalls is guaranteed fresh.

Along the Klong

From the Watergate: Near the overpass of Pratunam (Watergate) Clothes open-all-night-Market, long-tail boats begin to pass through Bangkapi. This rich foreign residential area contains houses that are often more traditionally Thai than many Thai homes. Continue along Klong San Sen for an hour and a half. The boat carries you past dark teak houses with orchids hanging from pots on the verandas. A woman in a bath-soaked sarong brushes her teeth in the canal. Children in uniforms wave down water buses to commute to school. To return via land, get off at Lat Karabang Market and hop on Bus 1101 to Bangkapi Market, then switch to Bus 26 to Phanom Phakon Yothin.

Down the River, Up the Klong: Begin at Saphan Phut Landing located under the Memorial Bridge at the end of Triphet Road. Long-tail boats leave on the fifty-minute ride to Wat Lao between 0600 and 2000. It's best to go early to see the morning life beside the canals. Riding down Klong Bangkok Yai, you pass floating petrol stations and several small *wat* and houses with steps down below the surface of the water. People in the canal wash their clothes in the mud and debris-filled water. From Wat Lao, take Bus 75 back to Wat Po.

Another route also begins from Saphan Phut and starts down Klong Bangkok Yai, but it ends on Klong Mon at Wat Bang Waek. On the way, the boat stops at Wat Arun where half-naked, dripping boys climb up into your speeding boat from the river holding wet, wooden elephants for sale. You get off to look around, your boat leaves without you. No problem, you'll catch another one later. Meanwhile, you practice essential Thai phrases such as *chahng mai ow!* (No, I don't want an elephant.) The best way to return from Wat Bang Waek is by boat, but if you'd rather not, catch a minibus to Charan Sanitwong, and from there take Bus 42 to Bangkok.

___Shopping

The Weekend Market: Every Saturday and Sunday until 1800, the field fills with canvas stalls that sell every manner of goods from cassettes (classical Thai next to caustic punk), to cosmetics (root-based cooling powder beside tubes of lipstick). You see mice with their fur dyed psychedelic chartreuse, posters of royalty and Donny and Marie, pink plastic dolls dangling from bamboo poles, purses with "pussycat" printed on the plastic, or fine tooled leather. Clothes form walls in a labyrinth of less-than-shoulder-wide aisles. Used books in English are let go for a few *baht*. Illegal portable stalls fill the centers of the walkways until a warning is given, and then these stalls fold up and disappear into the crowd seconds before a policeman strolls by, only to return seconds after he passes.

The food section displays blood-red meat, red chilies, piles of garlic, baskets of dried and salted fish, live spidery crabs, Easter color candies, and *yod nam mali* (jasmine extract).

In the middle of it all, a mongoose fights a snake near rows of army-surplus camouflage coats and camping gear. Less frequently, vicious grey fighting fish turn red with anger inside adjacent bowls, wagers are made, and they are joined in a churning duel to the death.

Nakorn Kasem Market: Located on Yaowarat Road, Nakorn Kasem is filled with "junque" piles tottering into the sidewalk. It's more of a treasure hunt than a shopping trip. Of course, the antiques are fakes. (Bargain for thirty to fifty percent off.) You'll spot nielloware, embossed silver bowls, bronze cutlery, jade figurines, jewelry boxes, hand-painted pages from old Thai scriptures, large brass drums, stuffed rabbits, and carved wood canes.

Bangkrak Market: Where New Road (Charoen Krung) bends are several Indian spice booths. Farther south blooms a garden full of plants and flowers: orchids, herbs, even Japanese bonsai. You can watch women weave slender *poamalai* garlands of fragrant jasmine blossoms to be sold as lei-like offerings. Piles and piles of earthy-tone vegetables paint the air with pleasant aromas. This market supplies most of the Bangkok restaurants with fresh vegetables.

Gems: Along New Road and at the east end of Silom are several shops that contain glittering cases filled with jello-colored rocks, black star sapphires, rubies, emeralds, and "teak eyes" (tiger eyes). Associated Lapidaries on the fifth floor of the JAL building at 2 Pat Pong Road is an overplush establishment with free tours of their sterile grinding factory, a room in stark contrast to their opulent showroom. Or, tour the gem cutting factories at Royal Lapidary Company at 253 Ratchawithi Road or Bangkok Gems Lapidary at 170/2 Pitsanulok Road. Johnny's Gems, an old establishment at 199 Fuengnakorn (or Fuanfnakon) near the Big Swing, has trustworthy dealers who have served the likes of Nixon and Reagan. Buy black elephant leather goods at Jacobs Leather Goods nearby. On hot afternoons, gem shopping provides a way to escape to air-conditioned coolness and to enjoy free soft drinks while you pick through dazzling displays of expensive baubles.

Handicrafts: Thai Local Industries on Silom has some high quality merchandise. Suni, the owner, is helpful and friendly, but reluctant to lower her prices. The government-run Narayanaband Store on Larn Luan Road near the R.S. Hotel makes for a good one-stop shopping trip. Many of the items are touristy, but there's an excellent selection of handicrafts worth browsing over: silks, precious stones, ceramics, wood carvings, paper umbrellas, lacquerware, bronzes, masks, and northern tribal cloth and floor mats dyed in red and black designs. Prices are fixed and are higher than if you go to the people's markets and bargain for hours.

The Hillcraft Foundation, a better place to buy northern Thai handicrafts, is located behind the parking lot of the Siam Center; enter from Phayathai Road. You'll find it on the second floor, up a flight of circular stairs. The embroidery is incredibly fine; a panel may take up to a year to complete and the designs are excitingly ancient. The natural fiber fabrics are usually bright from artificial dyes, but there are some rare natural-dyed pieces. This store is a nonprofit organization under the patronage of the Princess Mother; the money goes directly back to the hilltribes. Estimate prices at fifteen percent more expensive here than in Chiang

Mai. Get papier mâché masks and miniature wicker baskets (for example, a finger size fish trap), at Padung Cheep on Chakra Bongse Road, around the corner from Ratchadamnoen Klang.

Miscellaneous: Tattoos are hot-needled on in the Malaysia Hotel Coffee Shop. There's a doll factory on Soi Moh Leng off Ratchprarop Road. Embossed silver-colored trays and bowls are light to carry and make inexpensive souvenirs. *Pintoh,* bowls stacked in a frame, make an excellent and unusual gift. The Thai use beach-towel size terry cloth as bedsheets. Buy some oil in small

Pintoh (Thai lunch boxes) are usually repousse; silver and often cheaper alloys are pounded on the reverse side to emboss the surface. When fitted into the frame, *pintoh* can carry separately several sauce dishes as well as rice.

bottles at cigarette stands; a few drops on a cigarette turns smoke to menthol. It's also good on long rides to freshen the mouth.

Beware: Bangkok shops open at about 1000 and close at 2000. There's no such thing as a green sapphire. Antique Buddha images can't be legally exported.

___Stay

Khaosan Road: Take Bus 29 from the airport to Hua Lumpong Railroad Station. Cross Rama IV Road and walk left past the Centre Hotel to the bus stop in front of Thai Sawan. Then take Bus 94 to the Democratic Monument. Numerous small Chinese-run hotels have begun to sprout in the older buildings around Khaosan Road, two blocks to the northwest. This street is fast replacing the noisy vicinity of the railroad station as the Mecca for budget travelers.

Democratic Monument

In about the middle of the long block is a narrow alleyway. At the end of this is the teak-wood Tums Guest House. It's managed by an old Chinese man who loves to sit and prattle his few words of English. The rooms are cramped and they're short on shared bathrooms. No prostitutes allowed. Next door, the similar Bonny Guest House is slightly roomier and slightly more expensive.

Out on Khaosan Road, Hotel New Sri Paranakorn has large air-conditioned doubles with private baths. The mirrors, placed low and strangely near the bed, indicate the type of clientele they cater to. Up the road, Nith Charoen Suke Hotel has private baths. The old lady has the sheets changed every day. Leave your bags with the sweet old woman—how could you doubt her?

The VS Guest House has two locations, one at the Tanao Road-Khaosan Road intersection and one next to where Pra Sumen Road crosses the *klong* where rooms in the front overlook the black water. The VS people are beautiful. There's free ice tea all day long as a delightful compensation for sleeping on a mattress on the floor. Many people come back every time they return to Bangkok. It's the kind of place where you watch gecko lizards above your bed for a few minutes before you fall asleep.

You can get cheaper places near the railroad station if you bargain: "How much?" "Eighty *baht*." "Can't be! How about thirty-five *baht*?" "No." "Alright then, fifty *baht*." "OK," says the shrewd Chinese proprietor, "fifty-five *baht*."

Faded Flash Hotels: The Swan Hotel in the old tourist district at 31 Former Customs House Lane, not far from the famous Oriental Hotel, has clean air-conditioned rooms with hot running water in their private baths and a swimming pool you're not afraid to swim in. Its low price for such fine service attracts many middle-class Indian businessmen looking for top value on their *baht*.

โรงแรม

Rohng Raam,
Thai for "hotel"

The YMCA on Sathon Tai Road has a wide range of rooms, from hostel beds to air-conditioned doubles. Expensive? Yes, but the Christian cleanliness, the new sparkling swimming pool, the health club, and the sauna spa all make it tempting.

By way of contrast, the Privacy and Malaysia on Soi Ngam Phli are far from Christian or clean. The Privacy gets its name from the neat little curtains they pull around cars in its parking spaces so that no one will know who is there. The rooms are fairly well kept and about the same as those in the sleazy Malaysia Hotel, although the latter has a swimming pool. Be prepared—the police must have a drug raid permanently written into their weekly schedule book. The area is filled with hamburger shops, taxi drivers hassling high-rate rides, hookers (renting the delights of Venus and throwing in VD), and *Mang Da* (parasites usually found in rice paddies, but one species hangs around hotel lobbies in slacks, sport shirts, and sunglasses scamming a tour or a trip).

The Atlanta on Soi Phasuk off Sukumvit Road is about the same as Malaysia. A safer alternative is the homier Phasuk Guest House just up the *soi* from Atlanta. In the rainy season, the downstairs air-conditioned room can easily be bargained down, but it's better to stay upstairs where it doesn't flood. The Crown Hotel on Soi 29 off Sukumvit Road is a fair-priced place with fans and private baths. Farther out Sukumvit, at the dead end of an alley left off Soi 22, is the Starlight Hotel. It has the cheapest air-conditioned rooms in the city. But the air-conditioning doesn't always work and screaming Indians fight nightly in the hallway.

Dorms: The Boy Scout Hostel on the fourth floor of the National Executive Board Building on Rama I Road doesn't require Scout membership and welcomes all ages of either sex. You get one cot in a military row of six in a barracks full of similar bed halls. Girl Scouts have separate rooms. Even though this place is inspection-passing clean, it's on one of Bangkok's noisiest streets. Bring your own padlock for the locker provided.

The Patumwan Hostel (ask for "yuse hotel"), is slightly more expensive but less regimental. It's located on the quiet lotus-pond-filled campus of Triam Udom Suksa School and College of Education between Phayathai Road and Henri Durant Road. International Youth Hostel membership is preferred. Cafeterias on campus and across the street serve cheap food. There's a family room with its own private bath for the same price per person, but it's only for married couples. Dorms are segregated by sex. The toilets are a disappointment.

Kay Guest House is a gamble. It's hard to find and it's the only place in the area, so if it's full you have a long ride into town to find another place. But it's worth the risk. Kind Kay lingers over tea with her guests for friendly chats. Ask her where the nearby market is for the cheapest food in the city. The dorms in a spacious, modern-Thai suburban home are shining clean. You feel you're either in the wrong place or the perfectly right place. Take Bus 29 from the airport or train station to Intharamara Road. Change to Bus 24, 74, or 54 for Soi 55. Cross the street, walk up Soi 44, and turn left at the first street to 53/9 Soi 44.

Wat Mahathat near the National Museum will allow men to sleep in their novice quarters if they're sincerely interested in Buddhism. Strict monk-like decorum is expected; donations accepted.

____Food

Thai Food: *Kwey teow* carts wait in almost every alley. You point-nod an order and the tittering mama spoons boiling water over noodles and fish balls. Some *rote ken* (carts) have their boiling pots displayed in the middle of a boat-on-land, as if to say the food is as good as the old days when all was cooked, served, and eaten along the *klong*. Other *rote ken* wheeled out into the streets at night disappear by dawn. Still others linger, quasi-permanent in the shoulder-wide space between build-ings. At tea stalls, you sit at formica folding tables. The tea comes two-tone, reddish brown on top, condensed sweet cream on the bottom. An extra glass of hot colored water is served to thin your tea to a syrup.

Off the alleys are ubiquitous *kow pat* cubicles, workers dining halls with more permanent roofs. Here they fry the rice with chicken or shrimp, throwing into the wok stems of scallions and slices of cucumbers.

Near Silom Road, inside the gate to Lumpini Park, authentic lip-throbbing Thai cuisine is served. Sukol Bakery at 14 Silom near Rama IV cushions savory spring rolls in a plate-top forest of five different kinds of leaves, from cooling mint to sweet basil. The glass case along the wall snares you with its shelves of sugary pastries. Upstairs, the air-conditioned room has the same menu and prices as the bakery-hot room downstairs. Next door, the Saladaeng Phojana Restaurant serves very reasonably-priced meals with meat, vegetables, fruit, and beverage.

For someplace special, find the side street just up from the Ratchadamnoen Stadium. It's filled with *Issan* restaurants serving northeast Thailand's specialty, *gai yang* (BBQ chicken). Jan Chee See gets the greatest acclaim, but the food at the shop next door (no sign, yellow tiled walls), is as tasty and slightly cheaper. Order a *nam mannow* and some *kao mio* (sticky rice) to dip in the *jaeow* (spicy, sweet, hot sauce).

Not-So-Thai Food: Indian food ("Oh yes, we have curries, mutton *keema*, *nan* (Indian bread), lentil dahl . . ."), is available at Seema Restaurant on New Road around the corner from the G.P.O. They have a good vegetarian menu. Bharni's at 417 Sukumvit Road, between Soi 21 and 23, ladles up distinctively delicious bouillabaisse broth. The secret to the bouillabaisse sauce is Mekong whiskey. Their menu has near-gourmet food from all over the world—at gourmet prices. The tacos are spring rolls; the fish and chips are almost "spot-on" (perfect).

Also on Sukumvit near Soi 16 is a sign displaying a giant crab. "If it swims," they claim, "we have it." The seafood is fresh and served with baby corn, mushrooms, or morning glory greens. Pick your dinner from the tank. Tuxedo-wearing waiters wheel your supermart-cart around the cooling cases and fill your basket with whatever you point out.

In the modern New York decor (Thai style) of the air-conditioned Uptown Coffee Shop near Siam Square, hamburgers, or savory roast duck with ginger, or selections from the extensive Japanese menu are carried to your linen-covered table by waiters in tuxedos. Or go up to the Victory Monument. On its south side is a McDonalds-like fast-food restaurant conveying hamburgers and fries. You stand in line with locals in high-fashion western clothing for twentieth-century food.

Miscellaneous: Buy provisions at the Central Department Store on Sukumvit near the Erawan Hotel or at the Thai-Daimaru Supermarket just around the corner. Pick up a loaf of rich rye bread at the Danish Bakery on the north side of Sukumvit between Soi 17 and 19.

Entertainment

Dance and Drama: There are many dinner-dance combinations offered. Surprisingly, the Oriental Hotel has the cheapest offering. Take your camera to

the afternoon Kodak Siam Show. The Indra Hotel on Ratchaprarop Road hosts the Sala Thai Show every evening except Sunday.

Likay (comic folk opera featuring impromptu performances by singers, and bawdy ad-lib dialogues full of double-entendre), are performed in Thai at the stage outside the National Museum between November and May. The National Theater, on Chao Pha Road next to the museum, has classical Thai programs on the last Friday of each month at 1700. They occasionally have international artists performing here.

Sports: Thai boxing is a brutal contest in which two opponents beat the stuffing out of each other with their fists, elbows, heads, feet, and knees. The match begins with a *wai kroo* (reverent bow), as

Khon (person) mask used in Thai drama

the boxers thank their trainers for their assistance (and perhaps slip in a secret prayer for their own lives). Then the bout begins, accompanied by the frenetic clashing of cymbals. The normally passive Thai audience gets involved, releasing an amazing amount of hostility.

There are two stadiums in Bangkok that hold boxing matches. Lumpini Stadium on Rama IV has matches every Tuesday, Friday, and Saturday at 1800, and also at 1300 on Saturday. The Ratchadamnoen Stadium, just up the street from the T.A.T., has them on Monday, Wednesday, and Thursday at 1800, and on Sunday from 1700 to 2000. Or watch boxing free every Sunday night on TV.

Although not exactly a sport, there's a daily contest between man and snake at the Pasteur Institute (the Snake Farm) located on Rama IV Road. At 1100 daily, spectators see the deft extraction of poisonous venom.

NIGHTLIFE

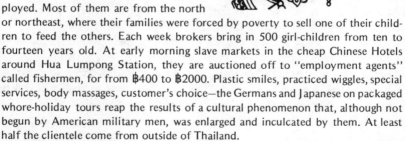

Bangkok deserves its reputation as the brothel of Asia. Between 200,000 and 300,000 women, about ten percent of Bangkok's female population, ply their trade in the 97 nightclubs, 119 massage parlors, 119 barber-shops-cum-massage and come-on teahouses, 248 illegal but hardly hidden whorehouses, and 394 disco-restaurants. Gawdy neon signs pandering sex messages knife through the muggy darkness of even some of the more respectable neighborhoods, and women sit in glass cages waiting to be selected. During their off hours many of them sleep imprisoned in guarded dorms upstairs.

Few of these women are self-employed. Most of them are from the north or northeast, where their families were forced by poverty to sell one of their children to feed the others. Each week brokers bring in 500 girl-children from ten to fourteen years old. At early morning slave markets in the cheap Chinese Hotels around Hua Lumpong Station, they are auctioned off to "employment agents" called fishermen, for from ฿400 to ฿2000. Plastic smiles, practiced wiggles, special services, body massages, customer's choice—the Germans and Japanese on packaged whore-holiday tours reap the results of a cultural phenomenon that, although not begun by American military men, was enlarged and inculcated by them. At least half the clientele come from outside of Thailand.

Seventy-five percent of the women-children have children of their own whom their culture calls bastards, almost twenty percent have had backroom abortions, illegal in Thailand on moral grounds, and there are strains of VD that would survive a nuclear attack. At night a foreigner walks down Pat Pong Lane wearing a T-shirt that reads, "I LOVE YOU MORE THAN I CAN PAY."

Movies: Sentimental to the extreme, sexual by implication, and sensational with hyped-up violence and improbable slapstick, the normal Thai movie plots involve slight variations on the poor-boy-meets-poor-girl theme. The cutout curves of a starlet form the outline for a gargantuan billboard outside a theater. The same theme and same face, but a different movie, is advertised at a nearby cinema. The top box-office attractions work on several pictures at once, making up to thirty a year.

In the older theaters, the "sound track" was provided by a narrator who spoke all the parts along with the movie. At the less expensive theaters, Hollywood movies still have a live translator who often interjects his own quips. Sometimes the British Council at the end of Soi 3 in Siam Square shows free films. Check the newspaper entertainment section.

___Practicalities

Services: Visitors with a problem can call the T.A.T. for assistance. (It's open from 0800 to 2400; phone 281-5051 or 282-0372. The red public phones on the sidewalk cost ฿1; shops will let you use theirs for ฿3. International calls can be made from the office to the right of the General Post Office. Bring small money—they rarely have change—and expect a forty-five-minute wait. On weekdays, the G.P.O. has an excellent, inexpensive packing service open from 0800 to 2000, Monday through Friday. The G.P.O. is open from 0900 to 1300 on weekends and holidays.

Health: Hospitals run by the government are the cheapest and most crowded. The Adventist Hospital at 430 Pitsanulok Road has European doctors. Clinic hours are 0900 to 1200 and 1400 to 1500, Monday through Thursday. At drug stores, buy Fansidar tablets, ฿4 each, for anti-malaria.

Learning: The World Fellowship of Buddhists has its headquarters at 33 Sukumvit Road. They hold meditation classes in English every Wednesday night. Ask for their list of temples where you can stay and where someone speaks English. They are the people to see for a sponsorship if you wish to be a student of Buddhism in Thailand. Then you don't need to deposit money with the government when you extend your visa.

For language classes, check the ads in the newspapers. About ฿1800 a month will get you a private teacher for three hours per day. You'll also be eligible for a three-month nonimmigration visa. The American University Association at 179 Ratchadamri Road has classes in Thai. They also have an English library open to the public. The Nelson Hay Library is in the British Council in Siam Square.

Bookstores: Books in Bangkok are expensive in comparison to Singapore or Manila. DK Bookstore near Soi 13 on Sukumvit Road has a much better selection and a helpful staff. Chalermnit Bookshop at 1-2 Erawan Arcade has an even wider range of books. The cheapest books are found at the weekend market.

Visas: Bangkok is a good place to pick up visas for Middle East countries and thus, avoid the hassles of bureaucracy later. Noncommonwealth citizens must pick up India visas at the Indian Embassy, Soi 23 off Sukumvit. Get a Nepal visa at the Consulate further out Sukumvit at 189 Soi Puengsuk. The Philippine Embassy is located at 760 Ban Kluey, Sukumvit. Burma's Embassy is on the north side of Sathon Road at 132.

Paranoia Corner: Some say *khamoy*, thieves, make a pilgrimage from other countries to train in Bangkok. There are certainly some excellent teachers. A common technique is the slash and grab, in which they slit through your leather bag. Either keep your bag in front of you on crowded buses—no guarantee—or pack some clothes around the perimeter of the inside. Steer clear of young Thai posing as students who offer cheap or free tours away from the crowds. In 1982, in honor of Thailand's bicentennial, the king declared a general amnesty for approximately 55,000 convicts, drug offenders not included.

Traveling From: Bangkok is the cheap air-ticket capital of Asia, although they no longer hold a monopoly on discount tickets. K Travel at 6 Sukumvit Road near the railroad tracks has discount prices, as does the agent in the Atlanta Hotel. Feel confident with the air tickets sold at TV Travel at 795 Silom Road. N.C. Travel near the Indra Hotel is Peace-Corp approved. To Laos or Vietnam, see Diethelm Travel at 544 Ploenchit Road.

Patras Travel at 174 Sukumvit raises prices before they give discounts. J's Travel sells highly fake Student International Cards, air tickets, and a lot of headaches. In one of their scams they sell you a one-year open ticket that ends up expiring three days later! They often are the cheapest in town. There have also been a few bad words floating around about Christian Travel. And avoid the agency working out of the Rich Hotel; it tends to disappear when ticket time comes.

At the air terminal, 485 Silom Road, reconfirm reservations, make baggage claims, leave luggage, and catch the shuttle service to the airport. If you go out on the city bus, get off near the ramp over the highway and take this to the second-floor departure lounge. There's a self-service coffee shop on the fourth floor of the airport. Buses to Chiang Mai leave from the North Bus Station on Phanon Yothin Road. Buses to Phuket and Penang leave from the South Bus Station in Thonburi. Trains to Penang with second-class sleepers are cheaper than buses.

Outside Bangkok: Daytripping

——*Kanchanaburi and the Bridge on the River Kwai*

History: During WW II, the Japanese army brought the bridge spans from Java and had them reassembled over the Kwai Yai River at the cost of 9000 POW lives. The bridge was bombed several times, and only the curved spans are part of the original; the newer sections were made in Japan. This famous metal bridge on concrete piles was only a part of the 425-kilometer-long Death Railway of Kanchanaburi where 116,000 men lost their lives.

Today, weeds grow between the ties over much of the line that ends at Three Pagoda Pass on the Burma border. Trekkers have recently begun to meet the mid-jungle hillpeople who had heard there had been a big war a while back. Tours of

Japanese file past the war cemetery on their three-kilometer journey from the Kanchanaburi Station. As they approach the bridge the Colonel Bogie March whistles through the loudspeakers on top of the souvenir shops.

Sights: The district has several waterfalls and some great riverside jungle hikes. Khao Phang Waterfall is located just two kilometers past the railhead, seventy-seven kilometers from Kanchanaburi Station. On the way to the falls, you pass the small village of Ban Kao. Here Dr. H.R. van Keekeren, a Dutch archeologist, was on field assignment in Thailand just before WW II. Before he could complete his research, he was captured by the Japanese and forced to dig rocks for the railroad bed. Some of the ancient implements he found as a POW are now at the National Museum in Bangkok.

Kanchanaburi is the home of 60,000 Mon, descendants of POWs from wars fought centuries ago. The Mon, who once ruled Burma, are now a people without a country. But many of their traditions have survived.

Getting There: Buses from Bangkok leave every twenty minutes from the South Bus Terminal (from 0530 to 1930). The last bus returns from Kanchanaburi at 1800. A train leaves Bangkok Noi Station at 0800 and arrives at 1030. On weekends and holidays a special bargain train brings streams of Thai to Nakorn Pathom, to Khao Phang Waterfall, to the cemetery, and then back to Bangkok's Hua Lumpong Station the same evening.

Stay: There are several hotels in Kanchanaburi, or check with the T.A.T. there for information about the tranquil farm on the river where you can stay.

___Nakorn Pathom

Thailand's oldest city, founded about 150 B.C., grew up around the world's tallest Buddhist monument. The mythological beginning of the stupa is an oedipal story: A man killed his father and was about to marry his mother when his grandmother told him who his parents were. In a fit of rage he killed her too, but then repented the double murders by building the tower.

At one time a powerful Mon port was here. Archeologists have speculated that Thaton, the Mon capital conquered by King Anawrahtha of Pagan (1057), was Nakorn Pathom.

Getting There: Buses from the South Terminal in Bangkok run hourly, beginning at 0600. For the slow scenic route, take the morning train from Bangkok Noi Station. The less-frequently used tracks and platforms of this station teem with fruit and vegetables brought for the morning market. As you leave the station, on your left is a graveyard of vine-laced steam engines. About a half hour out of town the train goes through *rong* gardens. These mounded fields, criss-crossed with irrigation ditches, are just above tidewater. The fluctuation of water levels brings in rich silt that is shoveled from the ditches to fertilize the vegetables.

The Monument: The giant 130-meter-high stupa still dominates Nakorn Pathom. Its bell-shaped dome, believed to contain a relic of the Lord Buddha, is surfaced with brownish-gold glazed tiles from China. The platform surrounding

the pagoda is cooled by gnarled bodhi trees. These were transplanted from a tree
in Sri Lanka which was, in turn, an offspring of the tree under which Buddha
reached enlightenment. The circular gallery can be entered through many moon
gates trimmed with green glaze. Beside several of these gates stand stern red-faced
warrior statues. Inside the gallery are stones etched with ancient Khmer script.
A fresco on the hall to the east shows a cutaway of the many layers on top of
the original Indian-style stupa of King Asoka's time (273-232 B.C.). A replica of
this first stupa stands on the outer platform, south of the main pagoda.

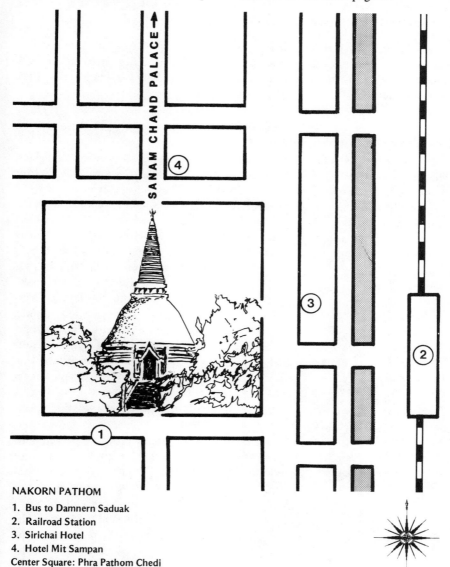

NAKORN PATHOM
1. Bus to Damnern Saduak
2. Railroad Station
3. Sirichai Hotel
4. Hotel Mit Sampan
Center Square: Phra Pathom Chedi

In a museum halfway down from the platform, *shambhala*, carved stone wheels, represent mankind's cycles of birth, death, and rebirth. Before 143 B.C., the wheel was used to symbolize Buddha's teachings. In November the parking lot is transformed into a three-day medieval fair where palmists, pickpockets, and pilgrims mingle.

Sanam Chand Palace: Two kilometers west of the stupa, the king's detached palace mixes Tudor with Thai style architectures. Here, Shakespearean plays translated by Rama VI (1910-1925) were performed before the court. There's a pleasant park beside the *klong* near the palace.

Stay: Sirichai Hotel has rooms with bath. The roof view at night is of the dramatically lit *chedi*. In front you see the lights of the food market, a supurb place for *kow lam*, sticky rice in a bamboo joint; Nakorn Pathom is said to have Thailand's best.

Damnern Saduak

The Floating Market: When the roads began carrying produce into Bangkok, the vast daily flotillas of fruit-and-vegetable canal boats ceased to flow. This market (at its peak at 0900), is one of the last of its kind to survive and shows a way of life as old as Thailand. As you stroll the two kilometers along the waterside walkway from the bus stop to the market, there's a family having breakfast on their polished wood veranda next to the plankwalk. The father offers you some rice. The mother teaches her child how to *wai* to you. A noisy tourist boat

disturbs the opaque green canal water. In a canal-side shed, men make boats with hand tools. You cross the high bridge to where women wear lampshade hats and royal blue blouses. They gather to barter fruits and vegetables from their long thin boats. You stop for tea and a coconut pancake. Farther down along a slippery plankway are the tourist shops.

Getting There: You can take Bus 28, 66, or 203 at 0600 from Bangkok's South Bus Station for the two-and-a-half-hour ride. But it's much easier to spend the night at Nakorn Pathom and catch the 0800 bus from the road east of the stupa. Or spend the night at the Long Rai Hotel in Damnern Saduak.

On her way to market

On the way you pass through the salt paddies of Samut Songkram. Field after field speed by, filled with seawater pumped into them by archaic windmills. The summer sun dries the liquid which is then raked into white stupas of sea salt.

Windmill in the salt paddies of Samut Songkram

___Beaches

Ban Saen: This beach resort was used by the Thai when Pattaya, now a tourist playground, was still a paddy field and fish dock. The staid canvas deck chairs stand under a row of shore-side palm trees near the shallow slope of muddy sand. On weekdays, Ban Saen is usually not crowded. At the far end of the beach, about a hundred meters from the shore line, the Saen Sabai has quaint wooden bungalows, each with its own porch and bath.

A bus leaves Bangkok's East Station for Ban Saen every twenty-five minutes and takes an hour and a half. Get off in town and take a bus to the beach. To get to Ko Chang for some excellent diving, go to Si Racha and catch the boat.

Ko Samet: This beach on an island is a fantasy world: tropical fish shoals off shore, bamboo bungalows by the ocean, sunlight on the sand, a lantern lighting your friend's face against the black sea background. And it's not crowded—yet.

Take a bus from Bangkok's South Bus Station and ride past Ban Saen and flash Pattaya to Rayong. Deluxe buses serve coffee and show movies during the two-hour ride. From Rayong take a *tuk tuk* to Bang Pei port and a boat to the island. Get off at the last stop, Bon Bin. The excellent Chinese cook keeps the bungalows full here, even when those nearby are empty.

___North Near Bangkok

Wat Phai Long: Thailand's undomesticated, open-billed storks survived extinction in the fifties when this *wat* agreed to become a bird sanctuary. Now there are more birds than tree branches. Normally monogomous male storks have taken second mates that share the same nests. As soon as one group of fledglings is old enough to fly, they vacate the nest in favor of new tenants. Around 0800, twenty-four thousand birds rise on the thermals. (They're accustomed to visitors and easy to photograph.) Take a bus from Bangkok's North Bus Station for the fifty-one kilometers to the Sam Khok district. Cross the river in a rented boat or wait for the less-frequent cheaper ferry.

Bang Pa-In Palace: About sixty kilometers north of Bangkok, this detached summer palace for the king is most famous for its Aisawan Thi Paya Pavilion, a copy of the Abhornpimok Pavilion at the Grand Palace in Bangkok. In the park, populated with trees carved like elephants, the Chinese-style Vehad Chumroom Palace north of the pond is open to the public. It is closed Mondays and whenever the king takes up his summer residence here. The palace is a replica of the Peking Palace built for the Thai monarch by the Chinese population of Thailand. Inside are two-meter-high pieces of jade carved into octagonal screens. There's a Gothic church by the river, Wat Nivet Thammaprawat, with a Buddha sitting on its altar.

Elsewhere on the grounds stands a memorial to Queen Sunanta and her child. Weighed down by regal gowns, they drowned when their boat overturned—in full view of a crowd of peasants. It would have been sacrilege punishable by death to anyone who had dared touch royalty, even in the act of saving them.

Buses leave Bangkok's North Station every thirty minutes from 0600 to 1800. The trip takes an hour. Every day, eight trains leave Hua Lumpong Station for the hour and a half ride. The train stops at Don Muang Airport midway between Bangkok and Bang Pa-In. On Saturdays and Sundays, the Mahari riverboat departs from the Thammasart boat landing near the National Museum at 0730 and returns at 1200, stopping on the way back at Wat Phai Long, the stork temple. Contact the Transport Company at the bus terminals for tickets, or else reserve a spot on the boat by calling 279-1424.

Chiang Mai: Ancient Capital of the North

A tribesman just in from the hills squats on the curb in front of a shop that sells his handiwork as tourist souvenirs. He watches the mild hubbub of provincial Chiang Mai. (The overgrown town has become Thailand's second largest city with 100,000 people.) His native garments shout colors where we would have them whispered.

Not far away, a tree-shaded moat protects the vanished fourteenth-century walls of the old inner city. King Mengrai commanded these ten kilometers of stone to be built in three months by ten thousand of his subjects. Some of them worked the night shift.

The Burmans overran the walls in the sixteenth century, and so ravaged the city that for twenty years only animals of the jungle lived here. Eventually, the former capital was rebuilt. Many of the temples around the town have a Burmese exuberance in their lacy stucco trim, their multi-tiered roof lines, their richly carved and lacquered doorways, and their impish spirit statues.

The altitude of three hundred meters above sea level sets Chiang Mai apart from the sauna plains of central Thailand. In the cool of every evening, travelers gather on the patios of the forty guest houses on the frontier of the twentieth century. They tell of a fellow trekker who insisted on buying a ceremonial pig from the hilltribe people because he wanted pork. You hear of someone who caught a glimpse of the opium smugglers, and of a near encounter with the warlord's bandit-army. The night outside is quiet.

CHIANG MAI

1. YMCA
2. To Rincome Hotel, Isra Guest House, and Wat Jet Yod
3. Chiang Mai Youth Hostel
4. Wat Koo Tao
5. Elephant Gate, Bus Station
6. Wat Chang Man and Banrai Steak House
7. To Vegetarian Restaurant
8. Wat Pra Singh
9. Police Station
10. Wat Chedi Luang
11. U.S.I.S. (United States Information Service)
12. Pao Come Guest House
13. Thai-German Dairy and Guest House, and Daret's Restaurant
14. Old Chiang Mai Cultural Center
15. Lacquerware factory
16. Silver factory
17. Wood carvers
18. Restaurants
19. Chiang Mai Tea House
20. U.S. Consulate
21. Je t'aime Guest House
22. Prince Royal School
23. Warorot Market
24. Tourist Office (T.A.T.)
25. Night bazaar
26. Chiang Mai Guest House
27. Bus to Bor Sang
28. General Post Office, Telegraph
29. Railroad Station

Getting There by Bus: At least ten buses, breezy, truck-motored vehicles with people packed inside like banana bunches, leave Bangkok's North Bus Station daily between 0530 and 2200 and take nine hours to bounce up to Chiang Mai. The government dispatches eight air-conditioned buses daily from the same station. These take seven hours. Many tour companies offer air-chilled transportation from your hotel door. Find them at any of Bangkok's travel agents or at the faded flash hotels. There are super round trip savings.

Seven hours on the bus! You had been riding four hours when your driver spotted a competitor's bus. He turned red, and the race began. The two giants of the road muscled down the two-lane highway, around curves, and up hills. The speed accelerated. An accident seemed inevitable. During the next three hours, time stops in shock. Inside this fearful eternity you recall one of the survivors of a Thai bus collision telling you how the advertised insurance couldn't quite cover the medical costs for his broken bones.

By Train: Safer and slower, the daily express leaves Hua Lumpong Railroad Station at 1800 and takes thirteen hours. The train is a luxurious way to travel. You can sleep away most of the long hours and wake up to the sight of mist on teak-topped hills. A row of flatcars loaded with logs waits on a siding.

By Air: There are at least three flights from Bangkok daily. The indirect jet takes four hours, and the direct flight takes an hour. There's also a direct flight from Hong Kong.

Getting Around: From Chiang Mai Airport, there's taxi and local bus service into the city. At the train station, look for people holding up signs to interest potential lodgers in their guest houses. They'll supply free bus service. If you miss these, most places will pay the *samlor* drivers to bring you there; just hop in and tell the driver where you want to stay. He'll be paid by the manager.

Town buses go all over the city for ฿1.5. Routes 1 and 3 together will provide a comprehensive view of all of Chiang Mai. The rates for mini-trucks can be bargained for groups of three or more people. Both motorcycle and bicycle rentals require a passport or large deposit.

Songkram in Chiang Mai: Chiang Mai is flooded by gushing hoses, overflowing buckets, and insidious squirt guns between April 13-15. The young relish this festival. Beauty queen contestants, futilely equipped with locally-made paper umbrellas, ride a wet gauntlet through the street. Even the sacred image of Buddha from Wat Pra Singh gets wet during its procession, but with much more respectful sprinklings.

There's a special breakfast of Thai food served at the Old Chiang Mai Cultural Center beginning at 0700. The T.A.T. sponsors special cultural performances: puppet shows, Thai *gamelan* (gong and drum orchestras), *khon* dramas (masked players reenacting exerpts from the Ramakien), and tribal dances from the hill clans nearby and from Thailand's northeast and south provinces.

Traditional Thai weaponry included an arsenal of silver, wood, and buffalo hide shields, as well as staff, swords, lances, rapiers, and knives. Court retainers were encouraged to learn martial arts and to display their prowess before the king. These routines developed into dances from which the calisthenics used by modern Thai soldiers were derived.

Temples and Sanctuaries

Wat Chedi Luang: There's ominous air under the hoary gum tree inside this temple complex. According to a legend as old as Chiang Mai, the spirit of the city dwells in the tree, and when the tree falls a great disaster will obliterate Chiang Mai. This has not been a luck-filled place. The founder of the city and builder of the *wat*, King Mengrai, was killed by a bolt of lightning near this tree. And in 1545, a tremendous earthquake toppled the nine-meter-high stupa and buried the Emerald Buddha beneath its rubble.

Wat Pra Singh: Busy Ta Pae Road ends abruptly at the *wat* gate. As you walk into the courtyard, you are met by a row of silent stucco maidens. They each give you a stoic *wai* while they nonchalantly support the building on their heads.

The portly Pra Singh Buddha, his legs folded in full lotus, sits in the next temple structure. This is northern Thailand's most venerated statue. It is said to have been made in Ceylon and shipped east in the fourth century. An identical statue in the National Museum in Bangkok and another in Wat Mahathat in Nakorn Si Thammarat also claim to be the original. The question of authenticity didn't deter the art thieves who stole the head of the Chiang Mai statue.

On Buddha days (they occur almost weekly; check the T.A.T. for exact dates), visitors are allowed to enter to see Pra Singh. But today it's closed. Instead, you study the deeply-carved doors to the chapel on the south side of the courtyard. An old monk comes up the steps and into the shade to join you. He gives you that same stoic *wai*.

Wat Chang Man: The oldest *wat* in Chiang Mai is set off in the northeast corner of the ancient capital. The steeply slanting roof outlines a high triangle of intricate designs. Two statues of Buddha are kept inside. The crystal Pra Sae Tang Tamani statue was captured from the Mon when King Mengrai expanded his domain over Lampoon. The other was sculpted from stone in the eighth century. According to local tradition, whenever the two images are placed in a certain relation to each other and activated by incantation, they attract rain.

Pre-Buddha spirit on stupa

Modern spirit in northern Buddhist art

In almost every Buddhist temple in Thailand you'll find representations of *naga*-serpents, mythical creatures from pre-Hindu days. Usually these *naga* appear as balustrades on the side of bridges or stairway entrances. According to one ancient myth, the gods on Mount Meru sent *naga* across the water to the shores where man lives. From here they were to carry all men wishing and worthy to be in the realm of the gods. Passengers were to walk the serpent's back while meditating on love and kindness. Thus, these statues symbolically take anyone entering the *wat* into the realm of the spirits.

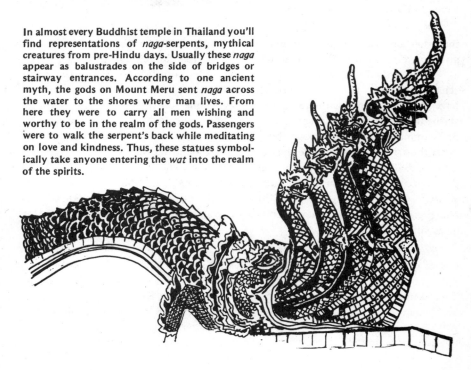

Outside, *naga*-serpents buttress the walls. Their embedded glass reflects your image in multi-colored fragments, an unfinished mosaic.

Wat Koo Tao: Rain is essential to life dependent on the rice harvest. When the months-long dry season reaches its parched climax, few peasants are willing to gamble that the lake *naga* in the north will just wake up and bring rain to the farmers. Thus during the Songkram Festival, a long alarm-drum at this temple explodes with sound. The drum is wheeled around the main chapel. The tympanum is made of leather stretched over an early cannon.

Koo Tao (five melon) Temple is named after its unusual stupa. A series of five stacked spheres, symbolizing the five elements of the cosmos, look like a giant electrical insulator. The *wat* is located on a side street near the Elephant Gate Bus Station.

Doi Suthep, Temple on the Hill: A *naga*-serpent slithers down the hill on both sides of the 219 steps. They lead to the temple at the top. You begin to climb. Some peasant pilgrims on the steps with you believe you're a pilgrim too and smile *wai* at you. A man halfway up the steps sells frighteningly accurate crossbows. He gives you a shot at his cardboard target. A young woman offers garlands of flowers for sale and a smile for free. You smile back and she follows you; she walks with you up the stairs until she spots a tourist at the bottom of the steps, remembers her blossom business, and runs down to make a sale. You turn to see the temple and it's just another *wat* wall. You walk around to catch a view of the city through the fog. Then you take off your sandals, and holding them in your hand you enter.

The stupa is gold, blackened with age. The prayer cubicles are almost Hindu. Fruit, cut to look like flowers, has been placed at the altar along with burning incense and real flowers. You see a saffron-robed monk and *wai* to him. Unfortunately, at the same time you show him the bottom of the sandals in your hands, the ultimate insult. He smiles, barely able to suppress a laugh as you quickly drop your arms. He knows foreigners, for here in one of the most sacred temples in all Thailand, the abbot is a foreigner.

To get there, take a mini-truck from near the Elephant Gate or Bus 3 to the end and try your luck at hitching the last nine kilometers. There's a pilgrims' steps up the hill; leave your valuables back at your guest house.

Phuping Palace: The winter home for the king and queen is five kilometers up the way from Doi Suthep. The house is open only on Fridays and Sundays, and only when their highnesses aren't staying here. The English-style garden, the best part of the palace, is always open.

___Shopping

Crafts: In a factory south of the city moat, an artisan still makes celadon pottery by a process brought back to Sawankhalok, Thailand from Chekiang, China in 1300. The better pieces give off a dull luminous glow, similar to light shining through precious jade. The lacquerware of north Thailand is usually made

From Sukotai era

by the *lai rod nam* process developed in ancient Thailand. *Lai rod nam* means "ornament washed in water." First, the artist paints the design in negative with water-soluble colors on the lacquered surface. The entire piece is then covered with a thin layer of lacquered gold. When it drys twenty hours later the piece is carefully washed, removing the watercolors. Only the gold remains. Containers, windows, doors, and wall panels are all lacquered in this way.

For the most part, teak carving has degenerated into a souvenir trade. Herds of brown elephants line up in display, from key-chain to baby-elephant size. However, some good pieces are still being produced at wood-carving shops. Good teak is recognizable by its pleasant aroma and its high price tag, although the latter is no guarantee. Better shops give a receipt with the purchase verifying the carving as teak.

Silverware, especially embossed bowls and elaborate Thai teapots, is also made in Chiang Mai. The silversmith pounds out the designs while he holds the piece between his feet. There is much variance in actual silver content. Bus 1 goes south of the moat near Walai Road to where most of the craft-making places are.

For contemporary art, yet still within the Thai tradition, see the *Ich Liebe Dich* gallery of painting and sculpture opposite the Chiang Inn Hotel near the night market. For hilltribe clothing, try the reasonably-priced shops just southwest of the main market. Items will be almost thirty percent cheaper than at many of the tourist shops on Ta Pae ("you pay") Road. The Center for Women's Home Products on Ta Pae is a delightful exception, with well made and reasonably priced clothing.

The Night Bazaar: Along the sidewalk of Changklan Road, vendors begin setting up temporary stalls at about 1700. The white light of pump lanterns shows the earth colors of handmade crafts. In a converted parking lot halfway down the road, you find hand-embroidered Meo bedspreads and dramatic black dresses with red and white trim. Along the street, highly-decorated opium pipes lie beside lacquered betel-nut boxes. A Meo woman in her tribe's traditional pleated miniskirt speaks only market Thai as she sells her artifacts. The man next to her in a knit shirt speaks fluent English as he pushes his teak toothpick holders. A man squats down on the ground to play his homemade *saw deuang*, a string instrument, to entice you to buy. Behind him, smuggled Burmese antiques are sold for a song and a traveler's check. Instant antiques, such as animal figure opium weights, stand in a file of diminishing size. Bargaining is the soul of the market. The stalls close about midnight, but the food places often stay open until dawn.

The Warorot Market: The main market in Chiang Mai is a multilevel building near the river on Witcha Yanond Road. One area is full of fabric and clothing stores run by the inevitable Indian cloth merchants. A man picks through the *pakama*, one-by-two-meter pieces of material worn as sashes, scarves, or shawls, or formed as bags for produce, or used as drying towels. You climb the motionless elevator to the balcony above the central floor. Below you is the ordered chaos of pickled fruits, curried peanuts, sugar-salted mangos, shrimp paste, crackers. . .

___Stay

There are more than forty guest houses. With competition so keen, prices are low. Je t'aime Guest House is out on Charoenrat Road, east of the Ping River, and twenty minutes walk from the heart of town. Lek is swamped running his art gallery, *Ich Liebe Dich*. His wife puts the same poetic soul into making this place pleasant. Rooms have big double beds with crisp-clean sheets. Abstract paintings hang on the walls. Each room has a private shower. Check out time is noon. Some long-distance buses don't leave until the early evening so Je t'aime provides showers even after guests check out.

This gold gilt panel of the Hindu god Indra riding Erawan, his many-headed mount, is on the back of the Buddhist temple near Je t'aime in Chiang Mai.

To find Chiang Mai Youth Hostel, turn off Manee Noparat Road north of the moat at the bowling alley and go fifty meters back. You'll see the hostel on your right. At the train station when you arrive, look for their minibus (or call 221-180 for free transport). Peter, the helpful manager, offers laundry service, motorbikes and push-bikes (for rent), a stereo with seventies rock on tapes, snacks, maps of the city, and sometimes free movies. In the morning there's often an impatient line bouncing outside the common toilets. The small rooms are clean.

Isra Guest House, located west of town, looks like a modern warm-climate suburban home. Take Bus 3, get off two hundred meters before the Rincome Hotel, and follow the winding road south for about four hundred meters. Ask locals for directions as you go. Eed is very accommodating. She goes to the market with you to help bargain prices, and works with your Thai while you work with her English. The rooms are well kept, the setting quiet, the food great, and the bikes are free to guests.

Pao Come Guest House, east of the moat, is on a quiet back street and is convenient to downtown. It's a beautiful teak structure and one of the oldest guest houses in the city. The Number One Guest House is a good value near Chaiyapoom Road on the east side of the moat—turn on Soi 1 at the Atami

Turkish Bath. Manit Guest House on Lampoon Road, following the east bank of the river, is a family-run place with palatial rooms in the quaint old house. Out in the cramped shed behind the house, the rooms are cheaper. Inexpensive food, laundry service, and a nonstop Thai-English-Communications-guessing-game are provided.

The Chiang Mai Guest House, located on the very touristy Charoen Prathet Road, has long been a favorite of those looking for low-hassle, high-class comfort. The rooms upstairs have hot running water flowing into the private western-size tubs. There's a peaceful lawn with lounge chairs next to the river in back of the guest house. The old gardener has had a fascinating life. He'll tell you all about it in fluent English as long as you want to listen.

The missionary clean YMCA is in a brand new building northeast of the moat. Orchid Guest House is relaxed and very young, as is the Patta next door. The Thai-German Guest House behind the Thai-German Dairy is a charming teak building, built and managed by affable guide, Sorn.

___Food

The Banrai Steak House is open from 0700 to 2200 and serves the best western food in town. They have whole wheat bread, percolated coffee, muesli with real yogurt, main dishes such as a super shrimp platter and, of course, steaks.

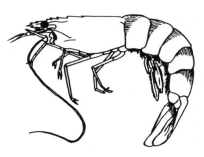

Set back from Pra Pokklao Road, between the Thai Airways office and Wat Chang Man, Banrai is run by a humble, friendly woman.

The dedicated couple at The Vegetarian Restaurant near Wat Suan Dok, out Cherng Doy Road, prove that meatless food can be delicious. With dishes so inexpensive, you can fill up on two to three plates and stay in budget. Try their coconut cream salad. The place has disappointingly short hours, it's only open from 1000 to 1400.

There are two other restaurants that serve western food, both located along the inside of the east moat on Moon Muang Road. The Thai-German Dairy has a corner shop where you can have anything from a cheese omelette to a hamburger. To the north, Daret's has a reasonably-priced European menu, but their Chinese food is expensive. Stop here for a mixed-fruit shake combo made to order. It's a good place to have a lazy conversation with other travelers and pick up trekking clues.

Across the moat, three outdoor restaurants serve excellent Thai food. Sorn-chand Restaurant at 23 Kotchasarn Road is the farthest north and the cheapest. They have a large menu of real home-cooked meals, including exotic dishes such as fried frog skin and cow intestines. Walk down the row of metal pots and point at what looks good. Aroon Rai, the next place south, serves very spicy *nam prik ong* (a tomato dish), or *gong hahng lay* (pork with cauliflower). You get a good size helping of food. The staff is super friendly. For atmosphere at a price, try Tura Restaurant. It's an open-air patio of dark wood. Be willing to pay a full meal price for a scrumptuous, small crab salad. The chicken in wine sauce is excellent.

Night Spots: There are several stands at the south end of the night bazaar. Choose your crab from several wriggling on the end of a string. One stall serving tasty seafood is run by transvestites. Not far away, a mother in pigtails says, "Heylow mista. Please come in and sit down." And, if you don't, she exhausts her English vocabulary with, "Hava looka round and comma gain." Get a milk shake at another shop or buy a beer at another and watch the vendors who are sizing up the tourists eyeing the merchandise.

Unlike most night food places in SE Asia, these stands stay open until dawn and serve beer as long as people want to buy. After the handicraft vendors close shop at about midnight, they come and sit around to celebrate the night's take. For a late night cup of coffee with candles and roses on the table, try the Chiang Mai Tea House (open until midnight). Sit next to a stream on Chang Moi Road; it's a delightfully romantic place.

In the evening at the stalls along Moon Muang Road, the prices are much cheaper. Sit next to the moat and eat the basic fried rice or noodle dishes. Buy fresh fruit here: *rambutan* by the kilogram, *lamyai*, a local specialty, and tart mangos.

A cultural show featuring the dances of six hilltribes is part of the Old Chiang Mai Khantoke Dinner. Save by skipping the meal. In neither case is it a bargain. Drink your meal at the Prince Hotel's Karen Hut Bar; they have live country-western music with no cover charge.

Budget Meals: Try the noodles at the Santeloht Restaurant (no English sign), a thatched-roof structure on permanent poles located at the first turn northwest of the moat. It's guaranteed fresh; the noodle factory is next door. During the day you'll find food at the Prince Royal School near Je t'aime. Moms bring cooked lunches for the kids, which are also sold to anyone who has ฿5 to ฿7 in his pocket. It's good, wholesome, cheap, homemade Thai eating. On the corner, just before the Nakhonping Bridge going out of town, a small shop sells savory *kow pat gung*, shrimp and fried rice. At the entrances to the footbridge get coconut pancakes and banana fritters coated with peanuts. There's a provision store with even canned cheeses on Ta Pae Road, next to building 35.

_Practicalities

Services: The T.A.T. dispenses maps and misinformation that encourages tours and discourages self-initiated travel. The luggage storage room in the Chiang Mai Railroad Station charges ฿1 per day per bag with a limit of fifteen days. It's open from 2400 to 1000 and from 1300 to 1900. Near the General Post Office is a shop that will wrap your packages for the mail. There's a similar shop near the Post Office downtown also.

Swim: Both the Rincome Hotel on Huey Kaeo Road and the Anodard Hotel on Rajmankha Road charge ฿15 for nonguests to use their pools. The former is more private but less conveniently located; take Bus 3. You must be checked by a doctor before you use the very clean University pool.

Books: U.S.I.S. (United States Information Service) on Ratchadamnoen Road has a library in an air-conditioned, carpeted room. Books can't be checked out, but it's a comfortable place to sit and read, and there are current American magazines and newspapers available. The YMCA has a paperback book collection with, for some reason, an excellent English section on Japanese culture. The Chiang Mai Book Center near Kotchasarn Road has travel and language books for sale.

Study: Thai classes are offered at U.S.I.S. and last four to six weeks. Buddhist meditation techniques are taught under monks' guidance at Wat Muang Mong in Chiang Mai or at Wat Umong near the University.

Work Opportunities: Qualified instructors earn up to ฿100 an hour teaching English; unqualified instructors earn almost as much. Both the YMCA and U.S.I.S. have classes; both occasionally hire. Language schools are often on the lookout for native speakers of English; no certification necessary.

Paranoia Corner: The decade of tourism has caused some of the normally honest people of the north to see a dollar sign where your face should be. Just being aware can help you avoid a lot of the hassles and risks. For example, shops arrange to have the bike you've just rented from them stolen as soon as you're outside of town. They know when your visa expires—they have your passport as deposit—and thus, when you must leave. You're forced to pay for the vehicle in order to get out of the country legally. The bike miraculously reappears in the shop a week after you're gone. To avoid this scam, it's best to have someone you trust from your guest house rent the cycle for you.

Drugs: The same person who sells you drugs gets ฿100 for turning you in. That's enough to tempt many of the dealers who have an unlimited source of fresh customers arriving. Some guest houses have planted drugs in traveler's luggage, and then reported the traveler to the police. Inspect your backpack carefully before you move on. Protect yourself! If they sell drugs at your guest house, don't buy; move! The police know who's dealing.

Police: The average upcountry government official earns only about ฿12,000 ($522) a year. To make ends meet, they charge for their services, such as investigating a crime. A police report costs ฿2 if you want a copy for insurance purposes; they'll try to charge ฿10. Drug holders who have been arrested are first offered a chance to bribe their way out of jail. The train police are in no way connected to the city police. If you have something stolen on the train, report it at the railroad station.

Theft: The Ping River footbridge near the market is dangerous at night. There have been robberies along the road east of the bridge. It's best to take a *samlor* if you're returning late to your guest house in that area.

____Neighboring Towns

Bor Sang: There's only one street in the village, and both sides of it are lined with cottage-shops where umbrellas are made. Rows of painted paper parasols dry in the sun, and skeletal frames of bamboo wait for the next step in production. Nearest the highway are the slightly more expensive and more toured shops. You roam to the other end and eat a plate of noodles at a roadside stall for a few coins. Bor Sang is nine kilometers from Chiang Mai; catch a bus or minibus from Nawarat Road.

Lampoon: Only the circular moat and a few scattered buildings are left as reminders of the former capital of the Mon Kingdom of Haripoonchai. Today, little seems to be happening here. The friendly villagers seem blasé about foreigners on day outings from nearby Chiang Mai. Few outsiders take the time to stroll the inner city. Even fewer meander along the tired, brown river east of town—down a dirt road past old wooden homes and past women draping laundry over bushes. Rarely does anyone happen upon the site of a secret factory that turns smuggled Burmese opium into heroin for the world market.

To get to Lampoon, wave down a white bus on the Lampoon Road east of the Ping River in Chiang Mai. One passes by every twenty minutes. Most of the twenty-six-kilometer lane is lined with giant trees.

THAI MUSIC

The *kong wong* is the main instrument in the *pibat*, a primarily percussion band. Only the musician on this instrument plays the basic melody. All other members of the band improvise. They create classic Thai jazz on a seven note scale with seven more halftones. Since all notes are evenly spaced, changing keys causes no problem in arrangement.

Traditionally, Thai singers also improvise. Their nasal voices often slide around the area of the note. To some extent this flexibility is made necessary by the tonal language. If the melody goes down the scale while the word must swing upward for meaning, the singer tries to do both. To the westerner, these indecisive notes make the melody difficult to pick out.

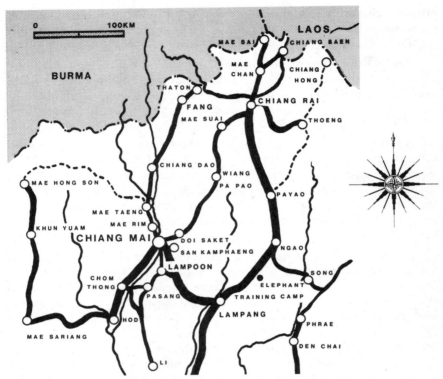

Mekong River: Flowing along 850 km of the Thai border, the "Golden Queen" originates in the Tibetan highlands. Between rainy and dry seasons the river level can change as much as 12 m, yet it rarely overflows its banks. It is one of the world's ten largest rivers; the third largest in Asia.

Wat Chama Devi, also known as Wat Kukut, is located one and a half kilometers west of the main street. The square-stepped sides of the stupa are honeycombed with niches sheltering sixty Buddhas. The building was built for Chama Devi, a princess from Lopburi. She became queen of Lampoon and bore two sons; one became king of Lampoon, the other, king of Lampang.

Wat Prathat Haripoonchai is between the river and the main street. The temple walls surround some structures more than a thousand years old. Beside a fifty-meter-high golden *chedi* that houses a relic of Buddha, there is a *sala* (tower), built around "the largest bronze gong in the world." The compound is alive with monks and students.

Across the street to the west, the National Museum has items clearly marked in English. At the east gate stand two large lions facing the river. Wander across the footbridge and to the left to a quiet spot near Wat Vieng Yong. You might manage to be alone for awhile. You roam the back streets to a bridge over which buses thunder on their way out of town. You let the syncopated thudding of the looms guide you to the silk factory.

Hotel Sri Lampoon, on the main street one block north of Wat Haripoonchai, has rooms with fans. The people are kind and playful, the building is an oven.

_Passage to the Northwest

The Trip: The White Elephant Gate Bus Station in Chiang Mai is a bustle of travel energy—people going places, people selling, looking, laughing. There are buses for Mae Hong Son at 0600, at 0800, and at 2000. The trip takes nine hours, so it's a good idea to break the journey halfway and take the 1100 bus to Mae Sariang instead.

You share the seat with a mountain of mailbags that threaten to tumble onto your shoulder. At each little hamlet there's a five-minute stop while the pile shrinks little by little to local post offices. After three-quarters of an hour of rumbling down the country highway, you see Wat Prathat Doi Noi crowning the rise above a rare hill in the Kuang River flats. The long *naga*-sided staircase invites you to the top. Eighteen kilometers past Hod, the highway skirts Thailand's only white-water river. It runs through the Obluang Gorge, a deep incision in rock cut by the Chaem River. Stepped rice fields blanket the valley floors and the rolling hills are hidden beneath reforested pine. Bamboo and wood shanty settlements brave the roadside where bewildered tribespeople come in from the woods.

At Mae Sariang, 200 kilometers from Chiang Mai, there's a chance to break the trip and enjoy the modern comforts of the Mit Alee Hotel, up the street from the cinema. Across the street from the hotel, a Karen family sells quality hand-woven clothes for far below city prices. You point and hold up six fingers; they shake their heads and hold up ten.

A bus heads north from Mae Sariang to Mae Hong Son at 1100. The tarred way turns to gravel and twists through the teak-wood wilds. The road widens briefly at Khun Yuam village, and passengers pile out for a sip of tea or some ice cream, and a stroll for men to the wall at the back of the building. Gee Tana Hotel provides minimum standard accommodations in a creaking teak structure. Two hours after leaving Khun Yuam you arrive in Mae Hong Son.

Planes fly from Chiang Mai to Mae Hong Son between 1100 and 1200 on Fridays and Sundays, returning the same days at 1300.

Mae Hong Son: Hidden in the valley of the Pai River, a tributary of the Salween, Mae Hong Son has been isolated for centuries. To the east, a range of mountains bars most of the commerce from the rest of the country. Thai are a minority here. The mountains separating Burma from the valley are not as steep, and the effect shows in the Burmese faces of the locals and the Burmese architecture of the *wat*.

The spire of one of these filigree temples points up to the clouds down in the lotus pond in front of it. Monks lie around like cats in the hot afternoon or recite sonorous segments of Pali scripture. At the foot of the steep hill on the city's perimeter, two giant *singha*, lions, guard a stairway overgrown with a camouflage of grass. You climb the zigzag path to the right of the *singha*, up to where Wat

Prathat Doi Kongmou overlooks Mae Hong Son. Perched next to the *wat*, a disk jockey in a hill's-edge gazebo broadcasts music and news over loudspeakers, spilling noise over tranquility.

At the early morning market, a Lisu woman is dressed in a brilliant blue dress. Two hilltribe Meo boys, dressed in subdued black pants and shirts, and magenta-tassled skull caps, inspect a hunting knife they can't afford to buy. They content themselves with the thought of the movie tonight—their first one!

Stay and Food: The Mitrniyom Hotel (for some reason read Min yom), rents rooms with baths, soap, towels, and clean sheets. From the back of the hotel, there's a view of Doi Kongmou with the space-ship stupa illuminated against the black sky. From the front balcony, you see the distant pond afloat with fog. The Sanguan Sin Hotel, adjacent to the market, has run-down rooms. After you see the deluxe room, you're afraid to ask for anything cheaper.

In the evening you have some food at the street stalls across from the cinema. For dessert you chance upon some delicious *kow neung* (warm, black rice pudding swimming in a bowl of coconut cream). The Burmese teenager scoops up your portion out of the large metal cooking kettle and brings it to your table. In English, he asks to join you. In halting but understandable English he tells you of the time he almost got caught crossing the border.

The Golden Triangle: Quiet Danger

Fields of white and pale-violet poppies, concealed Hindu-designed temples, and vast virgin forests lacquered with a permanent dew. These contrast with the robberies on remote paths, murder on the River Kok, smugglers, emaciated addicts, army shootouts, refugees under fire swimming for freedom, and remnant armies of defeated warlords. Mix in troops of tourists in air-conditioned buses, and country nights as quiet as an owl in flight. This is the Golden Triangle.

The hills of northern Thailand contain remnants of a dying culture: pristine land with thatched-roof bamboo dwellings, wide-eyed children and questioning adults in colorful homemade clothing, not-so-filthy pigs rooting unfenced on the compost-yard inside a village gate, men carrying crossbows or home-fashioned flintlock rifles.

These are people who have never heard of America and aren't sure what Thailand means. They are people who, with their own hands, can supply all their needs except salt. Some tribes use the ancient stick-poking method of planting, others use the older scatter technique. Almost all employ slash-and-burn to clear the land.

The impending lowland floods and the inevitable devastation caused by slash-and-burn, coupled with the government's discomfort at having nonpatriots (whose allegiance is more toward brother tribes in neighboring countries), has led to government efforts to shift the cash crop away from poppies and to stabilize the tribes in permanent villages. But the open fires still burn on dirt floors of thatched huts, within a day's trek from crisp sheets on king-size beds.

Akha grandmother

Yao

___Trekking

Tours: Groups leave from Chiang Mai, Chiang Rai, and Mae Hong Son. In Chiang Mai it's big business. Almost every guest house is affiliated with a trekking outfit. Although not required, things work smoothest if you use the tour connected with your guest house. Then you have more assurance that they will hold your bags safely until your return, usually four days and three nights later. Check what the price includes; services vary. It should cover all transportation expenses, all food for the trip, drivers and bodyguards when necessary, and all basic equipment, such as backpacks, blankets, medical supplies, and plastics during the rainy season.

Orbit Tours gives quality, safe trips, but they tend to go into heavily-toured areas. They have an office at Daret's Restaurant and also one out at Je t'aime. Sorn at the Thai-German Guest House has super-guide status for his Little Tribal Tours. Chan at Pao Come Guest House is an affable, high-energy guide.

Many people prefer to begin their treks nearer to the hilltribes by starting in Chiang Rai. Berm at the Chiang Rai Guest House is knowledgeable about hill hikes. Mr. Porn at Porn Guest House is possibly the most conscientious guide in the area, with an earnest concern for the tribes visited. His niece, Pimpa, is also quite capable.

In Mae Hong Son, Mrs. Lungnapa Lungow charges according to the distance traveled from town. She's sensitive to the tribal cultures as she teaches the Meo.

Seeds of Doubt About Tours: Mr. Nakhorn Pongnoi, a Fulbright scholar in charge of the Research Center in Chiang Rai, claims that nothing has done more damage to tribes than tours that sensationalize the tribes as primitives who sell opium and practice free love. Trekkers go there to buy the big "O" for a few *baht* a pipe. This severely affects the tribal barter economy.

Some trekking companies plan robberies. They have a suspicious number of recurring attacks by bandits. Many guides do not speak the tribal languages, and some can't speak enough discernable English to be of any value. Check with other travelers for up-to-the-minute information. Then decide for yourself whether or not the guide is someone you can live with during several days of intensive travel.

On Your Own: Go out for day walks from the Karen Coffee Shop, located eighteen kilometers north of Thaton. They have trekking maps, or ask Mr. Panga for specifics. Don't take your camera to Lisu village #2. Either sleep in the villages—clear it with the headmen—or at the Karen Coffee Shop. Great cheap meals are served at the Coffee Shop.

From Fang, several jeeps leave daily from 0800 to 0900 and travel the three hours to the Kuomintang village of Wawee. Nestled in a lush valley, this is the "Lost Horizon" home of Chiang Kai-Shek's scattered troops. There's electricity and even a refrigerator in the General's general store. If you're not invited into a house for the evening, go down to the stream where people from the village bathe. Kids climb trees to peek in at you as you wash behind shoulder-high corrugated metal stalls. The covered bridge with benches will suffice for an evening's bed. Take the pickup truck back to Fang on the following morning, or follow the road up the mountain past Yao villages. After four hours walking, most of it downhill, you come to the River Kok from where there are boats to Chiang Rai or back to Fang.

Notes: Needles, thread, zippers, aspirin, candy, nuts, cigarettes, baby powder, and salt all make good repayment for kindnesses, but don't expect to get good trade value on these for handicrafts. Think twice about going into an area that tour groups ignore unless your guide knows the tribes. You might be mistaken for CIA and get a split-second machete neck-massage.

Before you go trekking, visit the Tribal Research Center at Mahawitialai Chiang Mai (Chiang Mai University), on bus route 3. Ride through campus, or take a thirty-five-minute walk. Inside the museum are eerie life-like dioramas of tribespeople in their daily-life settings, authentic down to minutiae such as worn elbows on the clothes. You feel like an intruder in their home. There's a library next door with noncommercial, unsensational literature on the cultures you meet in the hills.

___The Tribes

In general, the twenty distinct peoples living above 800 meters are non-Thai speaking and, except for the Karen, raise opium as a cash crop. Inside Thailand's borders, they have a total population of about 300,000, of which the Karen, Meo, Akha, Yao, Lahu and Lisu make up eighty percent. Each tribe can be identified by the elevation at which they live: The Karen are valley people; then come the Akha, Lisu, and Lahu; then the Yao; and finally, the Meo live nearest the top. Since opium grows best in upper altitudes, the higher the tribe lives, the "higher" on opium they normally get. Many tribespeople now live in permanent government-sponsored settlements where their distinctiveness fades slowly as they become assimilated into mainstream Thai culture.

Karen: Although they make up almost forty-five percent of all northern Thai tribespeople, the Karen aren't really a hilltribe people. Rather, they prefer to build their hardwood and thatched houses along creeks in valleys. The Yang (as they are also known), live mostly along the Thai-Burma border south of Mae Hong Son. However, some have migrated as far south as Malaysia.

According to their folklore all people came "from the same gourd." The Karen, being the first-born race have a duty to welcome their younger brothers in other tribes—the Akha, Lisu, French, Americans, and so on. A flexible race, the Karen have adapted their basic animism to both Buddhism and Christianity. Both offered free food and education. Some Karen still follow a nineteenth-century tattoo cult called the *Cekosi* Rite. A sacred symbol is burned into the skin while holy words are chanted. The resulting tattoo serves as a perpetual appeasement of the bothersome ancestral spirits who previously required noisome daily sacrifices.

Karen

The clans' clothing is straight cut and made from black, red, or white hand-loomed fabric. Men wear jackets, women tunics. Unmarried girls wear white ankle-length dresses that have a waxed surface. This surface gives the dress the appearance of a flower petal, a symbol of purity. Married women wear black tunics, short and loose-fitting for comfort during pregnancy and to facilitate nursing. Tunics are often embroidered with shell-like hard seeds of grain, *coyx lacryma*, stitched into flower patterns on the cloth.

Courting is covert. A man sneaks beneath the house of his intended and pokes a stick through a hole in the floor (quite possibly put there for that very purpose by the girl's father). This signals her to join her fiance in the bushes.

The Karen raise wet rice in paddies. They husband pigs, buffalo, chickens, and occasionally elephants.

Akha: Dogs yelp as you enter the village, in which pigs roam freely on the grassless hillside. The *taw mah lok kaw* (gate) is flanked on both sides by stick statues, a woman on one side, a man on the other. These images are there to

Akha

ensure the fertility of the village, a necessary precaution as death comes often and early. Don't touch. Off to the side is a four-spoked ferris wheel that is *never* tampered with except during festivals when the fun has a religious significance. The Akha (or Ekah or Ekaw), migrated from Burma to Thailand about forty years ago and live at an elevation of 1100 meters along the Kok River and in Mae Hong Son.

The women wear short, knee-length dresses and often wear shin guards to protect their lower legs from scratches. They wear helmets decorated with stalks of grass, bamboo, dyed feathers, squirrel fur, strings of Job's tears, tassels of cotton and silk, and silver coins that dangle on their foreheads. Married women's headdresses are higher than those of the unmarried.

During the day the village is buzzing with insect sounds. At night at the rendezvous spot, girls sing songs, dance, and joke with the boys until one leads the other off for love *alfresco*. A male announces his engagement by wearing a filigree silver flower.

The Akha's favorite meat is dog. They hang the dog's head and feet along the path as food for the spirits.

Lisu: They are related to both the Akha and the Lahu. There are approximately 20,000 Lisu scattered in hamlets throughout northern Thailand north of the Kok River. They hunt with crossbows, smoke opium, drink tea, eat with chopsticks and chew betel nut. Women wear rainbows of colors on beautiful knee-length blouses. On formal occasions, the women cover their breasts with elaborate silver ornaments and wear enormous black turbans. After her first menstruation, a woman must go through *soom chiang*. A *tongpa* (exorcist) repurifies her and presents her with a "moon flower" talisman in the form of a silver disc. Then she is free to choose her husband. If he accepts he must pay a huge sum of money as bride price for what will become his chattel-bedmate.

Lisu

The Lisu have a reputation as linguists. They usually can speak Thai and use it when talking slang, joking, and also as a courting language.

Labu: The Chinese call them "Lohei," the Thai and Shan say "Muhsur," and they call themselves Lahu. About the turn of the century, they migrated from the narrow strip of Tibetan land between the Mekong and the Salween Rivers to escape pressure from the Han people of China.

Ecologically minded, they poke holes with sticks to plant their crops and leave rice stalks to protect the earth from erosion. After harvest they leave the field fallow for three to five years. Excellent farmers, they claim the largest per capita production of opium.

Three major subgroups account for 17,000 of the 23,000 Lahu. Lahu Nyi (Red Lahu), are perhaps named for their main cash crop of flaming chili, or perhaps from the red clothing the

Lahu

women wear. The steps to their crude dwellings are hewn from logs and serve a double use as pig feeders. Children are encouraged to smoke. They have great tasting banana-leaf cheroots (huge cigars, mixed with tea leaves for aroma). The trim on their clothing is a broad band of red, white, and blue.

Lahu Na (Black Lahu), have only narrow strips of white trim on their clothing. Surprisingly, the men work as hard as their women and are excellent in caring for their children. They marry at about age fifteen, after which the husband moves in with his in-laws for three years.

In the Lahu Shi (Yellow Lahu) villages, a man lures a woman out of the house with an unusual mating call—he blows on a blade of grass. The couple meet in the mating pavilion set away from the village. There, she joins him in a jungle vocal duet that ends in dalliance. She reports the incident to the village chief. If the partner promises to marry her, there's no fine. The promise is the wedding ceremony.

Yao: This "primitive" tribe makes paper from pounded bamboo roots and their medicine man must be literate in Chinese. They live in huge bamboo houses with dirt floors and raised sleeping platforms. Semi-nomadic, the Yao move every ten years.

Women wear distinctive boas of red yarn and shave their eyebrows. With lukewarm wax, they fix their hair in a primitive permanent. Over this they wear a stately turban. Skilled in embroidery, they have elaborately-stitched designs on their pants, a panel of which can take up

Yao

to a year to complete. A woman is valued by her skill of embroidery. During courtship, the man sneaks into the woman's home for an evening together on the mat, but must be certain to leave before her parents wake up. (Only with the aid of opiates could such a method of mating hope to succeed.)

Don't take pictures of the elderly or of children; their souls are considered too weak and may follow the image instead of the original.

Meo: Their name, meaning barbarian, was given them by the Chinese when they settled in the Yellow River Valley about 2700 B.C. They call themselves "Hmong," meaning free. Only a small segment of the tribe's five million people

Meo

live in Thailand. Many are communists, a security nightmare for the Thai government. They also have a reputation as warriors. An uprising in the 1960s was known as the Meo War.

Although both men and women wear pants made of hemp, women more often wear heavily-pleated short skirts with dyed designs.

Many Meo are opium addicts. It's virtually part of their culture and is as acceptable as alcohol is in the West. The poppy is also their chief cash crop, earning a family an average income of ฿3500 annually. The women do all the work; the Meo chauvinists stay home with their pipes. If one woman can't support her husband's habit, he is free to marry again—if he can afford the bride price of ฿400. When a girl reaches puberty, married men and boys compete to arouse her from her bedroom and seduce her.

The Meo are paranoid animists whose spirits are in constant need of gifts. They wear amulets to protect them from the ghosts they can't be sure to please and frequently employ exorcists to free them from harmful enchantments.

Phi Tong Luang: The "Spirit of the Yellow Leaf" move on when the leaves of their crude lean-to shelters begin to change color. Most of the time they have no shelters at all, and they never live in villages. No one knows where they came from. Until the sixties, they were believed to be a local myth.

The Phi Tong Luang are hunters, using spears to kill only enough food for the day. When no game is available, they forage for wild vegetables and roots, cooking and eating them in throw-away bamboo dishes. After a meal, they break into spontaneous, unchoreographed dances

Phi Tong Luang, Spirit of the Yellow Leaf

of celebration. The women blacken their faces before strangers arrive to protect themselves by ugliness. Fewer than twenty separate sightings have been recorded, most of them around Nan.

_Long Way to Chiang Rai

Until the road was built in 1952, Fang could only be reached on horseback. Today, the four-and-a-half-hour bus ride begins at the Elephant Gate in Chiang Mai. At marker #94, fifty-eight kilometers north of Chiang Mai, the road passes a training camp for elephants. It's a show with the pachyderm performers at their best in the bath at 0800. (There is a real elephant training camp in Ngao.)

Chiang Dao: This small town, fourteen kilometers farther north, is noted for an underground vault filled with images of Buddha. The deep cave is located five kilometers outside of town.

The way into the cavern is lit by electric bulbs. A guide will take a group even farther in with torches. Back in town, the Chiangdao Hotel has rooms without private baths. Last bus back to Chiang Mai leaves at 1800. About ninety-five kilometers north of Chiang Mai, the road passes a Meo village. Still in their traditional dress, the Meo sit looking out their rude huts at the traffic screeching around the turn.

Fang: The lethargic village huddles in the corner of an oversized city wall. The wall is the only remnant of the days when monarchs called Fang their "center of the universe." Around the corner on Main Street and across from a sign reading "Ueng Kham Bangalo," the Seen Sukit Hotel has rooms in a granary-like shed. They have nicer clapboard bungalows in the back. The Ueng Kham Bangalo is cleaner and quieter. There's street food at the bus station. Every half hour a bus leaves for Thaton, twenty-three kilometers north. A bus just as frequently returns to Chiang Mai.

Thaton: Food shacks, souvenir sheds, and basic bungalows edge the south side of the Kok River. They vie for the tourist business at the start of the river trip.

The River Kok: It flows across the Burma border along the base of the Golden Triangle. Since the Opium Act of 1959 banned the smoking or growing of opium poppy in Thailand, the Kok has been a mainline for smugglers. Swift, long-tailed craft sneak over the border and deposit the contraband along the river. From there, it's transshipped to secret heroin-producing factories.

From Fang, the river continues west to Chiang Rai and seventy kilometers later empties into the Mekong River near Chiang Saen. When you join the other five foreigners you just met on the boat, prepare to wait: Wait for the rice sacks to be stacked on board. Wait for eight or nine other passengers. Wait for the boatmen to have their lunch. The daily drift to Chiang Rai takes five hours or five days depending on the river depth or unforseeable hangups: "What do you mean you forgot the gasoline!"

The dwarfish forest and long broom-like *pong* grass give way to minor mountains rising alongside the river. Rapids begin to cut deeper into the brownish-red soil. At one point near Mae Salak a soldier with a gun orders everybody out of the boat. You must walk so the boat can maneuver among the rocks. The soldier hops on with you to ride shotgun and discourage armed robbery from the hill bandits. Movement in the bushes catches your eye. An old country monk in burgundy robes waddles down the bank to wave for the ride owed anyone who wears the robe. The driver can't look away in time and has to stop.

A family wades across the river. The sun makes you glad you remembered a hat. There's silence outside the sound of your long-tail engine. There are trees, and birds, and many clearings. Civilization is coming. You round the bend to the Chiang Rai dock at sunset.

___Chiang Rai

According to legend, King Mengrai was chasing a runaway elephant when he came upon the Kok River and decided to expand his kingdom to the south. More likely, he was the one being chased—by the threat of an invasion from Kublai Khan. For the thirty-six years between 1262 and 1298, Chiang Rai was his capital. Today, the downtown streets are on a western grid. But down by the dock during the last few moments of the day, silhouetted oarsmen pull across the silver water of the Kok River. You know you're in Asia.

Getting There: Air-conditioned buses leave at 0900, 1000, and 1200 from the Chiang Mai White Elephant Gate for the three-hour trip. A regular bus leaves every thirty minutes between 0600 and 1730. A bus via the old route through Lampoon takes six hours. It's a more folksy run where you share a seat with a family of four, and have a pig at your side in the aisle and chickens squirming in a bag at your feet.

Air-conditioned coaches depart Bangkok's North Station at 1930 and 2020 for the direct twenty-three-hour, 884-kilometer marathon. There's also a daily plane from Bangkok.

Getting Around: On your first trip to a guest house, the *samlor* is paid for by your hosts. From the Chiang Rai Airport, you can ride a minibus the 4.8 kilometers into town. It's an easy town to walk around in.

Wat Pra Keo: The Emerald Buddha's travels began from here in 1434. A streak of lightning cracked open the pagoda to reveal the buried Buddha figure covered with stucco and gold leaf. It was moved to Wat Pra Singh next door where the stucco fell away from the precious lime-colored image. Before long the king of Chiang Mai heard of the find and sent for it. But elephant trouble again, the beast headed down the wrong path to Lampang. Not until thirty-two years later did the statue finally reach Chiang Mai. On Ngam Muang Hill to the west lie the bones of King Mengrai, monarch of Chiang Saen, Chiang Rai, and Chiang Mai.

VILLAGE LIFE

Broad flat irrigated fields of rice surround the hamlet waiting for the yearly, or perhaps twice yearly, harvest. A small morning market sells recently adopted vegetables such as garlic. *Longan* fruit and lemons, coconuts, bananas, and mangos grow in the house compounds, where dogs, chickens, ducks, and pigs are also raised. Water, cooled by slow evaporation through the walls of earthenware jugs, stands at the front gate of each home. The bamboo dipper beside it is for any passerby to use.

Every Wednesday, the "Cow Market" comes to town. Water buffalos and cattle change owners, or are exchanged for motorbikes. Medicine, charms, and amulets are displayed next to fishtraps and flashlights. Transistor radios blare saccharine tragedies in song. In addition to the market, peddlers occasionally pass through the village carrying tinker's tin utensils and sun shades.

The village has a tailor, a temple with cremation grounds, a rice mill, a grade school, a gas station, and an auto repair area marked by oil spots on the gravel. Monks are invited to rites of passage celebrations, but only for a cursory blessing. Women consult shamans and mediums, usually other women, to guard family spirits. The diviner known as the "rice swinger" is invariably a woman. The herbalist, on the other hand, is always male, as is the "blower" who heals wounds and broken bones with incantations.

In the mornings, locals linger over the newspapers at the coffee-shop shed. In the evenings, the dirt streets are white with ghostly light spilling from black and white TVs airing American situation comedies, Japanese cartoons, and Hong-Kong-made dramas of ancient China.

Carrying cows to market

Shopping: The Chiang Rai Market is a covered area near the town center. Pick up a *gahn gehn chow nah*, a pair of indigo-blue cotton wraparound pants used by farmers in the area, for ฿40 after some playful bargaining. The stiffness goes after a few washings, and they then make great beach pants. Get top-quality handicrafts at the Tribal Research Center. Although the prices are slightly higher than in other shops, the money is certain to go back to the tribespeople.

Stay: Porn Guest House (no prostitutes allowed), is across from the courthouse on Ratanaket Road. It's a country palace of satiny teak floors and walls. At the station, one of their sweet-faced children peeks in the door of your bus before it stops and says, "Please stay in my house."

The slightly cheaper Chiang Rai Guest House provides mosquito nets. Meals are also available here. Berm is trying to run the best place in town. The teak building is a bit tough to find, so it's best to take a *samlor* the first trip there. Hotel Pao Patana, on the main road next to the barber shop, was built surrounding two courtyards in a squared figure eight. All the rooms have fans and attached baths.

Food: You get a large helping of chicken in a potato-peanut curry sauce served on rice in the small shop across from the flower market on Sanambin Road. (It's next to a motorcycle shop.) The people speak no English, but they are proud to have you as a customer; you're royalty. Thai food at the Ruam Mit is delicious and inexpensive. It's located on Ratanaket Road across from the Rama Hotel. The Petchburi Restaurant is a bit more expensive. It offers tasty Chinese dishes. Boy Ice Cream Shop has vases of roses on linen-covered tables and serves Foremost ice cream. The adventurous try the durian ice cream—it tastes like creme de aqua velva. Next door, the provisions store on the main street sells great banana bread.

From: Planes return to Chiang Mai from Chiang Rai at 1300 daily. Buses leave for the south at 1830 and at 1930. Four hours later they stop at Pitsanulok; six and a half hours later at Sukotai. A boat leaves upriver for Thaton at 1030. No one knows when it will arrive.

____Chiang Saen

History: The first Thai drifted over the mountains and rivers the same way the hilltribes do today. Eventually the farmers agreed to meet and trade their rice for hammered iron tools. Some stayed in the emerging market-town, and through the years, it grew into a city, and then a state.

Chiang (fortifications), three meters thick were built around the capital, leaving enough fields inside to outlast any seige. The walls were breached during the sixteenth-century Burman invasion, and the city became a base for further attacks against Chiang Mai and Ayuthia. The walls were brought down by Rama I so that Chiang Saen would never again harbor the enemy that threatened to become overlords of his people.

Toppled Temples: Outside your bus window, the crumbling Chedi Luang, a sixty-meter-high stupa sneaks from behind the trees on the right just past the city wall. The museum next to the ruin is filled with decapitated statues. The woman curator practices her religious chants while she's at work. There's a sparkling crystal Buddha on the shelves among all the dusty heads. You ask if you can leave your bag with the woman, and she says, "OK. Now, I'll be closed for lunch, you come back after that." She speaks in perfect Thai and you understand all of it by her gestures. At the road, another woman at her stall dips out *kwey teow* soup.

Just outside the wall is Chedi Wat Pasak, weeds high against its toppled stones. Statues in niches are veiled with spider webs. You follow the dirt road just inside the city wall for three kilometers and walk up the moss-cushioned steps. At the top of the hill, the tenth-century leaning stupa of Wat Prathat Chomkitti overlooks the Mekong Valley.

Laos looks deceptively peaceful in the distance. Saffron, like sunshine, catches your eye. Down behind you, a giant Buddha in the middle of the trees beckons you and a path leads toward you from out of the forest.

Center of the Golden Triangle: At the T in the road in Chiang Saen, a sign points left to Sam Ruim Tom Kam, the Golden Triangle. Take the hourly minibus that runs between 0800 and 1400. As you bounce down the rutted dirt road that hugs the Mekong River, the vehicle fills with homespun locals gossiping a singsong mixture of Laotian and Thai. At the point where Burma, Laos, and Thailand meet, are the Golden Huts of bamboo. Hastily put up years ago during the Triangle's golden days, they are still up. You can pay to stay the night. Lying on a wood plank on top of a thin mat, you can look up at the stars through holes in the thatched roof. It's a bit uncomfortable during rainy season. Candles light the way in the dark for mosquitos. On full moons, the Golden Queen, *Mekong*, is a breathless beauty flowing within five meters of your threshold. A crude gazebo near the bank is a perfect spot for late night solitude.

At sunrise, watch as life along the river wakes up. In this water lurks the world's largest freshwater fish, the *pabeuk* (or *pla buk*), a giant catfish two and a half meters long and more than 150 kilograms heavy. Rowers squat at their boats' sterns to keep the blunt-ended prow from diving into the water.

Just upriver from the huts a young couple has set up a restaurant under a thatched roof. They'll tell you (in English), chilling tales of refugees shot while swimming for freedom, or of a solid gold icon found by a farmer whose village now has a road because of it.

Warning: The local constable frequents the Golden Huts looking for some extra cash from ensnared drug users. Buses coming back from the area are checked enroute for the same reason.

At the restaurant, not-so-clear maps hint at how to walk the two hours to Sun Chow Kow, an Akha village. The village of Ban Toung Liang is six kilometers farther and from there, minibuses go regularly to Mae Sai. Mae Sai, on the northernmost point of the Thai border, is noted as a center for shoe making and smuggling goods into Burma's insatiable black market.

From the Golden Huts, you can walk along the path upriver to Ban Wang Lao, a refugee camp for Laotians an hour and a half away. A boat that carried four to five people ran to Ban Rong until a Thai naval officer was shot by Laotian border snipers in 1980. Until relations are normalized, no boat.

OPIUM

Yao with her bong for smoking opium

The Golden Triangle is the source of sixty-five percent of the world's heroin, of which eighty-five percent finds its way to the United States. In New York City, it sells for $1 million per kilogram. The Thai peasant get $500 per kilogram. Opium travels via routes maintained by the combined efforts of mercenary capitalists, left-wing rebel freedom fighters, ultra-right Kuomintang troops, primitive tribesmen, sophisticated Chinese "mafia dons," corrupt police, bribed government officials, not-so-anti-narcotics specialists, U.S. military pilots, and travelers.

Covering an area of about 250 square kilometers, the Triangle produces 600,000 tons of opium annually. Government efforts to substitute beans and coffee crops for opium have had limited success in Thailand. Now ninety percent of the opium is grown in Burma and smuggled across the border into Thailand.

Beginning in late October, the poppy plant, *papaver somniferum*, blossoms. The harvest continues until March, peaking in late January or early February. Opium is the milky-white juice extracted from seed pods and dried until brown. The bitter-tasting goo is then scraped and boiled and formed into bricks or balls to be sold. A user doesn't actually smoke opium; direct flames destroy the euphoric effect. He will heat it indirectly and inhale its whitish-yellow vapors. The effects are dangerously magical: a detachment from stress, a fantasy world of dreams, a nonviolent world.

Opium was used to cure hunger pangs. Mahouts gave it to elephants to calm their nerves at the big game shooting camps. Tigers' drinking holes were spiked with the drug to insure success for the "great white hunters." In the nineteenth century, opium was used as a cure for alcoholism. It was sold in grocery stores of Victorian London to help teething infants. Laudanum, an opium derivative, was given to children to keep them quiet. Ladies would use headaches as a cover for tripping out.

Opium is severely addictive: Ten percent of the tribesmen, and 500,000 Thai (with an additional 6000 annually), have become addicts. An addict consumes fifty to seventy-five milligrams a day. He is faced with the problem of securing an ever increasing dosage. He is chasing the dragon, ever-disappearing euphoria. Otherwise he is tormented by the effects of withdrawal: appetite loss, chills, weeping, diarrhea, sweating, vomiting, abdominal cramps, and insomnia.

And he never loses his desire for euphoria just one more time.

Central Thailand: Ruins in the Rice Fields

The Thai migrated in tribal flocks south from China via valley passes in the mountains. Each influx of people erected a capital within earthen ramparts. Each left patches of stucco on crumbling brick walls and stone images of Buddha dreaming in niches. The power to rule, like fire driven by a northern wind, burned southward to Sukotai, Ayuthia, and finally Bangkok.

During the rise and fall of empires, the peasant's life has changed very little. He plants his rice and drinks his tea as he always did. He's suspicious of the farmer down the road who just got a motor-driven plow for his paddies. He figures the world will straighten itself out when people go back to doing things the way they used to—the way they did when that temple ruin in one of his own paddies was new. Central Thailand: Things turn slower in the center of a wheel and in the center of the land.

In the traditional method of wet rice cultivation in the central plains of Thailand, the paddy soil is less important to the farmer than the water. During dry season the parched paddy becomes a baked clay basin. Seeds are broadcast over the unplowed fields. There they remain as food for rats and insects until the rains come to germinate them. Then the stems grow fast to keep the crown above flooding waters as deep as 150 to 200 centimeters between August and October. When the water subsides, the grain is harvested.

Chiang Rai to Lampang

Payao: Hourly buses leave Chiang Rai for Lampang and arrive four and a half hours later. Ninety-four kilometers out of Chiang Rai you reach Payao, a city-state from 1096 until it was absorbed by Chiang Mai in 1338. Archeologists have discovered pre-bronze artifacts near the faintly discernible outline of the ancient city walls. The present town edges the east shore of the shallow lake.

Stay at Wattana Hotel in town or at the lakeside bungalows. Try the local delicacies—crisp-fried crickets, frogs, and waterbugs or locally caught *nin* fish.

South of Payao, the road climbs through a pass. For centuries, the sheer cliffs with their saber-toothed peaks inhibited invasion from the north. About eighty kilometers before Lampang, the bus passes the highest point in the road, a sacred spot at a turn in the road where everyone (including the driver), raises both hands to *wai* in respect for the *phi* (spirits of the departed and of the not yet born). The *phi* haunt the piles of unkempt old spirit houses that number in the hundreds—no one would dare destroy even an old broken spirit house for fear the spirit still lived there. Instead, they bring the *phi* house here. From this point, the road descends sharply, dropping more than a thousand meters in less than thirty kilometers.

Elephants may never forget but it takes six years for them to learn the ropes. A trained elephant is worth ฿90,000.

Ngao Elephant Camp: At Ban Lok, not far from the town of Ngao and fifty-four kilometers north of Lampang, is an authentic elephant training camp, *rong ree-un lu chang Ban Lok.* It's a five kilometer walk west from the road. If you arrive early, you might catch a ride with one of the mahouts (elephant drivers) on his way to work in a pickup. Most of the training is done before noon. Continuing south, the bus splashes puddles at the piles of pineapples along the road. At a stop, a sticky plastic bag of sweet pineapple passes through your open window for a *baht.*

Lampang

The village started at the side of the river and moved landward. The first houses were warehouse-homes. After three months of rowing and poling upriver, travelers and boat people from Bangkok would rest here before the former would continue up to Chiang Mai by land on elephants. The streets of this trade center grew parallel to the river as the town expanded. Up to sixty percent of the world's annual crop of opium once passed through Lampang, spreading wealth in its wake. Money meant jobs, and peasants came to make Lampang a small city. Then in 1921, the train tracks from Bangkok reached Chiang Mai and less trade filtered through Lampang's warehouses.

Now vintage teak mansions of the former rich lean on their stilts by the street near the river. On elegant teak-wood porches hang slatted wooden planters for orchids. There are temples that were constructed in the thirteenth century when Lampang was strong enough to keep the Emerald Buddha as its own despite the wrath of the mighty king of Chiang Mai. There are Burmese *wat*, built during the century-long occupation of the north in the 1600s. And when the din of traffic dims in the evening, there are horse-drawn carriages clopping down streets.

Wat Pra Keo Don Tau: The temple was ornamented with flamboyant filigree to shelter the Emerald Buddha in glory. In front of the stupa stands a pavilion that has a ceiling of mother-of-pearl inlay and a jeweled fantasy of mirrors. The museum is full of religious paraphernalia: a monk's fan which he hid behind in old times so he wouldn't be tempted by a pretty woman's face, and the old statue for the fifth altar. Among these sacred "attic-facts" is a comical puppet that waits near the entrance; his hands move in response to a donation.

Wat Sri Chum: From the temple gate on Sri Sham Road, Wat Sri Chum appears to be a typical Burmese-style *wat*—and it is. But there's one difference: Pra Kata Punno, "The Old Monk," as he jokingly calls himself in flawless English,

Wat Sri Chum, Lampang

Wat Pra Keo Don Tau, Lampang

enriches the *wat* with a noticeable tranquility. Pra Kata Punno speaks seven languages and has dedicated his being to the strengthening of his meditative powers for the benefit of others. He sleeps in a three-meter cube of copper mesh to help him transmit his Oneness with the universe to those in need, to attract these vibrations to him, and to protect himself from nighttime evil forces and mosquitos.

The shining interior of the *bot* has mirrored floors of polished teak. The pillars are covered with gold lacquer paintings. The bottom pictures show the casual, simple beauty of the Burmese; the top, the ethereal, refinement of the Thai. One pillar shows Buddha in a former life as an elephant-bird. Lacquered on the wall is a pictorial history of the *wat's* origin: A poor man came from Burma, started a lumber company, built wayside rest pavilions and bridges to earn merit, and down the path built this *wat*. On the road that weaves the scenes together pilgrims travel on foot, in oxcarts, and in automobiles.

The Golden Buddha, his topknot and ears accentuated in the Burmese fashion, shines beneath colored flourescent lights. Pra Kata Punno welcomes men who wish to stay and study Buddhism.

Wat Lampang Luang: Walled in like the medieval town it once was a part of, this religious sanctuary has a history of more than a thousand years. Just outside lives a venerable bodhi tree, an offspring of the divine tree under which Buddha received enlightenment. Its decrepit limbs are supported by hundreds of crutches, with new ones added each year.

The fortification was renovated three hundred years ago, before most of the old buildings in the area were built. Inside, gold glows from carved red recesses on pillars and lintels. Old paintings decorate the eaves of the open pavilion. A marked spot on the base of the pagoda shows the scar of the cannon ball that killed a Burmese general in an eighteenth-century battle for control of the temple-fortress.

To get to Wat Lampang Luang, take a *songtao* down Praisani Road to near the railroad tracks, and then change to a vehicle bound for Kohka, eighteen kilometers away. The *wat* is located three kilometers beyond Kohka.

Stay: On weekends, all the cheap hotels fill with Thai soldiers on rest-and-recreation from their base nearby. There's the old wooden whorehouse called Rongram Lampang across the street from Wat Suandawk. The Sri Sangar Hotel on Boonyawat Road is nearby. In the alley behind this hotel stands the Kelang Nahkorn Hotel, a reddish-brown teak building. Giggling women run around the halls in their bras and panties like sisters. The Sri Lampang Hotel on Boonyawat Road is very clean, with helpful management, and a price to match their superior quality.

From Lampang: The main station is a *songtao* ride from the city center. Catch a bus bound for Chiang Rai at the clock tower in town.

___Sukotai

When the Thai came from China, they were loose aggregates of refugee clans looking for land on the frontier plains of the Khmer Empire. As migrant workers,

Wat Mahathat, Sukotai

most of the rice they raised was theirs, but the land was not. Then in the daring uprising of 1258, two Thai princes banded together to drive out the Khmer overlords, and the first truly Thai kingdom was born.

Every man was free to confer with his king at a meeting spot just outside the palace gate. There was rice in the fields and fish in the streams. There was work only during planting and harvesting one crop a year. The rest of the time was dedicated to renovation of old Hindu temples and to the construction of a new city of stone populated with thousands of Buddha statues and thousands of Thai. They mortared the blocks of stone together and stuccoed them with a granite-tough mixture of sand, lime, buffalo hides, and molasses.

Meanwhile in 1253, the Khan's army destroyed the Thai city of Nanchao in China. The survivors fled to Sukotai and provided the Pra Rung Dynasty with troops to add more land to its domain.

Ramkamhaeng (1278-1318) wanted to free himself from dependence on his literate Brahmin Hindu court-advisors. He altered characters in the Khmer script and developed the refined, curved Thai script. He brought the art of making celadon pottery with him on his return to Sukotai, after he paid tribute to the Chinese emperor. During his reign local art flourished, reaching its peak in the graceful walking Buddha figures of Sukotai.

In 1350 the new city-state of Ayuthia was established to the south. It was peopled by another group of Thai. The soil to the south was freshly turned up from under centuries of wild growth, and therefore much more fertile than the older, tired land around older, tired Sukotai. Before long, the princes of Sukotai were bowing to Ayuthia's kings.

New Sukotai: The glory days of Muang Kao (old town) Sukotai are gone. But the ruins are in good shape compared to the modern city that has grown up along the Yan River twelve kilometers to the east. Buses make brief stops here on their way between Bangkok, Chiang Rai, Chiang Mai, and Korat.

It's an informal place. The cook at the ground-floor coffee shop of the Chinese-owned Sukotai Hotel comes to sit at your table to see if you like gingered pork. At night the covered stalls near the bus stop have quick fry meals and also desserts such as muskmelon topped with coconut cream, cooled with a mountain of ice, and sweetened with raw sugarcane juice. *Aroi mahk!*

Across the street, the Pong Prasert Hotel sits on the river bank. The upstairs corner room has a view out two sides, or you can sit on the veranda to watch pink clouds of sunset as they float on the surface of the river. In the early evening you can smell the aroma of pound cakes as they come out of the oven at the home-bakery nearby.

Next to the bridge on the opposite side of the river from the Pong Prasert Hotel is Cham's Restaurant. You sit at a table and watch the life on the riverboats. The men behind you want to pour you a drink of Mekong whiskey. Cham's wife stirs up some fried crab and rice or a succulent whole roasted chicken so sweet and crisp, you could eat the bones. Cham, a Thai veteran of the Vietnam war, talks to you while you wait. Across the river the bright-white Buddha of Wat Rachthanee helps you imagine what old Sukotai was like when it was new and white.

Wat Sra Sri, Sukotai

Old Sukotai: In a parking lot west of the river wait antiquated vehicles with homemade wooden roofs. The truck-buses fill with vegetables from the morning market, chickens, sacks of rice, and passengers. Then you're off down the road to the ruins at a breakneck speed of twenty kilometers per hour; plenty of time to pick out details in the countryside.

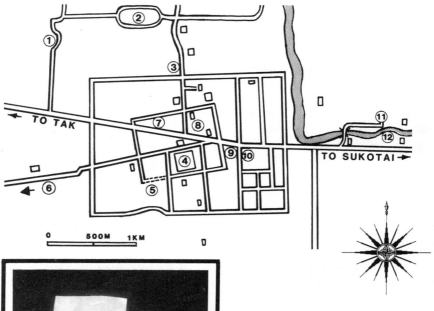

Wat Sri Chum, Sukotai

OLD SUKOTAI

1. Wat Sri Chum
2. Wat Pra Pai-Luang
3. Sam Luang Gate
4. Wat Mahathat
5. Wat Sri Sawai
6. To Forest Temple
7. Wat Sra Sri
8. Monument of King Ramkamhaeng
9. Ramkamhaeng National Museum
10. Wat Trapang Tong
11. Wat Chang Lom (Elephant Temple)
12. Boonchoo Antique Store

Outside, under a tree in the compound, a hairless *acharn* (teacher) in saffron robes points at a map leaning against a tree and instructs young *nen* (novice monks) in European geography. Opposite the main gate, dancers in stupa-like hats and sparkling gold-embroidered pants honor Buddha with graceful movement. In their midst, an infant girl in costume concentrates her fingers into precise position and yawns.

In the gallery behind the *viharn*, the Buddha Chinaraj National Museum displays weapons used by the Japanese during WW II along with uniforms tailored for elephants.

Stay: The Sri Jeun Hotel has a small sign over its entrance written in Thai:

โรงแรม

The manager speaks absolutely no English. It's a delightful experience.

Classic yawn of dancing child, Pitsanulok

Kamphaeng Phet

Rust-iron red laterite is a basalt rock, the closest thing scientists have found to the composition of primeval magma. In the fourteenth century, it was carved into stones and used to build temples, stupa, and the great 5300-meter-long oval wall (*kamphaeng*) with crenulations shaped like diamonds (*phet*). These iron-rock walls and weathered statues rest in the almost haunted surroundings of toppled temples only a ten-minute walk from the center of the present village of Kamphaeng Phet.

The Ruins: In twilight, the broken head of a sitting Buddha pierces the sky above the crumbled block of the vanished temple walls. Nearby, another Buddha-head lies face down in the grass; the stucco profile is aged with lines. A man pedals his steaming dumpling shop on a push-bike up to tempt you.

A road outlines the interior of the wall, now an overgrown hill surrounding rice and sugarcane fields. The highway crosses the moat almost overgrown with hyacinth. Just past the bridge a gravel road leads off to the left. It passes a broken-down farmhouse with a stupa in the backyard. Soon the remnants of a several kilometers long fence appear beside the road as thin shoulder-high slats of laterite stick out of the ground. The lane leads all the way past several forest temples, such as the roofless Wat Pra Nam and Wat Sri Iriyabot, to Wat Chang Rob. The

Wat Sri Iriyabot

stupa has vanished, only the base remains. Mayan-like steps lead to the top of its terraces to the exposed, once-hidden stupa crypt.

Like the other temples and monasteries on this dusty lane, Wat Sri Iriyabot was built by a sect of forest monks. They preferred to isolate themselves from the too-much-with-us world and live in the forests. They were a sect separate from the court, separate from the Sangha, the Thai brotherhood of monks. Their temples have crumbled like those of the other monks inside the wall. But their ruins have lonely majesty in the woods. Behind Wat Sri Iriyabot stands a Buddha figure with an enigmatic smile. He appears emaciated because the stucco has fallen away from his chest seeming to expose his ribs of laterite brick.

The Museum: The exhibits have explanation cards in English, but you won't need them if the curator, who speaks English, has free time. The collection is one of the best organized in the country. Study the relief map at the door and ask to leave your bags here while you look around the ruins.

Stay: The Niyaprapa Hotel is a rabbit warren of wood on the corner of the main turnabout. The children in the family buff the shiny teak floors by skating on them with coconut husks. The beds are long enough for an average-size western man to stretch his legs; you don't even have to dangle your feet over the end. Out the window of room 22 is a small, wild lily pond.

A poor alternative is the Rajadamnern Hotel on the street by the same name. It's modern; it's sterile. The staff counts your money potential when you walk in the door.

Food: Two doors toward the river from Niyaprapa Hotel, the restaurant cooks up a great plate of *mee kow* with big chunks of chicken in noodles. They also have a great *gai tom yam*, a thick chicken soup. In the evening the main road attracts street stalls. Fried rice and fried noodles throw steam up at the electric bulbs strung from the closed nearby shops. A hefty mama with a rolling smile scatters raw sprouts on a field of fried noodles and sprinkles salt and sugar mixed with ground peanuts on top to make *pad thai*.

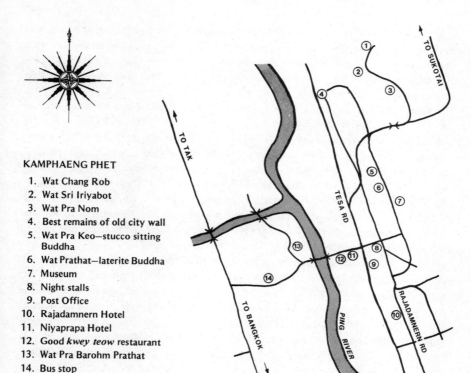

KAMPHAENG PHET

1. Wat Chang Rob
2. Wat Sri Iriyabot
3. Wat Pra Nom
4. Best remains of old city wall
5. Wat Pra Keo—stucco sitting Buddha
6. Wat Prathat—laterite Buddha
7. Museum
8. Night stalls
9. Post Office
10. Rajadamnern Hotel
11. Niyaprapa Hotel
12. Good *kwey teow* restaurant
13. Wat Pra Barohm Prathat
14. Bus stop

At about the same time that the street stalls begin to set up, the sun sets down subtle cloudless colors on the shallow Ping River. You can watch the sunset while you rest your teacup on a patio table at the Navarat Hotel at the south end of Tesa Road.

From Kamphaeng Phet: Take a mini-truck across the Ping River to the bus station out of town. You pass the stupa of the vanished Wat Pra Barohm Prathat on your way there. The form of the lonely spire is echoed in the watery rice fields that surround it. This side of the river is the sight of the even older city of Chakangrao.

——Ayuthia

History: In the middle 1300s, the village of U-thong was scorched by the fever of epidemic. Those who could, fled into the forest for safety. The king sent word that all should gather at his camp near the Chao Phraya River. Here he told them of his dream of a great city-state where he would be a humble Buddhist god-king with Hindu court magician-sages. He would call the city Ayuthia after the glorious island-state of Ayodhya praised in the Ramayana legend.

The king's scout had told him of a suitable location where the Lopburi River neared the Prasak River before it emptied into the Chao Phraya. Here, a *klong* could be dug to create an island protected behind a river moat. It would look like Buddha's footprint. The canal was excavated. The king promised to the peasants the land that fronted the canal that they dug. Over the years, a network grew like silver threads loosely woven over the land until there were more than two thousand kilometers of canals.

Wealth began to flow along the *klong* to Ayuthia. Gifts of large bronze Buddhas were floated down from Sukotai and up from Nakorn Pathom. Rajahs in Malaysia and on the island of Singapore and city-kings in Thailand as far east as Angkor Thom in Kampuchea would make sure Ayuthia would stay neutral before they warred with their neighbors. Ships arrived from the ocean, sailing into the muddy mouth of the Chao Phraya River. Arab dhows, Japanese sampans, Chinese junks, English frigates, Portuguese carracks, and Spanish galleons all merged in the forest of masts at Ayuthia's wharfs. The spires of the French cathedral rose south of the island. On the island was a city of temples and *chedi*. Seventeenth-century London was a village by comparison.

Then, in the middle 1760s, news came that the angry Burman army had taken Chiang Mai. Each garrison city tried in turn to stop their advance; all of them failed. By 1766, the Burmans were camped across the river from Ayuthia. Ayuthian women cut their hair short in an attempt to trick the invaders into thinking there were twice as many men inside the walls. Finally, after fourteen months of fires and epidemics, the Burmans poured in. Remembering the destruction of their fathers' bamboo homes by Thai soldiers, the invaders torched temples and homes. Large Buddhas were hacked to rubble or tossed into the fire to melt off the gold leaf. Five hundred temples were left in ruin.

Getting There: In Bangkok, the Oriental Queen pulls away from the dock at the Oriental Hotel and glides upriver. Passengers sit at the air-conditioned bar and watch bare-backed men work the wharfs. After a stop in Bang Pa-In, the lazy four-hour cruise ends when the luxury barge enters Ayuthia. Carved elephants and key chains await the disembarking passengers.

Don Muang Airport is halfway between Bangkok and Ayuthia and is on both the bus and train routes. Many travelers schedule a trip to Ayuthia for their last few days in Thailand.

Buses leave Bangkok's North Bus Station every half hour. They arrive in downtown Ayuthia two hours later. Trains take an hour and a half from Hua Lumpong Station in Bangkok. Aisle vendors sell spicy, grilled chicken and fresh green lotus pods. The other passengers show you how to peel out the nut-like lotus and before long the floor resembles the bottom of a bird cage. (Thai can litter in public without a second thought, but they keep their homes and temples immaculate.) From the railroad station, take a three-wheeled *tuk tuk* to Chandrakasem Palace near the cheap hotels.

The regular *tuk tuk* routes across the island don't go to some of the more remote ruins. So, you must spend several days sightseeing, or see less, or hire your own vehicle. A round-the-island boat rents for about ฿200 at the pier next

to the U-thong Hotel. (It's twice as much at the Oriental Queen dock.) You go from pavilion pier to toppling dock, past homes on stilts along the bank and majestic temple ruins.

The Village: Modern Ayuthia huddles near the northeast corner of the island, along a noisy street. There are three hotels: Kasem, Cathay, and U-thong. From your window at the U-thong Hotel you can watch traffic weave back and forth along the river.

A woman wearing a broad hat sits behind her baskets and motors her small craft downstream. She dips a metal dish into the green river for a drink. You sit in the riverside stalls next to the U-thong Hotel, where a vendor mixes her special *buoy yen* (a salty-sweet fermented plum drink). She wants to teach you Thai. Men make amulets at a cart near a stall serving dumplings and milk tea. A Thai man comes cap in hand to give you a shred of paper on which he has struggled a message: "You want boat how muck *baht* Mr. Pa-Yun." He smiles. Maybe

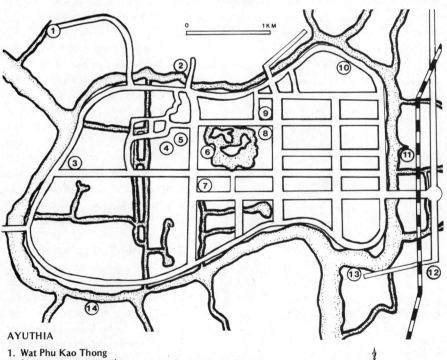

AYUTHIA

1. Wat Phu Kao Thong
   (Golden Mount Chedi)
2. Wat Na Phramen
3. Wat Lokaya Su-tha
4. Wat Pra Mongkol Bopitr
5. Wat Pra Sri Samphet
6. Wat Pra Ram
7. Chao Pya National Museum

8. Wat Mahathat
9. Wat Raj Burana
10. Chandrakasem Palace
11. Railroad Station
12. Wat Yai Chai Mongkol
13. Wat Panan Cheong
14. St. Joseph's Cathedral

tomorrow. Right now you want to walk down the pier by the park and watch an old man load his bicycle into a boat for the crossing. Or you may stroll to the corner food shops that have Chinese cooks. Or you may roam among the broken statues that stand inside the courtyard museum of the nineteenth-century Chandrakasem Palace.

Ruins on the Island: In the center of the island, Wat Pra Ram was built over the crypt containing the ashes of Ayuthia's first king, Rama Tiboldi. The swamp surrounding the temple on three sides was dredged to create a pond-garden and was planted with fire-orange flame trees.

Inside Wat Sri Samphet, to the northwest, birds build nests in the holes where roof beams once rested. In the sharp-shadowed sun of daytime, you can't feel the ghosts here amid the devastation of restoration. You find a secluded spot in the shade of a broken-down wall to meditate. When these walls were new, King Songharm would come here to do the same. Once while he was in meditation, five hundred Japanese mercenaries staged an unsuccessful assassination attempt and the rafters echoed with their death cries.

Wat Pra Mongkol Bopitr to the south shelters an ominous black Buddha giant, one of Thailand's largest bronze statues. The roof has twice crashed in on him, gashing his head and tearing off his topknot and right arm. The white eyes stare out from the black Buddha as if from behind a mask. Weekend worshipping Thai bow before him dressed in their double-knit sport shirts and designer dresses.

East of the pond-garden, the many spires of the once majestic Wat Mahathat now stand like gargantuan eroded anthills.

To the north, Wat Raj Burana was built to house the ashes of two brother princes who killed each other in their quest for Ayuthia's throne. A third brother, who became king, ordered them to be buried together. During restoration in 1959, a workman moved a slab and there, among the rubble, he discovered the secret vault. Inside were found the toppled stacks of 100,000 votive tablets (merit prayers), and gold—gold ingots, gold Buddhas, and jewels embedded in gold.

Women share the dirty work of carrying cement at reconstruction sites in Ayuthia.

The long reclining Buddha of Wat Lokaya Su-tha rests near an obscure road on the west side of the island. It's a first-century memorial to Queen Suriyothai. She convinced her husband to let her dress as a male and join him in battle. She rode her elephant-fortress into the breach and saved his life by losing hers.

Ruins North of the Moat: The driver beeps his horn for grace as he passes a roadside shrine of distorted statues. You bump down the lane along the rice plains about three kilometers from the northwest corner of the island. Then the Golden Mount Chedi towers over you and splits the road into a circle around its base. This base was built by the Mon during their brief reign (1565-1583). The Thai raised a stupa on top and, in 1954, on the Buddha's twenty-fifth-century anniversary, they placed a heavy orb of gold at the pinnacle. It was stolen. As you climb the sharply-inclined steps, the sun glares off the age-grayed stucco walls. It must have been blinding when new and white. From the top terrace, you can survey the nearby village. The people in the harvest-ready fields are changing the level of the land with each stroke of the scythe.

THAI BOXING

In the mid-1500s, so the legend goes, Prince Naresuen of Ayuthia was captured by the Burman invaders and carried off to Pegu. There he was given a chance to win his freedom by fighting the champion of his captors. In a fair fight he wouldn't have stood a chance, but he was inspired to use what since has come to be known in Thailand as the "science of the eight limbs." Fists and feet, elbows and knees directed anywhere at the opponent are legal. When the prince returned victorious from his captivity, the fame of Thai boxing spread. It was taught by monks in monasteries, until the advent in modern times of the professional fighter with camps, show fights, and dives. Today there are more than fifteen thousand professional boxers in Thailand.

To get to Wat Na Phramen north of town, take the wooden bridge that crosses over the river moat. In their country-church surroundings, the white stucco Thai temple buildings are shaded by trees. You pass from day to darkness as you enter the small chapel next to the main hall. Sit down on the cool stone floor next to a bar of dusty light beaming through slits in the wall. The heavy tenth-century Buddha in front of you was floated all the way from Nakorn Pathom, and perhaps from as far away as Ceylon. A monk appears in the shadows (or did your eyes just adjust to the darkness?). His smile is the same as that of the statue.

Ruins Southeast of the Moat: Wat Yai Chai Mongkol was built in 1529 by King Naresuan to celebrate his victory over Burma. His generals, the commanders of his elephant fortresses, had all run out on him, leaving the king to fight the crown prince of Burma one on one. He was furious when he got back home, and quite ready to chop off a few heads. His advisor-monk cooled him down with hints about reincarnation and killing: "You'll come back as a temple dog craving meat and being fed only rice if you wipe out your generals, Your Highness. Build a *chedi* instead and let it continue to rise until your temper is gone." The stupa is still one of Ayuthia's tallest structures.

Near the stupa is Wat Panan Cheong. It was built in the fourteenth century, twenty-six years before King Tiboldi moved his band of survivors across the river to begin building the city-state-empire of his dream.

At the entry corridor an old nun in white with shaven head prays vacant-eyed with her Buddha rosary of 108 beads. Shoes off at the door! Inside, Chinese monks work for your money. One points at you and then at the donation box. Another plays a violin-like instrument to elicit alms. The massive Buddha in front of him is the largest single-cast bronze statue in Thailand. It was donated to Ayuthia by the fourteenth-century emperor of China upon the death of his daughter, who had been politically married to a Thai monarch. When Ayuthia fell, so the legend goes, the statue wept. On Chinese New Year, song, dance, and straw-hat-and-incense stalls fill the grounds like a country picnic.

Issan: Plateau of Poverty

The land of *Issan* (Sanskrit-Thai for northeast), undulates ever so slightly, rising only 150 meters from Korat all the way to Nakorn Panom in the northeast corner. The land isn't rich. A farmer, like his father's father, slaves to coax the reluctant soil into raising mostly glutinous rice, the strain best suited for the absurdly dry paddies. Or he hand-broadcasts maize on the dusty earth cracked by his wooden plow. He leaves a tree growing in the middle of his fields so that

Country life

the spirit inside will sprinkle his ground with the stardust of fertility. Scientists say the roots of a tree carry up nutrients from deep in the earth and then give the nutrients to the topsoil in the form of falling leaves. Same thing.

The farmer knows enough to keep a termite mound in his fields. He can flatten out the top and, on the little circle of soil almost as rich as the central plains, he can grow nearly enough vegetables and fruit to feed his family.

There's plenty of land in the brush. Almost eighty percent of Issan is wild with thorny shrubs, bamboo grass, and midget forests only occasionally disturbed by a grazing cow. But to the farmer, it doesn't seem worth the effort to burn out the stumps and turn up the sod when the yearly rain festivals are not regularly able to ward off the drought at the end of the summer. And by then, the farmer is praying that the drought won't be followed by yet another September flood.

Besides, there's barely enough people to work his land as it is. He has one son who is a monk. His youngest son is indentured to an abbot—he will be carrying the old reverend's alms bowl in the morning. His daughter went to work in Bangkok and he hasn't heard anything of her since.

ISSAN FESTIVALS AND ELEPHANT ROUNDUPS

Every year in the second week in May, the Rocket Festival is celebrated in Yasothorn. Homemade rockets are marvelously decorated and paraded past the judges. On the following day, they are fired to wake the sleeping serpents in a mythical Himalayan lake so that the serpents will attend to the rains. *Bong*, as the larger rockets are called, are made of bamboo and may be as tall as a two-story building and hold up to a kilogram of gunpowder. The owner of a dud gets dunked and almost all the men get drunk.

The Candle Festival is held in Ubon about the middle of each July. Huge carved candles are carried down the city streets on floats. The four thousand participants—dancing girls, beauty queens robed in silk, musicians in marching bands of bamboo flutes—parade past the city's mostly new buildings. The old ones were destroyed by fire.

In Ubon, stay at the Rajtani Hotel on Khuan Thani Road or at the Siam Hotel at 84 Phalochai Road.

The elephant roundups are held in Chaiyapum, annually in April, and in Surin on the third Saturday of November. The stars of these shows challenge a hundred men to a tug of war, tramp over a row of children lying equally spaced on the ground, play soccer, reenact war dramas, and disco! The Bangkok T.A.T. arranges special bus tours to these roundups, but it's cheaper to take a short ride to either town from Korat.

In Chaiyapum, stay at the Phaiboon Hotel on Yuttidam Road. In Surin stay at either the Amarin Hotel on Tesaban 1 Road, or the Krung Sri Hotel on the street of the same name.

The Candle Festival of Ubon

Korat

Getting There: Just past Saraburi the train from Bangkok begins searching right and left for the pass up to the Korat Plateau. The pass is one of three breaches in the cliff wall that has barred the northeast from the rest of the country. Ayuthia's conquering army followed this path. You quit counting stations, quit watching other passengers watching you, and keep your eyes on the turning, widening world outside your window. At the top of the climb the land levels once more. The colossal alabaster-white Buddha of Wat Teppitakpunnaram appears in the distance and stays in view for forty-five minutes.

At a small station, you buy a banana leaf of vegetable salad from the window vendor. Eyah! The pungent Issan food sears your lips with spice. You croak out a request for some sticky rice to quell the blaze.

Five and a half hours after leaving Bangkok your oven-car pulls into Ratchasima (Korat). Over the centuries it has been a frontier garrison-city for Laotians, Khmer, Thai, and Americans during Vietnam. When the train stops the heat pours in the window. Take a *samlor* or Bus 2 into the inner city two kilometers away.

Khunying Mo

Statue of Khunying Mo: Mother Mo stands with head held high as she looks over the city park. Khunying Mo saved the city from the Laotians, but at a terrible price. In 1836, the men of Korat had all left to quell a revolt, and the city was taken by Prince Anuwongse of Vientiane. It was hopeless. The men didn't dare attack for fear of the lives of their families, and the Laotians were preparing to gather the townspeople together and walk them back to Laos as slaves.

Khunying Mo, wife of the absent governor, took control. She told all the women that they must be willing to defile their bodies now for freedom or else their bodies would be defiled forever. On the night before they were to be taken on the road, she ordered her plan into effect and the city saw a night of ribaldry. Every desire of the hungry enemy soldiers was indulged. Special meals were fixed by flirting women. Wine was poured by sensual, attentive maidens in their finest jeweled dresses. Then, in the moments after love-making, the enemy were put to death by poison or stabbed with kitchen knives.

The City Park: Across the street from the statue, the lawn area blossoms with people who come at dusk to catch the first of the evening's cool breezes. Fortune tellers spread out their tarot cards. People lie on straw mats to receive twist-massages. An adept masseuse can set bones by causing muscles to tense and hold the break. They find it difficult, however, to heal a patient who has seen an x-ray, and therefore, knows what his arm looks like broken. Farther in the park, a circle of young men and boys stand around a five-meter-high *dalacourt* hoop trying to butt, kick, knee and elbow the rattan ball through it. Everyone works together so nobody wins and everybody does.

Across the street to the north are stalls with *nam mannow yen* (lemonade). Young women vendors flash big 4-H smiles. The aroma of home-cooked food mingles with the fragrances from the flower stall.

Stay: Thai Pokaphan Hotel at 1484-86 Asdam Road looks like a hotel that would cost three times its price. Rooms have showers, but not toilets.

Crafts: From Din Fark Moon (Moon River), comes the particular clay that fires into the distinctive metallic-gray Dan Kwain pottery. The kiln and the rows of geometric-patterned pots are fourteen kilometers from Korat, along the road toward Surin. *Mut mee*, a traditional Thai silk with intricate repetitive patterns woven into the fabric, shimmers and turns into its own negative image at the slightest change in the light. It costs almost a third again as much as standard Thai silk. The village of Pak Tong Chai, twenty-seven kilometers south of Korat, is the weaving center for this Issan specialty.

Dan Kwain pottery

From Korat: Frequent buses bound for Pimai or Surin stop for fifteen to twenty minutes inside the north side of the moat, to the east of the center gate. Board there instead of going to the Bawkawsaw Bus Station.

___Pimai

The Ruins: At the entrance, the geometric arrangement of the buildings draws your gaze inward through a series of diminishing arches. The effect is like the infinite regression of a mirror reflecting a mirror. The first set of walls was the gallery. The Khmer never mastered the arch, and as a result of an architectural compromise, these passageways are narrow with high peaked roofs.

The sacred ponds in the corner of the courtyard could once be seen through gallery windows. The windows were barred with round stone mullions that looked as if they were carved on a lathe. From the ponds, priests drew water to pour over the phallic rock sheltered in a small pavilion west of the main tower.

The central *prang* (Khmer tower), of pale pink sandstone is shaped like a lotus ready to bloom and is covered with a kaleidoscope of carving. High on the darkened interior walls of this Hindu Holy of Holies, beside etched tantric-magic symbols, Buddha meditates under the protection of seven *naga* heads. Below him, sensuous dancers cavort and minor deities stomp out the demons of ignorance beneath their feet.

KHMER RUINS

The Khmer, like all other plains people in Thailand, were once mountain people. Their village headman lived on the highest spot on the hill except for the sacred spot on the summit where he would go to receive his powers. Eventually the headman moved up to live at the hill's peak as god-king, and his advisors and nobles fell in around him, their rank determining how high up on the hill they lived. The hill was a temporal model of Mount Meru in the land of the gods, and the advisors and nobles represented the minor gods. At the center of the cosmology were at first the abstract male-female figures of *lingam* and *yoni*. Later, these were combined into the image of the soft-featured Buddha.

Lingam and *yoni* **form and Buddha outline**

When the Khmer moved to the flat plains, nature quit participating in their cosmological metaphor by providing no hills for the god-king. The king needed a symbol that would stand for his Mount Meru, so he had his cities built as artistic abstractions of the mountain. In the capitals of the central plains, temples were built with concentric galleries of Buddhas surrounding the center of worship. Thus, from the tenth through the fourteenth centuries, the Khmer used heavy stone walls to build a contour map of the universe.

The grand temple at Angkor, near the Khmer capital, was the most magnificent ever built in this *prasat hin* pattern. Today, Wat Pra Keo, the main temple in Thailand, located behind the walls of the Grand Palace in Bangkok, shows the same basic design.

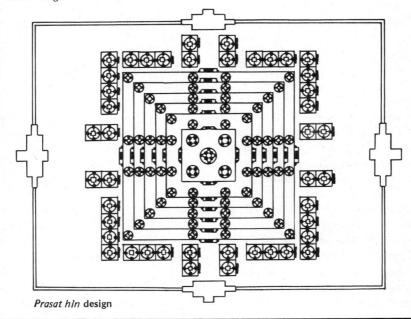

Prasat hin **design**

The central *prang* (Khmer style tower), at Pimai contained the *lingam-yoni*. Each year the god-king representative would come to this tower to pour water over the *lingam*. This symbolically lubricated the phallic stone to help the male and female principals of the universe unite.

According to the mythology of the Funan (pre-Khmer, circa 100 to 700 A.D.), the king participated much more directly during the ritual in his capital. Each year he was required to mate with the daughter of the *naga*-king to prove his right to rule. Failure to perform his sexual duties resulted in drought, famine, and the loss of his throne and his life. However, priests were kept on hand in case a substitute king became necessary for the night.

This temple predates Angkor Wat by more than a century; the earliest inscriptions are from 1036. The sanctuary was placed in the exact center of the ancient town of Vimayapura. A three-sided moat together with the Moon River surrounded the city with water. Eventually a paved road led out the south gate all the way to the Khmer capital of Angkor Thom, 150 kilometers away.

Before excavation began in 1951, roots of giant trees twisted through the windows and pushed up through the gallery roofs. It took eighteen years to untangle the jungle from its hold on the stone.

Just before the bridge over the river to the north is an open-air exhibit of stone craftsmanship from the tenth, eleventh, and twelfth centuries. Most of the exhibits are from the ruins of Pimai. Each piece is labeled in English.

Sai Ngam: This three-hundred-year-old "beautiful banyan tree" is located about one and a half kilometers east of the bridge. Each time a branch droops to touch the ground, a new trunk takes root to create this single tree grove. It covers a lot of sky.

Stalls sell *pad thai* at a great spot for lunch beside the river. Take a *samlor* from Pimai to Sai Ngam. The pedaler will wait while you eat, certain of a return fare to town.

Stay: The Pimai Hotel is located two and a half blocks south of the ruins, near the remains of the old city gate. It's modern, spotless, and inexpensive, and has accommodating managers (they watch your bags during the day even if you don't stay the night).

——*Panom Rung*

Getting There: Amazing, the bus conductor understood English. Just as you asked him to, he let you off at the turnoff for Tapak, eighty-four kilometers east out of Korat on the highway to Surin. From his pickup, a man waves you over to ride with him the six kilometers into Tapak. He'll take you six kilometers farther to the ruins and back for a price. You decide to try your luck at hitching a ride instead, and take the road to the left at the only T intersection in Tapak. The last part of the walk is three kilometers uphill. As you climb the easy slope, the ocean flatness of the Korat Plateau unfolds. By the time you get to the top you're happy for the water given to you by the Thai soldiers guarding the gate at the radar base.

Hilltop Temple: At the ruins, about five hundred meters past the radar post, a curbed avenue now green with weeds leads to the sharply rising staircase. On each side of the stairway a *naga* serpent slithers. They are somewhat segmented but still capable of transporting you to the ethereal world at the summit.

The temple was dedicated to Siva, the creator-destroyer, in the tenth century, to become a temple for Vishnu, the preserver, during the eleventh and twelfth centuries.

Sculpted rocks stand like gravestones at the periphery of the flattened hilltop. Some of the images on them

Hindu dance carved in rock at Panom Rung

were inspired by a fantasy-mind light years away from western norms. You look at the central temple. Slowly you realize that the rose petals you're looking at are made of stone chiseled thin with a hand tool centuries ago.

___Ban Chiang

The Trip North: Few travelers get up this way where the hills are knolls covered with brush and the fields are dry with dust smoking behind a buffalo-pulled plow. The train goes through Khon Kaen, a town as exciting as an intersection. *Kenaf*, the jute-like fiber in silver-gray gunnysacks, is made in Khon Kaen.

At Udon Thani, the local *samlor* drivers go crazy when they see a foreigner. "Maybe you are American GI like in the 1960s. You like girls?" The prices for everything shoot sky-high and the language is alive with decades-old servicemen jive.

Into the Country: Truck-buses load on the roadside near the Charoen Hotel on Hokanuson Road in Udon Thani. They're bound for thirty small villages, one of them is Ban Chiang. As you head east out of town, a long overdue rain bathes your face with mist. There are smiles of relief on the people's faces, for now there's hope for this year's crop. Outside the truck children and women line the irrigation ditches with their fishnets. An hour after leaving Udon Thani you pull into timeless Ban Chiang.

The Village: The saleslady in her company uniform is pushing lipstick to a woman with lips stained ruby-red by betel nut. A country maiden draws water from the well in the soft focus twilight. An ox cart creaks over a log bridge. A young mother dressed in a hand-knit sweater and store-bought Bermuda shorts feeds her baby home-grown food in a plastic cup.

Things have changed only a little in Ban Chiang since the day in 1967 when an American named Stephen Young tripped on a root in the jungle. He fell and cut his lip on a piece of pottery with an enlarged ochre-colored thumbprint on it. He asked the villagers about the pottery, but they were unexcited. There were many such pieces lying around, and some perfectly good pots, too. But when Stephen showed the pieces to the museum in Bangkok, they caused quite a stir. They were carbon dated from twenty-five centuries before the birth of Buddha (563 B.C.).

The digging began. The findings have been astounding; eighteen tons of artifacts have been unearthed. Some of the six-thousand-year-old jar designs have led archeologists to speculate that technology and art spread north to China (1766-1121 B.C.), and not the other way around as previously suspected. Other earthen vessels dated from the eighth century B.C. and proved to be the world's oldest pottery except for some unearthed in Japan. But the most remarkable finds were pieces of bronze forged in 3000 B.C. They are six centuries older than any other bronze yet discovered in Mesopotamia, previously believed to have been the birthplace of civilization because of their metallurigical skills.

The conclusions reached from the excavation: The people who once lived in the area around Ban Chiang farmed rice, wove fabric of silk and cotton, built

Ban Chiang pottery, more than
five thousand years old

homes on stilts and made pottery. They also taught their neighbors, who taught their neighbors, how to make bronze. And without leaving home, they spread civilization to China and the West. Civilization has now returned to Ban Chiang: The betel nut chewing woman buys the lipstick from the saleslady to give to her daughter away at school.

Stay: The old woman smiles and tries in vain to offer you her house, but before you can understand, Praky Suttiboon arrives with her three-word English vocabulary. Two of the words mean welcome—"food?, sleep?"—and the third is "Thank You." Nice folk. She sells high-quality textiles woven in the village and imitation Ban Chiang pottery. Praky wants no money for the meals she prepares or for the night's lodging, so you bargain poorly on the silk sarong and it all evens out—you're both ahead.

Museums: About thirty foreigners arrive here each month to see the village's two museums. The modern one has an excellent display, and is roomy and well lit. But the excavation site at Wat Po Chin Nai near the log bridge has the darkness and dirt hole under a shelter that gives the feeling of antiquity. Shards of earthware are encrusted in the mud-made-rock along with a skeleton lying where he was buried millenia ago. In a filthy glass case next to some of the world's first bronze pieces, the vacant eyes of a skull look back at you from centuries past.

South: Searching for the Perfect Beach

It's so godawful hot in the bus heading south out of Bangkok. Even that pink sugar drink in the sweating plastic bag looks good. The bag drips cold wet on your skin. Wet! Within the day you can be totally submerged, swimming through a garden of coral off Phuket. Or you can be lying just where the waves roll and be tickled by the sand in Ko Samui. Or you can be closing your eyes to the powerful double-dose rays of sun reflecting off the powder sand at Hua Hin. Or perhaps you'll just rent out a canvas beach chair in the cotton shade of a casuarina tree on Songkla beach, eat some fresh fish, and sip dull-sweetness out of a coconut. That coconut would be better than this pink sugar drink. But the cold and wet feel good on the hot bus.

___Petchburi

Pra Nakorn Khiri, the Summer Palace: King Mongkut was intrigued with some of the strange ways of the English foreigners who had come to his court. He particularly liked the model steam engine given him by Queen Victoria. And some of the sciences such as astronomy were actually as good as the readings given him by his Brahmin magician-sages. Mongkut learned the knack of predicting eclipses. (His Hindu sages were none too pleased that he knew the trick.) So when it came to designing a palace, King Mongkut decided to be frivolous and incorporate some of those happy ideas of nineteenth-century England.

Just past the tourist stalls at the base of the hill, the cobbled stone way leads up the hill toward the palace. Stone lanterns were regularly spaced on each side for the convenience of chariots that arrived late in the day with news from Krung Thep. The road, speckled with the shade of magnolia trees, branches like an Alice-in-Wonderland maze. Some paths end at battlements where guards once stood watch in some of the first western trousers in Thailand. Other lanes eventually make their way to the one-hundred-meter-high summit where the newly-refurbished Petchbumiroj Hall displays some of King Mongkut's scientific equipment and furniture. Perhaps this desk is where he penned his letter, in creative English, to President Lincoln, offering a battalion of elephants in military aid for "King" Lincoln to use in his civil conflict. Lincoln politely refused the offer.

From the top of the tower nearby you survey the land all around. To the west, abrupt limestone outcroppings surprise the eye. On the other side of the tower's terrace, your gaze roams past the Khao Wang extension of the palace at the far end of the hill, through the city streets, and beyond to the white-gold glare of the ocean fifteen kilometers to the east.

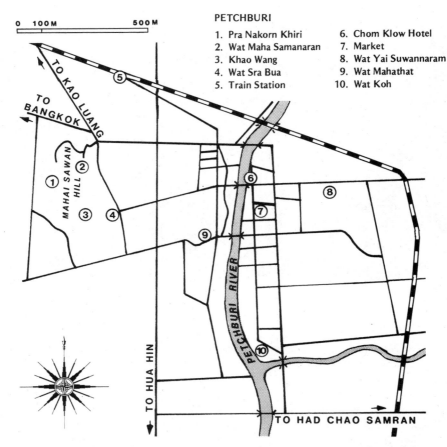

PETCHBURI
1. Pra Nakorn Khiri
2. Wat Maha Samanaran
3. Khao Wang
4. Wat Sra Bua
5. Train Station
6. Chom Klow Hotel
7. Market
8. Wat Yai Suwannaram
9. Wat Mahathat
10. Wat Koh

Kao Laung Cave: According to official history, in 1782 King Taksin was clubbed to death under a velvet blanket. Thus, no royal blood was spilled and Rama I became King. In Petchburi, some older locals tell a different tale passed on to them by their great grandmothers. The executioner, they say, couldn't bring himself to kill the general who had driven off the Burman invaders. He substituted a man willing to sacrifice himself in the king's place, and secretly whisked the insane monarch to Kao Luang Cave. Rama II heard rumors that the hermit-monarch was alive and sent troops to kill him. The soldiers found Taksin, but the insanity of the old man alone in his cave world was too sacred to defile and they left without harming him.

Today, you reach the cave via a *samlor* from the summer palace or a three-kilometer walk north down the hot dirt road. You descend the stairway at the end of the cement walk and enter a chamber of elephantine stalagmites honeycombed with niches filled with golden Buddhas. The noonday sun pierces through an opening above and beams on the glittering Buddhas below. A boy hands you a burning torch and walks with you through the several chambers. In the darkest corner he asks for money.

Stay: The Chom Klow Hotel beside the bridge of the same name is a new Chinese family establishment with terra-cotta floors and walls decorated with simple Chinese designs. The rooms on the top two floors have balconies that look down on old buildings along the river.

Had (Beach) Chao Samran: The screen hangs loosely from the corner of the window on your clapboard duplex cottage set up on stilts. In the morning, monks with black alms bowls file across the wide, low-tide beach. It's early, plenty of time to go back to the squeaky frame under your mattress. There's plenty of time today or tomorrow to walk along the sand. You'll probably have the beach all to yourself unless it's a weekend. You fall back to sleep before you decide what day today is.

Pickup trucks leave for the fifteen-kilometer ride east when full. From downtown Petchburi, the starting point is difficult to find the first time; consider taking a *samlor.*

Hua Hin

In Hua Hin the king can get off his special train at his private station, a little gingerbread Thai pavilion. It was built in the 1920s for Rama VII to come to his beach retreat palace named Klai Kangwon (far from worries). He was at this palace when the bloodless coup of 1932 relieved him of his governing responsibilities.

The Hua Hin Railroad Hotel was built in the same Edwardian era. It hasn't changed much. Two giant bushes carved to look like elephants form an arch over the approach. On the beach side was once a toy train that tooted around the perimeter of the croquet court now full of Hua Hin's powder sand. Near the lapping waves, canvas beach chairs sit under umbrellas and locals come to sell coconuts, take photographs, and rent horses for an oceanside ride. Back on the polished hotel veranda, the terrace sitters sip beer while they watch the three-week-old NFL football game on TV.

The king's private railroad station in Hua Hin

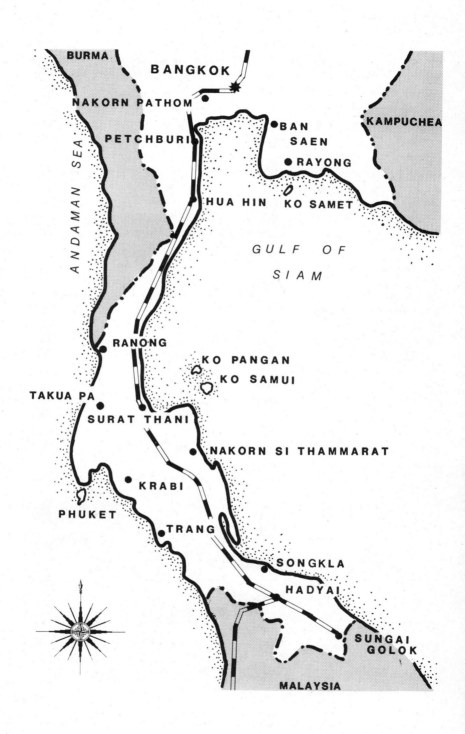

A fifteen-minute walk brings you to the oceanside fishermen homes built half out onto the water. The fleet shoves off at twilight. Later, in the darkness you might see firecrackers exploding out at sea to ward off the evil believed lurking in the dark water.

Bangkok to Surat Thani by Train

The train jerks out of the glass and steel of Bangkok's Hua Lumpong Station. You go over bridge after bridge over *klong* and stream, picking up speed as the tracks turn southward. The train goes through Nakorn Pathom, Petchburi, and Hua Hin. Most of the travelers stay on the train.

You pass flats of paddies punctuated by a lonely palm tree here and there. To your left are the lands leading to the sea, to your right rise limestone out-croppings, the vertebra of the peninsula. One such limestone massive edges the Gulf of Siam at Prachuab Khirikhan. The sand coast sweeps in a broad arch around Manao Bay, hundreds of meters below. Most travelers stay on the train.

Some of the old sleepers were once luxurious; now they're humbled to second class with tarnished brass fittings, as air-conditioned cars take over first class. The seats were made when spaciousness meant elegance. The fans were made during the same era, and the motors complain of their age. When crowded, the third-class cars seem like refugee camps on wheels with more passengers than seats and more packages in the aisle than standing room.

During the long sleepless night of travel, you escape to the diner and sip a drink. The lights of the little towns ripple by outside the open window. After thirteen hours, the train arrives at Kun Pun, the station for Surat Thani. Most of the travelers get off the train.

Ko Samui

Fresh from the ocean, you fall exhausted into the sand. A drop of water trickles down your leg like a fly dragging its feet. The sun warms; the breeze blows polka dot cool on your drop-spotted body. Up above you on the slope is your bamboo hut. Inside the bungalow, a mouse passes on the rafters and punc-tuates your letter home: "We've been swimming a lot lately. The other day we had a seafood orgy." Splot! The next day you got sick and were on nothing but tea and plain rice for a week.

Your body still feels tossed by the waves even as you lie basking on the dry sand like a luxuriating reptile. Down the beach a couple of bikini pants chase after a frisbee. "Une ciggy?" oozes the man in loose white cotton standing over you. He mimes his request with his fingers in a tight V over his puckered lips and scowls disapprovingly when you have none to offer.

As you move to the hammock, you ponder the idea that life should be dedi-cated to the gratification of your senses. You open your book and close your eyes.

Getting to the Islands: Buses leave from just left of the railroad station to Ban Don where speed boats and passenger ferries leave for Ko Samui. Or change to Cheap Charlie's transport company bus, and ride through farm and field, village and valley between the fingers of limestone on your way to the harbor at Kanon. From Kanon you take the air-conditioned ferry across to the island an hour away. You lean against the rails as the boat draws away from the pier. Moslem men in their caps bow their prayers to Mecca on the prow of their fishing boat. You slide over the surface of blue, out past the land and toward a mountain range sticking out of the ocean horizon, the island group called Angthong. There are forty-eight small outcroppings with beaches sheltered in the mouth of limestone caves, or an emerald lake surrounded by tree-supporting cliffs, rock bridges over the ocean, and palm-shaded lonely beaches. And there is the largest of all the islands, Ko Samui, island of coconut growers and shoreline of bungalows.

On the Island: About twenty Thai teenage cowboys and cute girls hawk and herd new arrivals off the boats and into the backs of pickups bound for Chaweng Beach, Lamai Beach, or Bo Phut Beach. Your first trip to the beach is generally paid for by the owner of the bungalow where you stay.

Lamai has the smoothest, whitest sand and slants steeply. In the middle of its long curve stands the temporary pier built in the seventies, during construction of the concrete road that now girdles the island. Sunrise Bungalows, on the

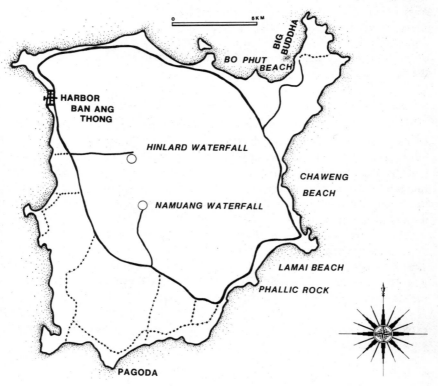

right end of the beach next to the rocks, serves big shrimp with lots of vegetables. Those who don't stay here often come here to eat. Over the hill behind, a phallic-like natural erection of rocks rises from the headlands above a turquoise cove.

Chaweng Beach eases into water turned gray-silver-gold by the rising sun. The beach belongs to foreigners. The food at Liberty Bungalow draws the biggest crowds, especially large during peak season in August. The most colorful coral around the island is off the left end of Chaweng Beach.

The grain-size sand of Bo Phut doesn't get carried into your bamboo hut as easily as powdery sand does. Bo Phut is a short walk from the big Buddha sitting out in the bay. Occasionally, excursion boats from Bo Phut go to Pangan Island for the day (or there's a daily ferry from the Ko Samui town harbor). Ko Pangan has very few bungalows and a beach so white, shallow, and warm it's like sitting in a hot mineral bath.

Back on Ko Samui, you sit and listen to the latest gossip. A traveler heard a car backfire last night and was sure the south was rising in armed revolt against Thailand. A sign next to the boat and train schedule advertises an all-you-can-eat seafood party. That sounds good. Food sounds good. You order an orange-colored milk-tea and fruit salad while you decide whether a banana pancake or fried rice shrimp would be the right brunch.

A MASSAGE

Mr. Ko of Ko Samui appears next to your hammock, and takes off his cap which reads "Massage." He holds up five fingers for ฿50. You counter offer three fingers and he agrees. Just relax. If it hurts, you, not the masseuse, are doing something wrong. Just relax.

His grip is firm and he seems to know beforehand those places on your leg that are not right. He finds muscles long ago forgotten. His feet are as sure as his hands when he bends your leg to the limit and works the back of your thigh. He seems to be chasing out evil spirits and he won't let them hide between your bones. His fingers dig in there with full-body pressure to rile the spirits to pain and then—snap!—they're gone.

He twists you and forces you into a near lotus position while you lie on your stomach. There goes an ache left over from the thirteen-hour train ride down here.

Your neck and head are all pressed in turn. He squeezes your scalp so hard, you see the shadows of his fingers from the inside with your eyes closed. Then he bends your ears forward and grabs your eyes. Lightning!

He smiles and holds up five fingers. You agree.

___Two Routes to Phuket

From Bangkok to Phuket: You're an air-conditioned gypsy zooming over nine hundred kilometers of highway while you sit in a cushioned seat in a luxury coach. The music coming over the speakers is vintage rock; the snacks are vintage tea cakes. This is the kind of luxury that attracts highway robbers. They force the coaches to stop and strip the passengers of their belongings—"Yes, they want the watch. No, you can keep the underwear." You figure if it were too dangerous, nobody would be on the bus. The bus is full of foreigners, and it's a fast overnight ride.

Crossing the Isthmus of Kra: The bus from Ban Don is overfull by the time it begins to climb the hills. Still, the driver pulls to a stop whenever another potential passenger waves at him from the side of the road. Dust pours in your open window.

The road weaves across the peninsula through the gaps in the hills cut by rivers. You near a bald cliff with ribbons of water flowing down its face. You see stalagmites and columns that were once part of subterranean cavities inside massive rock formations of decomposed sea creatures. What once was the bottom of the sea is now the summit of the land.

KING COBRA

The King Cobra, identifiable by its wide occipital shield, is the giant of venomous snakes. It grows largest on the Malay Peninsula. One of them shot in Nakorn Si Thammarat was over five and a half meters long. Normally they are only two to three meters in length.

A cobra bite is extremely potent and can be fatal. Once, a trainer at the snake gardens in Bangkok was bit. He was treated immediately and was released from the hospital after a month.

However, there are few deaths recorded as a result of the King Cobra bite. Perhaps few who are bitten make it to be treated medically and therefore records are inaccurate. More likely, the snake is just too slow to be effective. Natives leave the cobras' bamboo nests near jungle paths with little concern. There is a story that the first white person in the area hired natives to walk in front so if the snakes were angered, the locals would receive the strike. The natives knew the cobra rarely bit the first person down the path.

This jagged land of limestone is honeycombed with cavities. Wat Thamwaran was built in one of these caves—about halfway on the six-hour, cross-peninsular trip. A monk discovered this cave, placed an image of the Buddha inside, and the cavern became a chapel. If you break your trip here don't expect a seat on the bus when you continue on.

At Takua Pa the bus joins the highway coming south from Bangkok via Ranong. Not long before you cross the causeway into Phuket, you pass the Kao Lak National Park. Here grassy, tree-spotted hills roll into the sea far below.

The causeway is a long bridge over muddy shallows. After the bus reaches the other side, it dives back into the center of land without even a whiff of sea. Rows of rubber trees blink by. Latex pads hang over lines outside shanties like old bath mats. As you come to the first main intersection, you see the statue of two women, grim with determination. They greet you with swords in their hands.

Phuket

Small noodle shops in the main town serve *khanomchin* (read kon jean), a local specialty. On the table before you is spread an alchemist's selection of condiments, eggs, and vegetables for you to mix with your noodles.

Like each bowl of *khanomchin*, the population of Phuket is a unique mixture. First there were the Chao le, a race of seafarers who lived their whole lives on the sea, coming to shore only to obtain food in trade for fish and to bury their dead. Their language most closely resembles that of the Cham, rulers of ancient Vietnam. Today, they have moved to houses on land. They moor their fishing boats in the low tide mud of Rawai Beach.

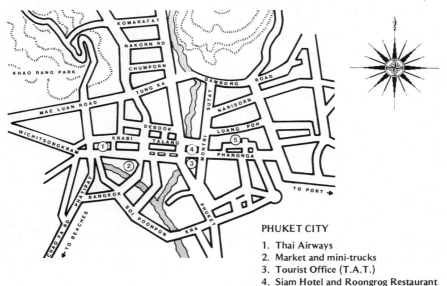

PHUKET CITY

1. Thai Airways
2. Market and mini-trucks
3. Tourist Office (T.A.T.)
4. Siam Hotel and Roongrog Restaurant
5. Bus Station

The Thai-Malay people who live on the island speak a chopped off Thai as compared to the melodic Bangkok dialect. It's almost as if the language were an indication that life in the south is rougher than on the rice rich central plains. It took a lot to survive.

In 1785 it looked as if no one would. The governor of the island had just died and a Burman naval force of three thousand men were threatening an attack. The governor's wife, Khunying Chan, took control. With the help of her sister, Muk, she devised a stratagem to stop the invaders: She called everyone on the islands into the stockade walls and burned all the fields outside. To make it appear there were more men than there actually were, she borrowed a trick from Ayuthia. She armed five hundred crew-cut female recruits with sticks carved as guns. The enemy held back and after a month-long siege, the starving invaders from the west left. (The two sisters' statue immortalizes their courageous deed.)

During another attack only one year later, the people of Phuket weren't so fortunate. The marauding bandit, Phia Tak, "Tyrant of Siam," fought his way to control the island and beheaded the raja and his son. They were lucky. All the population that didn't run or hide—Chinese, Malay, Portuguese—were tied together in the town square and trampled by elephants. It was a year before the Thai troops arrived to regain control of the island. In the meantime, the Sultan of Kedah was so nervous about this menace to his north that he offered the English two islands: the disputed island of Phuket and Penang. The English chose the latter.

The island was repopulated when tin was discovered. Thirty thousand Chinese came and most died young. The silt from the mines clogged the harbor, and many of Phuket's finer beaches on the eastern side were destroyed. Besides the hazards of the mines, many Chinese dropped from malaria. During one devastating epidemic, a troupe of vagabond actors arrived from Kwangsi province in south China. They exorcised the harmful malaria spirits with a festival. In order to purify their island, no one was to eat meat for nine days.

Now on the first day of the waxing moon in October, the festival begins once more. Typical of Chinese celebrations, there are firecrackers and lion dances. And a procession of priests and images march from each of the islands five Chinese temples. But there are also feats of self torture that resemble the Indian festivals of repentance, Thaipusan. Chinese men in trances run barefoot across red-hot coals. Others stick iron rods through their tongues and cheeks. Others merely abstain from eating meat for the whole nine days. And a few Chinese consider the whole thing superstitious nonsense. If you have malaria, they think, you should simply do what's practical. Go to the Chinese apothecary where they sell ground deer antlers and brown creosote tablets and other such medicine.

Modern Phuket: Since the early 1970s, a new group of people have altered the island's flavor. You see evidence of this influx walking down the five-foot colonnade outside a Chinese hotel. At the entrance to a shop that sells locally-grown cashew nuts, a sign warns that beach wear in town isn't permitted. Standing at the counter inside are tanned foreign bodies in bikini pants.

At 73-75 Phuket Road is one of Thailand's finest tourist offices. They hold your mail addressed to you in care of them. They'll keep your bags safe. And they have an up-to-date price list on every legal bungalow from baronial cottage to budget hut.

The Beach: Waves that have ricocheted off the east coast of India, undulate across the Bay of Bengal and crash against the stubborn rocks below where you stand. You watch part of the white breaker sneak past the island that guards the mouth of the cove. The wave passes behind palm trees and slides up the powder sand.

It's crowded on the main beaches of Ao (Bay) Patong, Karon, and Kata. Not that it's much worse than it was five years ago. Few new bungalows are being built even on the more popular beaches. The number has reached a plateau, perhaps because people have been frightened away by the armed robberies on the highway, on the beaches at night, and on the remote trekking trails that roam along the island coast.

Bamboo huts are for rent on the beaches of Ko Samui and Phuket

You found a place to stay on a wind-swept hill. It's pretty basic with candles (and no noisy electrical generator motor). The outhouse is down a steep slippery slope. The lock on your door could be picked by a two-year-old. The people who run the place keep their distance. You get meals of fresh fish at John's, far down the hill in the middle of the beach. It's always worth the walk.

The view out your window draws your eye once more. A line of white glides across the deep gray-blue toward the azure cove.

Ko Hi: Fifty meters offshore from this small island south of Phuket, the sea floor drops sharply. Coral has turned the cliff into an iridescent wall. The sun shining through the waves above, draws a moving mesh of gold across the jagged surface. Opalescent flakes of light flash from the tropical fish. Sharks pass close by. The locals say they never attack swimmers in the coral gardens. You decide to float very quietly for a while.

The islanders on Ko Hi aren't necessarily happy to see you, especially if you arrive on a tour boat that provides lunches. Most visitors stay only for the day so they won't have to pay again for the ride back to Rawai or Laem Ka Beaches in six-passenger fishing boats. (It's a rough crossing when a monsoon blows in any time between May and October.) Many of these day-trippers leave Ko Hi nothing but their garbage.

When you buy a meal from the family near the beach, they begin to become friendly. When you come in from the day, sunburned so you clash with the color of the lobster on your supper plate, they show honest concern. They provide a bed for a fair price.

The second morning on the island, you have to argue in order to pay for your breakfast.

From Phuket: If you catch the first of four morning buses for Hadyai, you might arrive in time to catch the last bus bound for Penang. But that's scheduling it too tight in the loose time of Thailand. It's more practical and easier on the nerves to figure at least two days to Penang with a stopover for a night in Krabi.

Phangnga

Camel-backed mountains, spearheaded peaks, pedestals of rock, and pyramids of stone dance around the landscape and scamper into the sea to the rhythm of rock-geologic time. One of the grandest rock orgies in which nature

has ever indulged herself occurs along the southern coast of Thailand. The town of Phangnga rests right in the heart of it. Three of the countless caverns that catacomb the limestone are located within five hundred meters of the main road of Phangnga. Nine kilometers before this village is Suwanna Kuha, a cave and a Buddhist chapel.

Roht tadan (long-tailed boats in south Thailand), can be rented at the ports of Kasom, Surakul, or at the Customs Pier for a four-hour cruise around the fantasy islands. The boat owners hawk you with their rudimentary vocabularies, "Double O Seven. You. Boat." (Portions of the James Bond movie, *The Man With the Golden Gun*, were filmed on location in these waters.) The islands can also be visited as part of several package tours from Phuket. These usually include a bus ride to Phangnga Bay, the boat ride, a stop at the Buddha in the cave on the way back, and a few snacks. It's convenient.

As you skim out into the bay, you'll spot Ko Ping Kan, an island consisting of two giant blocks of rock leaning against each other. Your boat turns into Ko Kain and is swallowed by the island as you float through a subterranean passage.

Tharn Bokharanee Botanical Gardens

Halfway between Phangnga and Krabi are the two town centers of Ao Luk. They are located three kilometers from each other. Between the two hamlets is the entrance to the gardens. The pathway squeezes through a crack in the limestone wall to a hidden meadow. After a half-hour walk you come to where an underground river surfaces inside a cave. The water spills out, down a natural steps into an emerald pond banked by a cliff and a strangle of roots.

Krabi

The bus waltzes through the gnarled landscape past Ao Luk. On a wide turn in the road eighty-nine kilometers from Phuket, it stops at the Krabi intersection, and from there a pickup takes you the last five kilometers into town.

Kaho Kanarb Nam (Waterside Mount), Krabi

Like a misty Chinese scroll painting, the rock formation called Kaho Kanarb Nam (Waterside Mount), rises out of the river near town. It marks the port where Indian ships once landed to tranship their cargo on its way to Ayuthia. Today, the tiny port harbors vessels bound to Penang, Malacca, and Singapore with gunnysacks full of mangrove charcoal.

At Suan Public Park, one kilometer from the town center, you can lie on a knoll and watch the dock workers fret the bundles on board while carefree sea hawks dive for fish in the river. At night one of the stalls on the river bank serves peanut sauce with roast beef on rice, while juke boxes blast out sad Thai ballads on top of Thai versions of Beatle tunes.

The Vien Thong Hotel along the main road is neat and plastic. A hundred meters back toward the highway is a red building with a red sign that reads Sam Ran Hotel in two languages—Thai and Chinese. The folks here communicate friendliness without a single word of English. There's one drawback: The shop next door begins chopping blocks of ice before sunrise for their morning deliveries.

Boats can be hired for the forty-five minute trip upriver to a cave that opens onto the bank. You might have to wait several days for other travelers to come along and join you on a chartered boat to Ko Phi Phi. On the walls of the cave on that island are prehistoric paintings of boats, fish, and skeletal men.

——*Hadyai*

Sin City: Fifty years ago the first few buildings were built beside the tracks at a point where three rail lines converge. Today, it's a city of fifty thousand people, forty percent of whom are Chinese money-money-work-work.

On weekends Malaysian males dash the seventy kilometers across the border to the mainly manly attractions of this sin city of the south. There are bullfights and gambling the first and second Sundays of each month; two angry bulls meet in a head to headache contest. And every Saturday the TV stadium hosts Thai boxers and more gambling.

But the males from Malaysia and the Chinese from Bangkok also come to Hadyai for the carnal pleasures. The Emperor Disco grinds live music, featuring an echo-chamber Elvis imitator. The Nora Hotel has a nightclub and a massage parlor. The Sukhontah Hotel has two nightclubs and a massage parlor.

The Chinese mafia come to mix a little business with pleasures. Life here is cheap; a murder can be commissioned for a mere ฿3000. This is not a good place to make enemies, nor to hold loosely onto your travel bag.

HADYAI

1. Hospital
2. Market and Bus to Songkla
3. Bus to Phuket
4. Post Office
5. Immigration Office
6. Railway Station
7. Sri Taksin Hotel
8. Bus and Taxi to Penang
9. Ton Nun Hotel
10. Tourist Office (T.A.T.)

From Hadyai to Penang: Taxis make the trip the fastest. They leave when full. On Saturdays and Sundays the driver wants an extra ฿20 for overtime pay. In Thailand, taxi drivers have their own political party. It's a strong union to try and bargain against.

Several air-conditioned bus companies compete for your fare for the five-hour trip. There's an express train to Butterworth, Penang. A slower, cheaper train leaves right after the express and arrives in Butterworth an hour after the express. (There are trains daily creeping south along the east coast to the border-line town of Sungai Golok.)

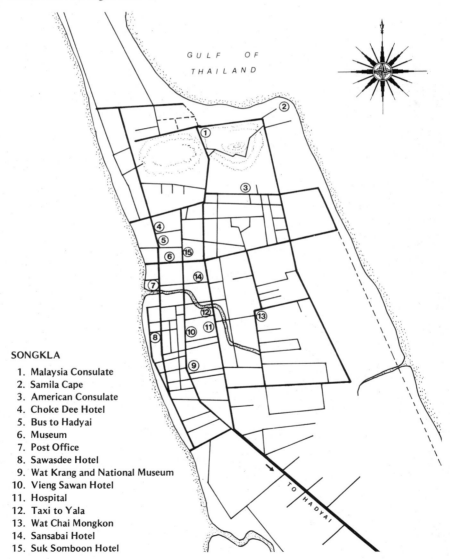

SONGKLA

1. Malaysia Consulate
2. Samila Cape
3. American Consulate
4. Choke Dee Hotel
5. Bus to Hadyai
6. Museum
7. Post Office
8. Sawasdee Hotel
9. Wat Krang and National Museum
10. Vieng Sawan Hotel
11. Hospital
12. Taxi to Yala
13. Wat Chai Mongkon
14. Sansabai Hotel
15. Suk Somboon Hotel

SONGKLA AND A CHANGE OF PLANS

The gecko lizard on the ceiling of your hotel room is calling out its name in Thai *"dtook-gaa, dtook-gaa, dtook-gaaaaaa."* With a last bit of effort it drags out the final syllable.

It must be past midnight. You remember that your watch hasn't worked since Hua Hin. It's strange how things you thought were essential have proven to be only excess baggage. Like the long-time traveler told you; if you don't use something for a month, it probably doesn't belong in your pack. Well, after today, you'll be traveling much lighter.

You can't blame Songkla. Actually it's a beautiful setting, if a bit touristed. You recall the view from the cooling pavilion perched on top of Kao Tang Kaun, a hill at the edge of town: The islands and the white sand pointing into the water.

Down by the beach, the canvas chairs didn't tempt you. Instead, you headed south along the sand toward a shoreside clutter of rocks and the water-village beyond. That was when the plans changed.

You saw the motorcycle cowboyed by a couple of teenage boys dust down the gravel road toward you. Your shoulder bag flew away with them when they passed.

Now what? Tomorrow you make your way toward Bangkok to claim your traveler's checks and get your plane ticket reissued. That's a long way to go on the little money you have left.

Your mind drifts to a conversation you had with a station master a while back. He invited you to his house while you waited for your train. He offered you a place to sleep. Later, he showed you a photo of his guru, a bald old man with a surfaceless smile. The station master explained how he had been taught that you create your own world perspective, your own attitude. He watched a mosquito bite his arm. "It's up to you what you want to matter," he explained. "Thai Buddhist believe *mai pen rai,* I choose not to worry."

The gecko interrupts your thoughts. You count seven croaks. That's supposed to be lucky.

The crescent moon rising outside your window is as bright as you've ever seen it. You're going to remember this trip. Who knows what will come your way? You're ready for the ride.

Travel Data for Burma

_Transportation In and Around Cities

City	Transport	Cost	Comments
Rangoon	Bus in city	30 to 50 pyas	Average 25-minute wait
	Taxi from airport	Ks30	Four passengers maximum
	Taxi in city	Ks20 per hour	
	Bicycle in city	Ks2 per hour	Can be rented for Ks15 per day
	Thombey (three-wheeled cart) to Shwedagon	Ks5	
Day trip to Syriam and Kyauktan	Boat to Syriam	75 pyas	Boat departs at 0530 and 1300; last return to Rangoon at 1800
	Truck from Syriam to Kyauktan	Ks20	Military checkpoints along the way
	Boat from Kyauktan to mid-river pagoda	50 pyas round trip	
Day trip to Pegu	Bus to Pegu	Ks5	Buses depart every hour from 0600 to 1830; last bus returns at 1630; takes 2 hours
	Taxi to Pegu	Ks200 round trip	
	Bus in Pegu	25 pyas	
	Tonga (horse cart) in Pegu	Ks2	From Shwemawdaw to Shwethalyuang
Mandalay	Bus in city	25 to 50 pyas	
	Tonga in city	Ks3	
	Trisha (pedicab) in city	Ks3	
	Jeep in city	Ks10	Available at Mandalay Hotel
	Jeep to airport	Ks20	
	Tonga to airport	Ks5	Long, slow ride
	Bus 2 or 10 to airport	Ks3	Long, slow ride

City	Transport	Cost	Comments
Mandalay (*continued*)	Jeep for 6-hour rental	Ks100	
	Ferry to Mingun	Ks2	First departure at 0600; 1-hour ride to Mingun, 30-minute return ride
Day trip to Amarapura, Ava, and Sagaing	Truck-bus to Amarapura / Truck-bus to Ava	Ks1 / Ks1.50	Bus goes through Amarapura and Ava on way to Sagaing
	Tonga to Sagaing Hill	Ks3	Twenty-minute trip
	Rowboat from Sagaing to Ava	Ks10	One-hour trip
Maymyo	*Mindlay* (horse carriage) to waterfall	Ks20	
Pagan	*Tonga* in city	Ks10 per hour	Five passengers maximum
	Tonga to Nyaung U	Ks8	
	Jeep to Mount Popa	Ks200 round trip	
Inle Lake Area	Bus or jeep between Taunggyi and Shwenyaung	Ks4	Departs from down-hill side of market
	Ferry from Yaunghwe to Phaungdaw U Pagoda	Ks30 round trip	Ten passengers maximum
	Tourist Burma boat trip from Yaunghwe to Phaungdaw U Pagoda	Ks210	The Tourist Burma bus from Taunggyi plus the boat trip is Ks400; tour capacity is ten people
	Local boat charter from Yaunghwe to Phaungdaw U Pagoda	Ks110	Six-hour trip

Transportation Between Cities

From	To	By	Cost in Kyats	Comments
Rangoon	Mandalay	Plane	194 (plus 18 for jet)	Departs at 0750
		Train	76 (96 for upper class); 20 pyas for baggage check at Rangoon Railroad Station	Departs at 1845 and 0745; arrives at 0745 and 1845

From	To	By	Cost in Kyats	Comments
Rangoon	Nyaung U airport for Pagan	Plane	172 (plus 16 for jet)	Departs at about 1500; takes 1.5 hours; bus from airport to Pagan included
	Taunggyi	Plane and jeep	155	One hour flight to Heho, then 2.5 hour jeep ride to Taunggyi
	Thazi	Train	29 (82 for upper class)	Evening express departs at 1845; arrives at 0500
Mandalay	Rangoon	Train	76 (96 for upper class)	Morning express departs at 0500; arrives at 1800
	Maymyo	Jeep	12	Departs about every half hour between 0730 and 1500; takes 2.5 hours
	Nyaung U airport for Pagan	Plane	67 (plus 13 for jet)	Departs at 1200
	Pagan	Bus	17	Departs at 0330; arrives at 1400
		Boat	16 (deck class); 29 (cabin class)	Departs 0500; arrives 1 day later (hopefully)
	Heho for Inle Lake	Plane	70	BAC offers transport from Heho to Taunggyi or Yaunghwe
	Inle Lake	Bus	54	
	Taunggyi (Heho airport)	Plane	70	Ticket includes bus from Heho airport
		Bus	32	Departs at 0430; arrives at 1430
		Datsun	42	Takes about 8 hours
Pagan	Mandalay	Bus	17	Departs at 0430; arrives at 1400
	Rangoon	Bus and train	75	Tourist Burma bus departs Pagan for Thazi at 0400; train departs Thazi at 0900; arrives in Rangoon at 1800
	Thazi	Bus and jeep	10	Trip involves *tonga* to Nyaung U (Ks8 extra), 3-hour bus ride from Nyaung U to Kyauk Paduang, 2-hour bus ride from there to Meiktila, and 30 minutes by jeep to Thazi

From	To	By	Cost in Kyats	Comments
Meiktila	Thazi	Jeep	1.50	Takes half hour, but irregular schedule
Thazi	Shweyaung	Train	16	Takes 10 hours
	Taunggyi	Bus or jeep	28	Takes 5 to 7 hours

____Places to Stay

City	Hotel	Cost in Kyats
Rangoon	Dagon Hotel Garden Guest House Strand Hotel YMCA	Single: 18; Double: 26 Single: 17; Double: 22; Triple: 29 Single: 40; Double: 55 Dorm: 6; Single: 22; Double: 32; Deluxe: 40
Mandalay	Mandalay Hotel Man San Dar Win Guest House Man Shwe Myu Hotel Tunhla Hotel	Double: 50 with air-conditioning Single: 18; Double: 30 Single: 18; Double: 30 Single: 22; Double: 33; Triple: 44
Maymyo	Candacraig Hotel	Single: 18; Double: 33
Pagan	Burma Guest House Cooperative Hotel Irra Inn (front) Irra Inn (back) Thiripyitsaya Hotel	Single: 9; Double: 18 Single: 14; Double: 22 Single: 30; Double: 40; Suite: 65 Single: 15; Double: 20 First class commercial rates
Meiktila	Myuma Hotel	Single: 13
Inle Lake	Inle Inn	Single: 25; Double: 40; Triple: 60
Taunggyi	May You Hotel Sanpya Lodging House Strand Hotel	Single: 20 Single: 21 Single: 36; Double: 50

____Information About Sights in Rangoon

Diplomatic Store	Open 1000 to 1600, closed Saturday
Indian Market	Open 0700 to 1600
Jubilee Hall	Classical dance performance at 1400 on Saturday and Sunday, Ks2 admission
Karaweik Restaurant	Dancing at 2000, Ks1 admission, Ks11 for beer
Shwedagon Pagoda	Open 0500 to 2200
Zoo	Open daily 0600 to 1800, Ks1 admission

Chart below shows the days of the week and their corresponding characteristics for Burmese people. These days are represented by the eight directional posts in Konagama Adoration Hall in Shwedagon.

Direction	Day	Planet	Animal	Characteristic
South	*Bohddahu* Wednesday Midnight to noon	Mercury	Tusked elephant	Short-tempered, but soon calm
Southwest	Saturday	Saturn	*Naga*-serpent	Hot-tempered and quarrelsome
West	Thursday	Jupiter	Rat	Mild
Northwest	*Yahu* Wednesday Noon to midnight	Rahu, mythical planet	Tuskless elephant	Same as *Bohddahu*, only more so
North	Friday	Venus	Guinea pig and mole	Talkative
Northeast	Sunday	Sun	Galon (bird)	Miserly
East	Monday	Moon	Tiger	Jealous
Southeast	Tuesday	Mars	Lion	Honest

Travel Data for Thailand

Transportation In and Around Cities

City	Transport	Cost in Bahts	Comments
Bangkok	Taxi in city	20 minimum	Many cruising taxis
	Tuk tuk in city	10 minimum	Hard bargaining
	Air-conditioned bus in city	10 maximum	Runs about every 30 minutes
	Bus in city	1.50	Usually 15-minute wait
	Express boat in city	3 to 5	
	Rua hang yao (long-tail boat)	2 to 5	
	Rua kham fak (ferry)	0.50	
	Limousine from airport	75	To your hotel door, and if hotel full, to next hotel choice
	Taxi from airport	200	
	Air-conditioned bus from airport to Victory Monument	15	
	Bus 29 from airport to Victory Monument and on to Hua Lumpong Railroad Station	4.50	Hectic
Day trip to Kanchanaburi	Train to Kanchanaburi from Bangkok Noi Station	17.50	Departs 0800; arrives 1030
	Bus to Kanchanaburi from South Bus Terminal	20	Departs every 20 minutes from 0530 to 1930; last bus returns at 1800
Day trip to Nakorn Pathom	Train to Nakorn Pathom from Bangkok Noi Railroad Station	8	Departs at 0600
	Bus 28, 66, or 203 to Nakorn Pathom from South Bus Terminal	20	Departs hourly beginning at 0600; takes 2.5 hours; bus continues to Damnern Saduak

City	Transport	Cost in Bahts	Comments
Beaches near Bangkok	Bus to Ban Saen from East Bus Station	17 (40 for air-conditioned bus)	Departs every 25 minutes; takes 1.5 hours
	Bus to Rayong from South Bus Station	40 (60 for deluxe bus)	Trip takes 2 hours
	Tuk tuk from Rayong to Bang Pet port	12	
	Boat from Bang Pet to Ko Samet (Bon Bin)	50	
Day trips north of Bangkok	Bus to Sam Khok (Stork Temple) from North Bus Station	10	
	Bus to Bang Pa-In Palace from North Bus Station	12	Departs every 30 minutes from 0600 to 1800; takes 1 hour
	Train to Bang Pa-In Palace from Hua Lumpong Railroad Station	12	Eight trains leave daily; takes 1.5 hours
	Boat from Thammasart boat landing	50 round trip	Runs only on Saturday and Sunday; departs at 930, returns at 1200; stops at Stork Temple
Chiang Mai	Taxi from airport	40 to 60	Cruising taxis
	Bus from airport and in city	1.50	
	Samlor in city	5 for short trip	Can be rented for 25 bahts per hour
	Mini-truck in city	5	
	Mini-truck to Doi Suthep	25 to 30 one way	Takes 30 minutes for 16-km trip
	Bus or minibus to Bor Sang	4	
	White bus to Lampoon	5	Departs every 20 minutes
Chiang Rai	Minibus in city	4	
	Samlor in city	6	
	Minibus from airport	7	
Chiang Saen	Minibus to Sam Ruim Tom Kam	7	Departs hourly between 0800 and 1400
	Minibus from Ban Toung Liang to Mae Sai	20	

City	Transport	Cost in Bahts	Comments
Lampang	Minibus to bus station	4	
	Bus to Ngao	27	
	Minibus to Kohka	10	Only 12 bahts from Lampang to *wat* if bus will be heading out of Kohka to *wat*
	Minibus from Kohka to Wat Lampang Luang	5	
	Roht mah (horse cart) from Kohka to Wat Lampang Luang	20	
Kamphaeng Phet	Minibus from bus station to city center	4	They ask for much more
Ayuthia	*Tuk tuk* to Chandrakasem Palace	4	Departs from railroad station
	Tuk tuk across island	7	
	Tuk tuk for 4-hour rental	400	
	Boat around the island	200	Departs from pier next to U-Thong Hotel
Korat	Bus 2 from train station to city center	3	
	Samlor from train station to city center	14	
Petchburi	*Samlor* from summer palace to Kao Luang Cave	15 one way	One-hour trip; alternative is a long hot walk
Ko Samui	Truck from harbor to beaches	15 to 18	18 bahts to Chaweng or Bo Phut; 15 bahts to Lamai
	Bus from Surat Thani to Ban Don	4	Departs every 15 minutes
	Trisha from Ban Don bus station to pier	5	Only 1 km walk (1 stop before bus station is shorter walk to pier)
	Express boat from Ban Don to Ko Samui	50	First boat departs at 1100, last one at 2300; several boats during day
	Boat from Ko Samui to Ko Pangan	25	Departs 1540; arrives 1625

_Transportation Between Cities

From	To	By	Cost in Bahts	Comments
Bangkok	Chiang Mai	Plane	1100	
		Train	307 (2nd class, upper); 119 (3rd class)	Departs 1800; arrives 0700; takes 13 hours
		Bus	250	Takes 8 to 9 hours
	Chiang Rai	Plane	1240	
		Bus	330 (air-conditioned bus)	Departs at 1930 and 2020; takes 23 hours
	Mae Hong Son	Plane	1240	
	Lampang	Plane	830	
		Bus	164	
	Pitsanulok	Plane	630	
		Express train	100	
	Sukotai	Bus	170 (air-conditioned bus)	
	Kamphaeng Phet	Bus	132	Departs from North Bus Station
	Korat	Train	45 (3rd class)	Departs at 0600, 0820, 1205, 1330; takes 5.5 hours
		Bus	61 (74 with air-conditioning)	Regular buses depart every 15 minutes; air-conditioned buses depart every 30 minutes from 1000 to 1330; takes 4.5 hours
	Ayuthia	Train	14 (3rd class)	Takes 1.5 hours
		Bus	18 (62 with air-conditioning)	Departs every half hour from 0600 to 1900 (North Bus Station); takes 2 hours
		Boat	720 (Oriental Queen)	Takes 4 hours
	Petchburi	Train	14	Departs from both Bangkok Noi or Hua Lumpong Railroad Stations
		Bus	35 (66 with air-conditioning)	Departs every 30 minutes from 0540 to 1700 (South Bus Station); takes 3 hours

From	To	By	Cost in Bahts	Comments
Bangkok	Surat Thani	Train	218 (sleeper)	Departs from Hua Lumpong Railroad Station at 1610, 1730, and 2150; takes 13 hours
	Phuket	Plane	1340	
		Bus	134 (250 with air-conditioning)	Regular bus departs at 0730, 1505, 2030, and 2200; air-conditioned bus departs at 1530; takes 14 hours
	Hadyai	Plane	1530	
	Penang	Plane	2950	
Chiang Mai	Fang	Bus	30	Departs every half hour; takes 4.5 hours
	Mae Hong Son	Plane	270 one way	Departs between 1100 and 1200 on Fridays and Sundays
		Bus	110	Departs at 0600, 0800, 2000; takes 9 hours
	Chiang Rai	Plane	270	
		Bus	55 (80 with air-conditioning)	Regular buses depart every 30 minutes between 0600 and 1730; air-conditioned buses depart at 0900, 1000, 1200; takes 3 hours
Mae Sariang	Mae Hong Son	Bus	55	Departs at 1100; takes 2 hours
Fang	Wawee	Jeep	50	Departs at 0800; takes 3 hours
Chiang Rai	Chiang Saen	Bus	10	
	Thaton	Boat	150 (locals pay 90)	Departs at 1030; 6 hours minimum
	Lampang	Bus	40	Takes 4.5 hours
	Pitsanulok	Bus	80	Takes 4 hours
	Sukotai	Bus	105	Takes 6.5 hours
Sukotai	Swankhalok	Bus	20	
	Pitsanulok	Bus	17	
	Kamphaeng Phet	Bus	20	
Swankhalok	Si Satchan-alai (Muang Kao Papen)	Bus	14	

From	To	By	Cost in Bahts	Comments
Korat	Pimai	Bus	16	Get bus for Pimai and Surin east of the center gate on north side of the moat
	Surin	Bus	30	
Phuket	Hadyai	Bus	85 (140 with air-conditioning)	Four morning buses daily: 0530, 0740, 0900, air-conditioned bus at 1020
Hadyai	Sungai Golok	Train	40 (3rd class)	Five trains daily; takes 5 hours

Places to Stay

City	Hotel	Cost in Bahts
Bangkok	Atlanta Hotel	Double: 150
	Bonny Guest House	Double: 200
	Boy Scout Hostel	Single: 25
	Crown Hotel	Double: 200
	Kay Guest House	Single: 40
	Malaysia Hotel	Double: 260
	New Sri Paranakorn Hotel	Double: 200
	Nith Charoen Suke Hotel	Double: 120
	Oriental Hotel	Single: 240 to 340
	Patumwan Hostel	Single: 26 (15 for members)
	Privacy Hotel	Double: 290
	Swan Hotel	Single: 180; Double: 270
	Starlight Hotel	Double: 80
	Tums Guest House	Single: 50; Double: 70
	VS Guest House	Single: 30
	YMCA	Single: 180; Double with air-conditioning: 400
Damnern Saduak	Long Rai Hotel	Double: 80
Nakorn Pathom	Sirichai Hotel	Double: 80
Ban Saen	Saen Sabai	Double: 175
Lampoon	Hotel Sri Lampoon	Double: 65 to 100
Mae Sariang	Mit Alee Hotel	Double: 70
Mae Hong Son	Mae Tee Hotel	Single: 70; Double: 100
	Mitrniyom Hotel	Double: 70
	Sanguan Sin Hotel	Single: 60; Double: 70, 80
Thaton	Karen Coffee Shop (18 km north of Thaton)	Single: 20
Chiang Dao	Chiang Dao Hotel	Single: 30

City	Hotel	Cost in Bahts
Fang	Seen Sukit Hotel Ueng Kham Bangalo	Single: 30; Double: 70 to 100 Double: 100
Chiang Mai	Chiang Mai Guest House Chiang Mai Youth Hostel Je t'aime Guest House Manit Guest House Number One Guest House Orchid Guest House Pao Come Guest House Thai-German Guest House	Double: 95 Single: 40 Single: 50; Double: 65 Single: 65 Double: 55 Single: 55 Double: 55 Single: 55
Chiang Rai	Chiang Rai Guest House Hotel Pao Patana Porn Guest House	Single: 25; Double: 40 Double: 45, 85 Dorm: 25; Double: 40
Golden Triangle (Sam Ruim Tom Kam)	Golden Huts	Single: 30
Lampang	Kelang Nahkorn Hotel Rongram Lampang Sri Lampang Hotel Sri Sangar Hotel	Double: 40 Single: 35; Double: 50 Double: 95 Double: 70
(near railroad)	Kelan Hotel Thub Thim Tong	Single: 45; Double: 50 Double: 55
Sukotai	Sukotai Hotel	Single: 55; Double: 80
Sawankhalok	Muang Inn Sahamit Hotel	Double: 100 Double: 40
Pitsanulok	Champrasert Hotel Sri Jeun Hotel (in Thai script)	Double: 55 Double: 40
Kamphaeng Phet	Niyapraya Hotel Navarat Hotel Rajadamnern Hotel	Single: 35 Tourist class Single: 55; Double with air- conditioning: 130
Ayuthia	Cathay Hotel Kasem Hotel U-thong Hotel	Single: 80; Double: 120 Single: 80; Double: 120 Single: 80; Double: 120; 200 with air-conditioning
Ubon	Rajtani Hotel Siam Hotel	Double: 80; 160 with air- conditioning Double: 70
Chaiyapum	Phaiboon Hotel	Double: 80, 100
Surin	Amarin Hotel Krung Sri Hotel	Double: 90 Double: 70

City	Hotel	Cost in Bahts
Korat	Thai Pokaphan Hotel	Double: 60
Pimai	Pimai Hotel	Single: 55; Double: 80
Khon Kaen	Hotel Thanee Bungalow	Double: 45
Udon Thani	Mitrapacha Hotel Nakorn Udorn Hotel	Double: 45 Double: 45
Petchburi	Chom Klow Hotel at Had Chao Samran	Double: 70 Clapboard beach cottage: 150
Hua Hin	Hua Hin Hotel Hua Hin Railroad Hotel Meechai Hotel	Double: 110 Single: 140; Double: 270 Double: 55
Ko Samui	Bamboo beach huts	Double: 40 to 80
Phuket beaches	Ao Karon Ao Kata Nai Harn	Double: 120 Double: 80 Double: 60
Ao Luk Nua	Tatawan Hotel	Double: 65
Ao Luk Tai	Hotel	Double: 120
Krabi	San Ran Hotel (no English)	Double: 70
Hadyai	Sri Taksin Hotel Ton Num Hotel	Double: 50 Double: 70, 110
Songkla	Samila Hotel Sansabai Hotel Suk Somboon #1	Tourist class Single: 25 Double: 125

____Information About Sights in Bangkok

Dusit Zoo	Open 0700-1800; ฿6 admission
Grand Palace and Wat Pra Keo	Open 0830-1530, closed Sunday; ฿20 admission
Hillcraft Foundation	Open 0900-1700, Monday-Friday; open 1000-1900 on Saturday
Jim Thompson House	Open 0900-1530, Monday-Friday; ฿50 admission
Kodak Siam Show, Oriental Hotel	From 1100-1200, Thursday and Sunday; ฿60 admission; call 234-9920
Lumpini Stadium	At 1300 and 1800, Tuesday, Friday, and Saturday; ฿30 admission
National Art Gallery	Open 0900-1600, closed Monday and Friday
National Museum	Open 0900-1600, Tuesday-Sunday; ฿5 admission
National Theater	Open 0800-1630, Monday-Friday; call 221-8608
Pasteur Institute	Venom extraction at 1100

Ratchadamnoen Stadium	At 1800 on Monday, Wednesday, and Thursday; at 1700 on Sunday; ฿25 admission
Sala Thai Show, Indra Hotel	From 1930-2130; ฿78 and ฿157 admission; call 251-1111
Suan Pakkard Wang Palace	Open 0900-1600, closed Sunday; ฿50 admission
Tourist Authority of Thailand (T.A.T.)	Open 0800-2400; call 281-5051 or 282-0372
Wat Lao	Open 0600-2000
Wat Trimit	Open 0830-1730
World Fellowship of Buddhists	Located at 33 Sukumvit Road; meditation held in English on Wednesday evening

____Thai Words

one	*neung*	๑
two	*sawng*	๒
three	*sahm*	๓
four	*see*	๔
five	*hah*	๕
six	*hohk*	๖
seven	*jet*	๗
eight	*baat*	๘
nine	*gow*	๙
ten	*sip*	๑๐
ambulance	*roht pa-yah-bahn*	รถพยาบาล
baht		บาท
bank	*ta nah kohn*	ธนาคาร
beer	*bee-uh*	เบียร์
bicycle	*jahk-a-yahn*	จักรยาน
bus station	*sa tah nee roht meh*	สถานีรถเมล์
closed	*bpit*	ปิด
doctor	*maw*	หมอ
do not enter	*hahm kow*	ห้ามเข้า
east	*dta wahn awk*	ตะวันออก
elephant	*chahng*	ช้าง
embassy	*sa tahn toot*	สถานทูต
entrance	*tahng kow*	ทางเข้า
exit	*tahng awk*	ทางออก

female	*ying*	หญิง
full	*dtem*	โรคหนองใน
gonorrhea	*rohk nawng nai*	เรคหนองเน
hotel	*rohng raam*	โรงแรม
kilometer	*gih loh*	กิโล
little	*noi*	เล็ก
male	*chai*	ชาย
map	*paan tee*	แผนที่
museum	*pih pit ta pahn*	พิพิธภัณฑ์
near	*glai*	ใกล้
north	*neu-uh*	เหนือ
office	*tee tahm gahn*	ที่ทำงาน
OK	OK	โอเค
one-way street	*ya nohn duhn tahng dee oh*	ถนนเดินทางเดียว
open	*bput*	เปิด
palace	*wahng*	วัง
passport	*nahng seu duhn tahng*	หนังสือเดินทาง
person	*kohn*	คน
pharmacy	*rahm kai yah*	ร้านขยยา
police	*dtahm roo-ut*	ค้ารวจ
post office	*tee tahm gahn prai sa nee*	ที่ทำการไปรษณีย์
railroad station	*sa tah nee roht-fai*	สถานีรถไฟ
restaurant	*rhan kai ah-nahn*	ร้านขายอาหาร
sale	*loht rah-kah*	ลดราคา
sandy beach	*had sai*	หาดทราย
school	*rohng ree-un*	โรงเรียน
sick	*mai sa bai*	ไม่สบาย
slow	*chah*	ช้า
small	*lek*	เล็ก
south	*dtai*	ใต้
stop	*yoot*	หยุด
syphilis	*gahm-ma rohk*	กามโรค
tailor shop	*rahn dtaht seu-uh*	ร้านตัดเสื้อ
Thai	*Tai*	ไทย
ticket	*dtoo-uh*	ตั๋ว
toilet	*soo-um*	ส้วม
university	*ma hah wit ta yah lai*	มหาวิทยาลัย
west	*dta-wahn dtohk*	ตะวันตก

Bibliography

Culture

Draeger, Donn F., and Smith, Robert W. *Asian Fighting Arts*. Tokyo: Kodansha International Ltd., 1969.

Hollinger, Carol. *Mai Pen Rai*. Boston: Houghton Mifflin Co., 1965.

Hunter, Guy. *South-East Asia—Race, Culture and Nation*. New York: Oxford University Press, 1966.

Keyes, Charles F. *The Golden Peninsula, Culture and Adaptation in Mainland Southeast Asia*. New York: Macmillan, Inc., 1977.

Khaing, Mi Mi. *Burmese Family*. Bloomington: Indiana University Press, 1962.

Lowry, John. *Burmese Art*. London: Her Majesty Stationary Office, 1974.

Olsson, Ray A. *The Ramakien, A Prose Translation of the Thai Ramayana*. Bangkok: Praepittaya Co., Ltd., 1968.

Rajadhon, Phya Anuman. *Essays on Thai Folklore*. Social Science Association, Press of Thailand, 1968.

Rice, Edward. *Eastern Definitions*. New York: Doubleday & Co., Inc., 1978.

Southeast Asia Chronicle, Issues 65, 69, 78, 80. Southeast Asia Resource Center, Berkeley, California.

Srisvasdi, Boon Chuey. *The Hill Tribes of Siam*. Bangkok: Bamrung Nukolkit Press, 1963.

Than, U Aung. *Shwedagon*. 2d ed. Rangoon: Ministry of Information, 1957.

Tribesmen and Peasants in North Thailand. Chiang Mai: Tribal Research Center, 1969.

Waugh, Alec. *Bangkok, Biography of a City*. Boston: Little, Brown & Co., 1971.

History

Aung, Maung Htin. *Burmese History Before 1287: A Defense of the Chronicles*. Oxford, England: The Asoka Society, 1970.

Blair, Clay, Jr., and Joan. *Return From the River Kwai*. New York: Simon & Schuster, Inc., 1979.

Cady, John. *Thailand, Burma, Laos and Cambodia*. Englewood Cliffs, New Jersey: Prentice-Hall, Inc., 1966.

Coe, Douglas. *The Burma Road*. New York: Julian Messner, 1946.

Fuller, R. Buckminster. *Critical Path*. New York: St Martin's Press, Inc., 1981.

Groslier, Bernard, and Artaud, Jacques. *Angkor, Art and Civilization*. rev. ed. New York: Praeger Publishers, 1966.

Hall, D.G.E. *A History of South-East Asia.* 3d ed. New York: St Martin's Press, Inc., 1968.

Harrison, Brian. *South-East Asia, A Short History.* 3d ed. New York: Macmillan, Inc., 1968.

Khoo, Gilbert, and Lo, Dorthy. *Asian Transformation.* Kuala Lumpur: Heinemann Ed. Books, 1977.

Percival, Richard. *Marco Polo's Travels in Xanadu with Kublai Khan.* London: Lister, Gordon and Cremonesi, 1976.

Scott, Sir James (Shway Yoe). *The Burman, His Life and Nation.* London: Macmillan, 1910.

Smith, R.B., and Watson, W., eds. *Early South East Asia.* New York: Oxford University Press, 1979.

Steinberg, David Joel, ed. *In Search of Southeast Asia—A Modern History.* New York: Praeger Publishers, 1971.

Wales, H.G. Quaritch. *Towards Angkor.* London: George G. Harrap & Co., Ltd., out of print.

Woodman, Dorthy. *The Making of Burma.* London: The Cresset Press, 1962.

____Philosophy and Religion

Chan, Wing T., and Alfaruqi, Ismael R. *The Great Asian Religions.* New York: Macmillian, Inc., 1969.

Ling, T.O. *A Dictionary of Buddhism.* New York: Charles Scribner's Sons, 1972.

McGill, Ormond, and Ormond, Ron. *Religious Mysteries of the Orient.* San Diego: A.S. Barnes & Co., Inc., 1976.

Spiro, Melford E. *Buddhism and Society.* New York: Harper & Row, Publishers, Inc., 1970.

Spiro, Melford E. *Burmese Supernaturalism.* Englewood Cliffs, New Jersey: Prentice-Hall, Inc., 1976.

Tambiah, S.J. *Buddhism and the Spirit Cults of Northeast Thailand.* England: Cambridge University Press, 1970.

____Miscellaneous

Alden, Peter, and Gooders, John. *Finding Birds Around the World.* Boston: Houghton Mifflin Co., 1981.

Allison, Gordon H. *Easy Thai.* Rutland, Vermont: Charles E. Tuttle Co., Inc., 1969.

Keeton, Charles Lee, III. "King Thibau and the Ecological Rape of Burma." Ph.D. dissertation, University of Delhi, 1974.

King, Ben F., and Dickinson, Edward. *A Field Guide to the Birds of South-East Asia.* Boston: Houghton Mifflin Co., 1975.

Roop, D. Haigh. *An Introduction to the Burmese Writing System.* New Haven: Yale University Linguistic Series, 1972.

Index for Burma

Index for Thailand